THE FORCE
OF
FEW WORDS

*Poetry teaches the enormous force
of a few words. . . .*

RALPH WALDO EMERSON

from the Preface to *Parnassus*

THE FORCE
OF
FEW WORDS

AN INTRODUCTION
TO POETRY

Jacob Korg

UNIVERSITY OF WASHINGTON

HOLT, RINEHART AND WINSTON, INC.
NEW YORK   CHICAGO   SAN FRANCISCO   TORONTO

ACKNOWLEDGMENTS

Acknowledgment is gratefully made to the following publishers, agents, and individuals who have permitted the use of copyrighted material.

W. H. AUDEN · "Musée des Beaux Arts," "Voltaire at Ferney," "Herman Melville," and lines from "In Memory of W. B. Yeats," copyright 1940 by W. H. Auden. From *The Collected Poetry of W. H. Auden.* Reprinted by permission of Random House, Inc., and Faber and Faber, Ltd.

JOHN BETJEMAN · "In Westminster Abbey." From *Collected Poems,* by John Betjeman. Published in the United States by Houghton Mifflin Company. Reprinted by permission of John Murray (Publishers), Ltd.

ELIZABETH BISHOP · "The Fish." From *Poems, 1955,* by Elizabeth Bishop. Reprinted by permission of Houghton Mifflin Company.

ROBERT BRIDGES · "Low Barometer" and lines from "The Storm Is Over." Reprinted by permission of the Clarendon Press, Oxford.

HART CRANE · "The Air Plant" and "O Carib Isle." From *The Collected Poems of Hart Crane.* Copyright © R, 1961, by Liveright Publishing Corp. Reprinted by permission of Liveright Publishing Corp.

E. E. CUMMINGS · "anyone lived in a pretty how town," copyright 1940 by E. E. Cummings; "somewhere i have never travelled," copyright 1931, 1959 by E. E. Cummings; "i thank you God for most this amazing," copyright 1950 by E. E. Cummings; "since feeling is first," copyright 1926 by Horace Liveright, copyright 1954 by E. E. Cummings. All from *Poems, 1923–54,* by E. E. Cummings. Reprinted by permission of Harcourt, Brace & World, Inc.

WALTER DE LA MARE · "In the Dock." Reprinted by permission of The Literary Trustees of Walter de la Mare and The Society of Authors as their representative.

EMILY DICKINSON · "Success is counted sweetest," "There's a certain slant of light," "The soul selects her own society," "The bustle in a house," "I heard a fly buzz when I died," "A light exists in spring," and "Because I could not stop for Death" reprinted by permission of the publishers from Thomas H. Johnson, Editor, *The Poems of Emily Dickinson*. Cambridge, Mass.: The Belknap Press of Harvard University Press. Copyright 1951, 1955 by The President and Fellows of Harvard College. "After great pain a formal feeling comes" copyright 1929, © 1957 by Mary L. Hampson. From Thomas H. Johnson, Editor, *The Complete Poems of Emily Dickinson*. Reprinted by permission of Little, Brown and Company.

LAWRENCE DURRELL · "Je Est un Autre." From *Collected Poems*, by Lawrence Durrell. Copyright © 1956, 1960 by Lawrence Durrell. Reprinted by permission of E. P. Dutton & Company, Inc., and Faber and Faber, Ltd.

RICHARD EBERHART · "The Groundhog" and "Rumination" from *Collected Poems, 1930–1960*, by Richard Eberhart. Copyright © 1960 by Richard Eberhart. Reprinted by permission of Oxford University Press, Inc., and Chatto and Windus, Ltd.

T. S. ELIOT · "Gerontion," "Preludes," "The Love Song of J. Alfred Prufrock," and "A Cooking Egg." From *Collected Poems 1909–1962*, by T. S. Eliot. Copyright 1936 by Harcourt, Brace & World, Inc.; copyright © 1963, 1964 by T. S. Eliot. Reprinted by permission of Harcourt, Brace & World, Inc., and Faber and Faber, Ltd.

WILLIAM EMPSON · "Homage to the British Museum." From *Collected Poems of William Empson*. Copyright 1949 by William Empson. Reprinted by permission of Harcourt, Brace & World, Inc., and Chatto and Windus, Ltd.

ROBERT FROST · "Once by the Pacific," "Fire and Ice," "Reluctance," "Two Tramps in Mud Time," "The Gift Outright," "Desert Places," "Sand Dunes," and lines from "Birches" and "Stopping by Woods on a Snowy Evening." From *Complete Poems of Robert Frost*. Copyright 1916, 1923, 1928, 1934 by Holt, Rinehart and Winston, Inc. Copyright 1936, 1942, 1944, 1951, © 1956, 1962 by Robert Frost. Copyright © 1964 by Lesley Frost Ballantine. Reprinted by permission of Holt, Rinehart and Winston, Inc.

ROBERT GRAVES · "The Worms of History." From *Collected Poems*, by Robert Graves (Doubleday & Company, Inc., and Cassell & Company, Ltd.). © International Authors N. V. 1955, 1959. Reprinted by permission of A. P. Watt & Son.

DONALD HALL · "The Morning Porches." From *The Dark Houses*, by Donald Hall. Copyright © 1958 by Donald Hall. Reprinted by permission of The Viking Press, Inc.

THOMAS HARDY · "Channel Firing," "The Convergence of the Twain," "The Darkling Thrush," "Nature's Questioning," "In Time of 'The Breaking of Nations,'" and "Afterwards." From *The Collected Poems of Thomas Hardy*. Reprinted by permission of the Trustees of the Hardy Estate and Macmillan & Company, Ltd.

H. D. (HILDA DOOLITTLE) · Lines from "Orchard." From *H. D., Selected Poems* (Grove Press, Inc.). Copyright © 1957 by Norman Holmes Pearson. Part 1 of "Garden." From *Collected Poems of H. D.* (Liveright Publishing Corp.). Copyright 1925, 1953 by Norman Holmes Pearson. Part 2 of "Garden." From *H. D., Selected Poems* (Grove Press, Inc.). Copyright © 1957 by Norman Holmes Pearson. Reprinted by permission of Grove Press, Inc.

GERARD MANLEY HOPKINS · "Pied Beauty," "The Habit of Perfection," "God's Grandeur," "No Worst, There Is None," "The Windhover," and lines from "Felix Randal." From W. H. Gardner, Editor, *Poems of Gerard Manley Hopkins*, 3d ed. Copyright 1948 by Oxford University Press. Reprinted by permission of Oxford University Press, Inc.

A. E. HOUSMAN · "The Immortal Part," "On Wenlock Edge," "To an Athlete Dying Young," and "Reveille" from "A Shropshire Lad," Authorized Edition. From *The Collected Poems of A. E. Housman*. Copyright 1939, 1940, © 1959 by Holt, Rinehart and Winston, Inc. "Epitaph on an Army of Mercenaries" and "Stars, I Have Seen Them Fall." From *The Collected Poems of A. E. Housman*. Copyright 1922, 1936, 1950 by Barclays Bank, Ltd. Copyright © 1964 by Robert E. Symons. All reprinted by permission of Holt, Rinehart and Winston, Inc., The Society of Authors as the literary representative of the Estate of the late A. E. Housman, and Jonathan Cape, Ltd.

RANDALL JARRELL · "The Lonely Man." From *The Woman at the Washington Zoo*, by Randall Jarrell. Copyright © 1960 by Randall Jarrell. Reprinted by permission of Atheneum Publishers. "The Orient Express." From *The Seven-League Crutches*, by Randall Jarrell. Copyright 1951 by Randall Jarrell. Reprinted by permission of Harcourt, Brace & World, Inc.

ROBINSON JEFFERS · "The Eye," copyright 1948 by Robinson Jeffers. From *The Double Axe and Other Poems*, by Robinson Jeffers. "Hurt Hawks," copyright 1928 and renewed 1956 by Robinson Jeffers, and "Boats in a Fog," copyright 1925 and renewed 1953 by Robinson Jeffers. From *The Selected Poetry of Robinson Jeffers.* Reprinted by permission of Random House, Inc.

STANLEY KUNITZ · "End of Summer," copyright 1953 by Stanley Kunitz, and "Approach of Autumn," copyright © 1958 by Stanley Kunitz. From *Selected Poems 1928–1958,* by Stanley Kunitz. Reprinted by permission of Little, Brown and Company-Atlantic Monthly Press.

C. DAY LEWIS · "As One Who Wanders into Old Workings." From *Collected Poems of C. Day Lewis.* Reprinted by permission of Jonathan Cape, Ltd.

ROBERT LOWELL · "As a Plane Tree by the Water" and "The Crucifix." From *Lord Weary's Castle,* by Robert Lowell. Copyright 1944, 1946 by Robert Lowell. Reprinted by permission of Harcourt, Brace & World, Inc.

ARCHIBALD MACLEISH · "The Silent Slain," "You, Andrew Marvell," and lines from "Einstein." From *Collected Poems, 1917–1952,* by Archibald MacLeish. Reprinted by permission of Houghton Mifflin Company.

LOUIS MACNEICE · "Schizophrene." From *Collected Poems,* by Louis MacNeice. "Death of an Actress" and lines from "Snow." From *Eighty-Five Poems.* Copyright © 1959 by Louis MacNeice. All reprinted by permission of Oxford University Press, Inc., and Faber and Faber, Ltd.

JOHN MANIFOLD · "Fife Tune," copyright 1946 by The John Day Company. From *Selected Verse,* by John Manifold. Reprinted by permission of The John Day Company, Inc.

JOHN MASEFIELD · "The Downland." From *Collected Poems,* by John Masefield. Copyright 1917 by The Macmillan Company, renewed 1945 by John Masefield. Reprinted by permission of The Macmillan Company.

JOSEPHINE MILES · "Monkey." From *Poems, 1930–1960,* by Josephine Miles. Reprinted by permission of Indiana University Press. Lines from "Appointment in Doctor's Office." From *Poems on Several Occasions,* by Josephine Miles. Copyright 1941 by New Directions. Reprinted by permission of New Directions.

MARIANNE MOORE · "A Grave" and "Critics and Connoisseurs." From *Collected Poems,* by Marianne Moore. Copyright 1935 by Marianne Moore; copyright © renewed 1963 by Marianne Moore and T. S. Eliot. Reprinted by permission of The Macmillan Company.

EDWIN MUIR · "The Enchanted Knight" and "The Window." From *Collected Poems*, by Edwin Muir. Reprinted by permission of Faber and Faber, Ltd.

HOWARD NEMEROV · "The Snow Globe" and "Writing." From *The Salt Garden*, by Howard Nemerov. Reprinted by permission of Margot Johnson Agency.

WILFRED OWEN · "Anthem for Doomed Youth," "Arms and the Boy," and lines from "Strange Meeting." From *The Collected Poems of Wilfred Owen*. Copyright © 1963 by Chatto & Windus, Ltd. Reprinted by permission of Chatto & Windus, Ltd., and New Directions.

EZRA POUND · "The Garden," "The River Merchant's Wife: A Letter," and "Lament of the Frontier Guard." From *Personae*, by Ezra Pound. Copyright 1926, 1954 by Ezra Pound. Lines from *Canto LXXXI*. From *The Cantos of Ezra Pound*. Copyright 1934, 1948 by Ezra Pound. Reprinted by permission of New Directions.

JOHN CROWE RANSOM · "Parting, without a Sequel." Copyright 1927 by Alfred A. Knopf, Inc., renewed 1955 by John Crowe Ransom. From *Selected Poems*, by John Crowe Ransom. Reprinted by permission of Alfred A. Knopf, Inc.

HERBERT READ · Lines from "A World within a War." From *Collected Poems*, by Herbert Read. All rights reserved. Reprinted by permission of New Directions and Faber and Faber, Ltd.

HENRY REED · "Judging Distances." From *A Map of Verona and Other Poems*, by Henry Reed. Copyright 1947 by Henry Reed. Reprinted by permission of Harcourt, Brace & World, Inc., and Jonathan Cape, Ltd.

EDWIN ARLINGTON ROBINSON · "The House on the Hill." From *Children of the Night*, by Edwin Arlington Robinson. Charles Scribner's Sons, 1897. Reprinted by permission of Charles Scribner's Sons. "The Sheaves." From *Collected Poems*, by Edwin Arlington Robinson. Copyright 1925 by The Macmillan Company, renewed 1952 by Ruth Nivison and Barbara R. Holt. Reprinted by permission of The Macmillan Company.

THEODORE ROETHKE · "Dolor." Copyright 1947 by Theodore Roethke. From *The Lost Son and Other Poems*, by Theodore Roethke. "Epidermal Macabre," copyright 1932 by Theodore Roethke; "The Waking," copyright 1953 by Theodore Roethke; "The Adamant," copyright 1938 by Theodore Roethke; lines from "A Walk in Late Summer," copyright © 1957 by Theodore Roethke. From

Words for the Wind, by Theodore Roethke. All reprinted by permission of Doubleday & Company, Inc.

DELMORE SCHWARTZ · "The Heavy Bear Who Goes with Me." Copyright 1938 by New Directions. From *Summer Knowledge*, by Delmore Schwartz. Reprinted by permission of Doubleday & Company, Inc.

KARL SHAPIRO · "Buick." Copyright 1941 by Karl Shapiro. From *Poems 1940–1953*, by Karl Shapiro. Reprinted by permission of Random House, Inc.

EDITH SITWELL · Lines from "An Old Woman." From *The Collected Poems of Edith Sitwell*. Reprinted by permission of A. Watkins, Inc.

W. D. SNODGRASS · "April Inventory." Copyright 1957 by W. D. Snodgrass. From *Heart's Needle*, by W. D. Snodgrass. Reprinted by permission of Alfred A. Knopf, Inc.

STEPHEN SPENDER · "An Elementary School Classroom in a Slum," "Two Armies," "Port Bou," and lines from "Polar Exploration." Copyright 1942 by Stephen Spender. From *Collected Poems 1928–1953*, by Stephen Spender. Reprinted by permission of Random House, Inc., and Faber and Faber, Ltd.

WALLACE STEVENS · "The Snow Man," "Thirteen Ways of Looking at a Blackbird," "Peter Quince at the Clavier," "Ancedote of the Jar," and lines from "Bantams in Pine Woods." Copyright 1923 by Wallace Stevens; renewed 1951. "The Glass of Water." Copyright 1942 by Wallace Stevens. From *The Collected Poems of Wallace Stevens*. All reprinted by permission of Alfred A. Knopf, Inc.

DYLAN THOMAS · "The Force That through the Green Fuse," "A Refusal To Mourn the Death, by Fire, of a Child in London," "The Hunchback in the Park," "On the Marriage of a Virgin," and "Poem in October." From *The Collected Poems of Dylan Thomas*. Copyright 1953 by Dylan Thomas; copyright © 1957 by New Directions. Reprinted by permission of New Directions, J. M. Dent & Sons, Ltd., and the Literary Executors of the Dylan Thomas Estate.

EDWARD THOMAS · "The Cherry Trees" and "The New House." From *Collected Poems*, by Edward Thomas (Faber and Faber, Ltd., 1961). Reprinted by permission of Mrs. Edward Thomas.

ROBERT PENN WARREN · "Bearded Oaks." Copyright 1944 by Robert Penn Warren. From *Selected Poems 1923–1943*, by Robert Penn Warren (Harcourt, Brace & World, Inc., 1944).

VERNON WATKINS · "The Mummy." From *Selected Poems of Vernon Watkins*. All rights reserved. "The Heron." From *The Death Bell* by Vernon Watkins. All rights reserved. Both reprinted by permission of New Directions.

RICHARD WILBUR · "The Pardon." From *Ceremony and Other Poems*, by Richard Wilbur. Copyright 1948, 1949, 1950 by Richard Wilbur. "Mind" and "Lamarck Elaborated." From *Things of This World*, by Richard Wilbur. Copyright © 1956 by Richard Wilbur. All reprinted by permission of Harcourt, Brace & World, Inc.

WILLIAM CARLOS WILLIAMS · "The Poor," "The Red Wheelbarrow," and "Spring and All." From *The Collected Earlier Poems of William Carlos Williams*. Copyright 1938, 1951 by William Carlos Williams. Reprinted by permission of New Directions.

W. B. YEATS · "The Coming of Wisdom with Time," copyright 1912 by The Macmillan Company, renewed 1940 by Bertha Georgie Yeats; "To a Friend Whose Work Has Come to Nothing;" copyright 1916 by The Macmillan Company, renewed 1944 by Bertha Georgie Yeats; "The Second Coming," copyright 1924 by The Macmillan Company, renewed 1952 by Bertha Georgie Yeats; "Sailing to Byzantium," copyright 1928 by The Macmillan Company, renewed 1956 by Georgie Yeats; lines from "Song of Wandering Aengus." From *Collected Poems*, by William Butler Yeats. Reprinted by permission of The Macmillan Company, The Macmillan Company of Canada, Ltd., and Mrs. W. B. Yeats.

Preface

This book is intended for students who have begun to read and think about poetry purposefully for the first time. Hence, it joins the reader at the beginning of the subject, assuming little previous information. But it proposes to take him comparatively far, with the help of the instructor, to a point where he will be ready for the vigorous intellectual and imaginative activity that the intelligent reading of poetry involves.

Section 1 of this book is a revision of my *Introduction to Poetry* (Holt, Rinehart and Winston, 1959). The success this pamphlet has enjoyed has encouraged me to expand it by adding illustrative poems and a related anthology for those who may wish to use them in conjunction with the discussion. Profiting from the criticism of teachers familiar with my original text, I have revised and augmented it at some points and have changed the order of the material. But the most important change has been the inclusion of complete poems as examples within and at the ends of most of the chapters.

The second section, the anthology, is entirely new. In selecting the poems for it, I have kept in mind the needs of the intelligent but inexperienced reader, for whom the book is intended. I have tried to give some representation to the various periods and styles of English and American verse, as well as to illustrate narrative, lyric, dramatic, and other modes. I have also tried to strike good balances between the long and the short, the familiar and the unfamiliar, the traditional and the modern, the challenging and the accessible. One of the principles observed in selecting poems for the anthology has been that of supplying additional examples for the discussions in the first section. Cross-references within the chapters of Section 1 direct the reader to poems in the anthology that illustrate the topics discussed.

For guidance in preparing this book, I am indebted to Mr. Caleb Smith and Professor Richard S. Beal, and for numerous helpful suggestions and corrections, to Professor Fred A. Dudley of Washington State University, Professor Leonard Lief of Hunter College, Professor William A. Reynolds of Fresno City College, and Professor Charles D. Wright of the University of North Carolina.

I am also deeply indebted to my wife Cynthia for help and encouragement in writing this book.

JK

Seattle, Washington
February 1966

Contents

SECTION 2

AN ANTHOLOGY OF ENGLISH AND AMERICAN POEMS

AN
INTRODUCTION
TO
POETRY

Section 1

The Nature of Poetry 1

THE LIMITS OF LANGUAGE

Poetry attracts so little general attention today that it may be hard to believe that it has real importance. But anyone who studies the history of civilization will find it difficult to escape the conclusion that poetry has always held a central position in human culture. There is hardly any tribe so primitive that it does not have a poetic form of expression. Even the most backward savages, like the American Indians and the natives of Easter Island, produced chants and ballads that are unmistakably poetic. Poetry flourished in the remotest civilizations, such as the Egyptian and the Babylonian, and has been a prominent element in nearly every culture up to the present time. Wherever it appears it is used, not only as a means of entertainment but also as a medium for expressing such vital feelings and ideas as religious beliefs and moral principles. The holy books of the Hindus and such parts of the Old Testament as the Prophets, the Book of Psalms, and the Book of Job are written in poetry. The Greeks and Romans embodied their great contributions to civilization in epic, lyric, and dramatic poems. In China and Japan the art of poetry has traditionally been important in education, moral guidance, and even government. The lack of widespread interest in poetry does not mean that it has lost its importance. Its public is small in comparison with modern mass audiences, but it is responsive enough to support the publication of large numbers of new poems in books and periodicals and to stimulate active scholarship and criticism. When we consider that in the English-speaking world America alone probably has as many competent and interesting poets as any country has ever had, we can see that in studying poetry we are dealing with a living force.

It is reasonable to ask why poetry, which is more difficult to write and to read than prose, has nearly always occupied a more prominent place in world culture. This question can best be answered by a description of some of the special functions and characteristics of poetry.

Language is our most flexible and most sophisticated medium of expression, but everyone has felt its limitations at one time or another. For one thing, it is accurate enough to convey only the most commonplace distinctions. We have a word, "green," for describing the color of a leaf, and we are able to distinguish between light green, dark green, and a certain number of other shades. But a green leaf that is in the shadow has a very different appearance from one that is in sunlight. Yet our language provides no easy and familiar way of communicating this distinction. Similarly, we have an extraordinary wealth of words for sounds, such as *quaver, rattle, bump, squeak,* and *splash;* but there is no one expression for the phenomenon of a single loud sound followed by gradually diminishing overtones that is heard when a gong or a piano key is struck. These deficiencies do not reflect the inadequacy of language. They are simply consequences of a fact with which everyone is familiar, the fact that even the most ordinary experience is far more complicated than language can possibly be.

The limitations of language also become apparent when we try to communicate emotions and sensations. How would you explain to someone who has never had these experiences how an orange tastes, how a trumpet sounds, or how it feels to run your finger over velvet? To consider this problem is to realize that the primary experiences that make up the texture of life are, in the final analysis, incommunicable. In trying to convey them, a speaker seeks the most expressive words, but he is also likely to go beyond words, and to resort to exclamations, intonations, and comparisons. Poetry is language of this sort. Its natural subject matter is the kind of experience that ordinary language cannot communicate. Poetry works at the limits of knowledge, seeking to express the inexpressible.

The subtle and fleeting feeling is a common subject for poetry, and short poems that seek to capture the intense and peculiar sensations of such experiences as love, sorrow, and delight in nature are called *lyrics*. Most popular and well-known poems belong to this category. But poetry is also capable of narrating, philosophizing, dramatizing, describing, and other modes of expression. If it is well adapted to the expression of spontaneous feelings, it can also organize large areas of experience in an orderly and permanently meaningful way. John Milton's *Paradise Lost*, for example, is a long poem of twelve books with many characters, episodes, conversations, and descriptions, which makes use of great masses of learning and tradition. All this is carefully integrated into a single complex poem, a great expression of moral and religious philosophy.

POETRY AND PROSE

One of the first questions that naturally occurs to a reader who is trying to grasp the nature of poetry is, What is the difference between poetry and prose? Unfortunately, no clear distinction between the two has ever been formulated. The problem is as notorious in literature as the problem of squaring the circle is in mathematics. But we can learn something about it by taking as a point of departure a distinction that is useful, if not strictly true, and qualifying it later. It might be said that poetry characteristically expresses or evokes feeling and is addressed to the imagination, while prose characteristically conveys information and is addressed to the intellect.

The difference can be illustrated by a comparison between a prose statement and a passage of poetry. The statement, "I am falling asleep" depends entirely on literal meaning. Its purpose is to communicate a fact. But in Tennyson's lines

> To Sleep I give my powers away;
> My will is bondsman to the dark;

the fact itself is not as important as the feelings associated with it. For reasons relevant to the rest of *In Memoriam*, the poem in which these lines appear, Tennyson describes falling asleep as a matter of surrendering one's self-control and stresses the feeling of helplessness and subjection to something else involved in it.

A close examination reveals that the subject matter of the prose and poetic examples is not exactly the same, strictly speaking. The subject matter of "I am falling asleep" is a physiological event. The subject matter of Tennyson's lines is a particular emotional reaction to this event. Like poetry in general, Tennyson's lines treat the subject not as information but as felt experience. As a result, the two examples can fairly be said to be about different occurrences which take place at different times and involve different parts of the mind.

This brings us to the important point that the literal meaning a poem may contain and the poem itself are separate things. By comparing them with each other it is often possible to isolate the elements in the poem that differentiate it from prose, and to examine the way in which the poem builds feelings and attitudes on the foundation of its literal meaning. Let us apply this method to the following poem.

ONCE BY THE PACIFIC

ROBERT FROST (1875–1964)

The shattered water made a misty din.
Great waves looked over others coming in,
And thought of doing something to the shore
That water never did to land before.
The clouds were low and hairy in the skies,   5
Like locks blown forward in the gleam of eyes.
You could not tell, and yet it looked as if
The shore was lucky in being backed by cliff,
The cliff in being backed by continent;
It looked as if a night of dark intent   10
Was coming, and not only a night, an age.
Someone had better be prepared for rage.
There would be more than ocean-water broken
Before God's last *Put out the Light* was spoken.

Stated in prose, the main idea of this poem would be: The waves and clouds of the storm were so threatening that the land seemed to need all its solidity to resist them. They gave the impression that they were bound to be very destructive. Looking for reasons why the poem so obviously says more than this, we notice that Frost has opened an area of unstated possibilities by leaving some of the things he is saying indefinite. The waves are thinking of doing "something"; "someone" had better be prepared; "more than ocean-water" will be broken. If this were a prose passage, we would perhaps be justified in demanding more specific information. But the vagueness of the poem is essential in guiding the reader toward the meaning that lies beyond its literal sense. The storm embodies a "dark intent," and will express "rage." Further, this threatened violence is given some highly individual characteristics. It is unprecedented, for it will be something "That water never did to land before"; it involves vast space, for Frost skillfully widens the storm's area of influence by telling us that first the shore, then the cliff, then the whole continent will be needed to resist its force.

The last line expands the poem's scope still further, for it looks forward to the final event of all, the end of the universe. According to the third verse of the Book of Genesis, God began His creation of the universe by declaring, "Let there be light." By using the words "Put out the Light," Frost relates the destructiveness of the sea to the time when He will command this same light to be darkened. The careful reader will not overlook the fact that "Light" is capitalized. The light that will be "put out" is an absolute, that is, existence itself.

These touches, which would be exaggerations in an ordinary description of a storm, make us aware that the subject of the poem is not the storm, but something important enough to be thought of within the context of the universe as a whole. Since this could hardly be true, even of a very violent storm, we are led to the realization that Frost has in mind not only this scene but something bigger of which it is a part, the general violence of nature.

The specific words "Put out the Light" subtly suggest the poet's attitude toward this violence. They are quoted from the speech delivered by Othello in Act V, scene 2 of Shakespeare's play just before he kills his wife, Desdemona, in the belief that she has been unfaithful to him. In this impressive scene, Othello carries a candle into the room where Desdemona is lying asleep and says, as he looks from the candle to his wife, "Put out the light, and then put out the light." Obviously he means the candle by the first light, and by the second, Desdemona's life. In the remainder of the speech, Othello reminds himself that with the death of Desdemona something beautiful and worthy which can never be replaced will be lost. Frost's purpose in quoting his words is that of quietly attaching similar feelings to the destructiveness of nature.

In "Once by the Pacific" then, as in the case of the lines from *In Memoriam*, the meaning of *the poem* is quite different from that of its prose paraphrase. The poem is not, strictly interpreted, about a storm or nature, but about the poet's attitude toward these things. Frost shows that he knows that the emotional tone of the scene is not in nature, but in his own response, when he says, in line 7, "You could not tell, and yet it looked as if . . ." This interpolation may seem unimportant, but if it is omitted, and the passage beginning "The shore was lucky . . ." is read as a series of flat assertions, an overintense, melodramatic quality enters the poem. Frost's casual, conversational tone and the doubt he admits feeling have the effect of assuring the reader that he is listening to a level-headed, reliable observer; and that, of course, makes his report about the threatening element of nature all the more convincing and terrifying.

This way of distinguishing between poetry and prose requires many qualifications. For one thing, it does not seem to account very well for prose fiction, which is certainly imaginative and nearly always expresses feeling; but fiction generally gains its effects through the information it contains, which is not true of poetry. In addition, it should be said immediately that poetry is not purely emotional, but requires many talents of the intellect, such as a good memory, a sense of proportion, the capacity to think logically, and an ability to make subtle connections. It is safe to say that most good poetry offers more of a challenge and stimulus to rational thought than does good prose. It requires more feeling than prose, and requires more intellect too. The poet Coleridge said that poetic power consisted of "a more than usual state of emotion, with more than usual order; judgement ever awake and steady self-possession, with enthusiasm and feeling profound or vehement. . . ." (*Biographia Literaria*, XIV). However, the identifying characteristics of poetry, the qualities that make it what it is, are not logic, order, or accuracy (though these may be highly desirable) but imaginativeness and feeling.

A famous mistake made by the poet John Keats provides evidence for the validity of these criteria. Keats once stayed up most of the night to read a translation of Homer's works, which enabled him to appreciate their true grandeur for the first time. The next morning he wrote a sonnet describing his feeling of discovery, in which he compared his experience to that of a stargazer who sees a new planet and to that of the explorer who first discovered the Pacific Ocean (See "On First Looking Into Chapman's Homer," p. 150). However, he gave this explorer the wrong name, calling him Cortez instead of Balboa. Now, if the value of Keats's poem depends on the accuracy of the information it contains, this mistake would, of course, spoil it. But since it depends on evoking the wonder and excitement stirred by the experience of discovery as a general thing, the factual error seems irrelevant.

While poetry can generally be distinguished from prose by emotional and imaginative quality, it is more easily recognized by its secondary characteristics. It may use special rhetorical devices such as similes and metaphors, which, as we shall see, are particularly well adapted to its aim of expressing emotion. Also, because it expresses strong feeling, poetry is nearly always rhythmical. Rhythm may be supplied by the meter, the lines which divide the poem into units of meter, and such special effects as rhyme and alliteration. Because poetry is marked by one or more of these characteristics, it can go very far toward exchanging functions with prose without losing its identity, so that prose that is imaginative and full of feeling remains prose, while poetry may be comparatively factual or intellectual and still be poetry.

MISCONCEPTIONS ABOUT POETRY

Knowledge of the main characteristics of poetry enables us to correct three misconceptions about it that prevent many readers from understanding and enjoying it. These are:

1) The idea that poetry is an artificial and unnatural use of language.
2) The idea that it is an elaborate way of saying something that could be said more clearly in prose.
3) The idea that it always expresses exaggerated or sentimental emotions.

Poetry, far from being artificial or unnecessary, appears to be the oldest and most universal of the arts. In fact, the existence of well-developed poetic traditions among otherwise uncivilized peoples leads to the inference that what we call poetry may well have existed among prehistoric men before the form of communication called prose. The strongest expressive needs of primitive people are likely to be related to matters of feeling rather than to matters of fact, and their imaginations are likely to be far richer and more powerful than their intellects. The human race realized the value of accurate, objective description only comparatively late, as a part of the scientific attitude. Witches, goblins, and fairies came before molecules and light years, though both kinds of concepts serve the same purpose: they are ways by which man explains the realities of his universe to himself. The difference is that the former are imaginative, and the latter are intellectual. Primitive man does, of course, feel the need to describe the flash of lightning or the rumble of the earthquake, but in his description the factual element is likely to be submerged in the expression of the emotions he experiences. His account would be true to his feelings rather than to the objective reality. The result of expression under these conditions would be poetry. Thus, it is fairly obvious that poetry, whose primary concern is feeling, and whose primary instrument is the imagination, must have come earlier in human development than any but the most rudimentary prose. Prose, except for strictly utilitarian scraps of conversation, could not emerge until such a relatively advanced concept as an objective reality separate from the self could be developed. Poetry then, is not only older, but more primitive and more natural than prose.

We can also see, from our description of poetry, why it cannot be considered merely an elaborate and sententious way of saying things that could be expressed more directly. Poetry characteristically deals with subjects that cannot be adequately described in prose. It is a way of stretching the resources of language beyond their ordinary power, in order to communicate what language seems unable to communicate. In performing this minor miracle, poetry will often produce results that are difficult, and complicated enough to require close study. But to say that the idea of a poem can be communicated just as well through the simpler and more direct resources of prose is like saying that bread can be made of something less troublesome to procure than grain. The thought and feeling of a good poem depend upon the way in which they are expressed and cannot exist apart from the language of the poem.

Probably the most widespread and most harmful misconception about poetry is the belief that it is always overemotional and sentimental. It is true that the romantic tradition, which specialized in intense emotions and the praise of nature, has been dominant for many generations, and that it has been taken up by poets of little skill who write the sort of verse that is found in Sunday supplements and on Mother's Day cards. But popular verse of this kind has no more to do with real poetry than a hamburger prepared on a grill at a circus has to do with real cooking. Unfortunately the general public seems to form its idea of poetry on the evidence of these debased examples and concludes, quite correctly, that this sort of thing is not worth bothering about.

VARIETY IN POETRY

The belief that poetry is intrinsically sentimental or romantic is an obstacle that prevents many readers from liking or understanding the poems they encounter. The trouble is, that they look only for sentimentality when they read a poem; if some other feeling is expressed, they are unprepared for it and are likely to find the poem incoherent. Poetry, like every art, has a tremendous range of styles and subjects. It can be hard-boiled and bitter as well as sentimental, and it can be witty as well as rapturous; it can express fear or discouragement as well as ecstasy. The feelings of a poem need not even be exceptionally intense; many fine poems simply set out to express some familiar and ordinary experience in an authentic way.

Love is certainly one of the most hackneyed of poetic subjects. But the realism with which it is treated in this sonnet by Shakespeare will come as a surprise to the reader who believes that a poem about love must always be intense and idealistic.

SONNET 138

WILLIAM SHAKESPEARE (1564–1616)

When my love swears that she is made of truth,
I do believe her, though I know she lies,
That she might think me some untutored youth,
Unlearned in the world's false subtleties.
Thus vainly thinking that she thinks me young,   5
Although she knows my days are past the best,
Simply I credit her false-speaking tongue:
On both sides thus is simple truth suppressed.
But wherefore says she not she is unjust?
And wherefore say not I that I am old?   10
Oh, love's best habit is in seeming trust,
And age in love loves not to have years told.
Therefore I lie with her and she with me,
And in our faults by lies we flattered be.

7 *credit:* believe   9 *unjust:* unfaithful   11 *habit:* dress, costume

In this romance, we are candidly told, the woman is a liar, and the poet himself is too old. Yet each of the lovers pretends to be ignorant of the other's shortcoming. This situation could have been treated with pathos, but the tone of the poem is witty, ironic, even cynical. It concludes that falsehood has its value, not only for these lovers but in love in general, which, we are told, should be based on "seeming trust." The pun on the word "lie" in line 13 slyly suggests that love depends heavily on deception. Only a grossly imperceptive reader could mistake this sonnet for a romantic love poem; but even an attentive one will be puzzled by it if he expects all poems about love to be sentimental.

The attitudes expressed in poetry need not be pleasant, conventional, or even worthy. There are great poems whose greatness is accessible only if the reader accepts, at least for the moment, the spitefulness, sacrilege, or contempt for humanity they express. In "The Worms of History" (p. 351), for example, Robert Graves rewrites the Book of Genesis, saying that God died on the eighth day after the beginning of creation and was consumed by worms.

> Adam was buried in one grave with God
> And the worms ranged and ravaged in between.

Yet "The Worms of History" is more than a mere contradiction of the Biblical narrative, and even a reader whose religious sensibilities are offended by the apparent blasphemy of Graves's conception might well find, after considering the poem as a whole, that it is an imaginative way of expressing an idea that is far from impious. The point to be made here is that good poetry exploits the imagination; its effect lies in something new, some element of surprise. Consequently, it is important for the reader of poetry to avoid any preconceptions whatever about what a particular poem says or the way in which it says it.

At its best, poetry is a kind of exploration. It goes beyond the limits of our powers of expression, just as exploration goes beyond the limits of our knowledge of the earth's surface. When a poet has succeeded in saying something new in an intelligible way, or in saying something old in a way that makes it more accessible to our understanding, he has added to our capacity for experience, just as an explorer who discovers a new island does.

The comparison of the poet with the explorer helps to explain another fact about poetry. The poet, like the explorer, usually has to go far from the beaten track if he is to accomplish anything. As a result, the work of poets, especially significant ones, often seems difficult at first, just as a newly discovered country is hard to reach. It would be just as illogical to expect important poetry, especially if it is recent, to be immediately understandable, with little effort, as it would be to expect a place discovered by an explorer to have airline service, roads, hotels, and guides.

FURTHER READING

I. A. Richards, *Principles of Literary Criticism*, New York, 1950, Ch. XXI ("A Theory of Communication").

Eliseo Vivas, *Creation and Discovery*, New York, 1955, pp. 73–92 ("What Is a Poem?").

EXAMPLES

These examples illustrate the variety found in poetry through poems that express contrasting feelings about comparable subjects.

The first pair of poems is about the problem of breaking off a love affair. The attitudes they express are not entirely different, because each poet is satisfied that the affair is over and says so in a rather unemotional way. But there is enough of a difference to establish a contrast. Drayton begins with a mature willingness to accept the inevitable. But in the last six lines he reveals that he really prefers to continue the relationship and is hoping that his sweetheart will make it possible.

The speaker in Suckling's poem is not bothered by the pangs of love himself and can afford to take a joking attitude toward them. He is convinced that the love affair is impossible, because the aspiring lover is a hopeless case who will never interest the girl he loves. He concludes not with underlying hope, as Drayton does, but with an irritated impatience that suggests finality.

One might say that Drayton is trying to change reality, while Suckling is recommending that it be accepted. Drayton is perhaps overlooking the faults in himself or his sweetheart that have led to their disagreement; but Suckling suffers from no illusions about the unattractiveness of the young man and the indifference of the woman. Each of the poets has fixed his attention on different features of situations that are roughly similar, and thus has found reasons for adopting different feelings about them.

SINCE THERE'S NO HELP, COME LET US KISS AND PART

MICHAEL DRAYTON (1563–1631)

Since there's no help, come let us kiss and part.
  Nay, I have done, you get no more of me,
And I am glad, yea, glad with all my heart
  That thus so cleanly I myself can free;
Shake hands for ever, cancel all our vows,   5
  And when we meet at any time again,
Be it not seen in either of our brows
  That we one jot of former love retain.
Now at the last gasp of Love's latest breath,
  When, his pulse failing, Passion speechless lies,   10
When Faith is kneeling by his bed of death,
  And Innocence is closing up his eyes,
    Now if thou wouldst, when all have given him over,
    From death to life thou mightst him yet recover.

QUESTIONS

1) This poem obviously does not belong in the class of sentimental, gushing love poems. What evidence can be pointed out to show that the speaker is too realistic to be a victim of sentimentality?

2) Explain why it is not inconsistent for Drayton to allow the lover, who is characterized as sensible, to entertain the romantic hopes he expresses in the last six lines.

SONG

SIR JOHN SUCKLING (1609–1642)

Why so pale and wan, fond lover?
  Prithee, why so pale?
Will, when looking well can't move her,
  Looking ill prevail?
  Prithee, why so pale?   5

Why so dull and mute, young sinner?
    Prithee, why so mute?
Will, when speaking well can't win her,
    Saying nothing do't?
    Prithee, why so mute?   10

Quit, quit, for shame; this will not move,
    This cannot take her.
If of herself she will not love,
    Nothing can make her:
    The devil take her!   15

QUESTIONS

1) This poem is, of course, a satirical criticism of the conventional romantic belief, so often treated in poetry, that a lover must suffer in silence, admiring his lady from afar. What unromantic, common-sense recommendations does the poet make?

2) How does the advice in stanza 3 contradict that given in stanza 2?

3) Would you call this poem profound or moving? If neither, what is its value? Why has it remained famous since the early seventeenth century?

The two poems that follow are about unattractive natural scenery. However, after describing scenes that bear a strong general resemblance to each other, the poets move in opposite directions, arriving at different attitudes toward them, and expressing these attitudes in different ways.

NATURE'S QUESTIONING

THOMAS HARDY (1840–1928)

When I look forth at dawning, pool,
    Field, flock, and lonely tree,
    All seem to gaze at me
Like chastened children sitting silent in a school;

Their faces dulled, constrained, and worn,   5
    As though the master's ways
    Through the long teaching days
Had cowed them till their early zest was overborne.

Upon them stirs in lippings mere
    (As if once clear in call,   10
    But now scarce breathed at all)—
"We wonder, ever wonder, why we find us here!

"Has some Vast Imbecility,
    Mighty to build and blend,
    But impotent to tend,   15
Framed us in jest, and left us now to hazardry?

"Or come we of an Automaton
    Unconscious of our pains? . . .
    Or are we live remains
Of Godhead dying downwards, brain and eye now gone?   20

"Or is it that some high Plan betides,
    As yet not understood,
    Of Evil stormed by Good,
We the Forlorn Hope over which Achievement strides?"

Thus things around. No answerer I . . .   25
    Meanwhile the winds, and rains,
    And Earth's old glooms and pains
Are still the same, and Life and Death are neighbours nigh.

QUESTIONS

1) Explain the comparison in the first two stanzas. (See *simile* in the Glossary.)

2) What three theories about God's relation to the universe are suggested in stanzas 4, 5, and 6?

SPRING AND ALL

WILLIAM CARLOS WILLIAMS (1883-1965)

By the road to the contagious hospital
under the surge of the blue
mottled clouds driven from the
northeast—a cold wind. Beyond, the
waste of broad, muddy fields   5
brown with dried weeds, standing and fallen

patches of standing water
the scattering of tall trees

All along the road the reddish
purplish, forked, upstanding, twiggy   10
stuff of bushes and small trees
with dead, brown leaves under them
leafless vines—

Lifeless in appearance, sluggish
dazed spring approaches—   15

They enter the new world naked,
cold, uncertain of all
save that they enter. All about them
the cold, familiar wind—

Now the grass, tomorrow   20
the stiff curl of wildcarrot leaf
One by one objects are defined—
It quickens: clarity, outline of leaf

But now the stark dignity of
entrance—Still, the profound change   25
has come upon them: rooted, they
grip down and begin to awaken.

Questions

1) Where does the poet express his reaction toward the scene he is describing? How does this reaction differ from the attitude toward a similar scene expressed by Hardy in "Nature's Questioning"?

2) Both Hardy and Williams (in line 16–18) compare the features of the landscape to children. What quality do Williams' children seem to have that is lacking in Hardy's? How does the difference affect their attitudes?

3) The two poems offer contrasting views about nature, but they also employ very different ways of expressing these views. Compare these with each other.

4) Compare the vocabulary of the two poems.

5) Most of Williams' poem consists of fragmentary phrases rather than complete sentences. How does this compare with the sentence structure used by Hardy? What differences of effect result?

The subject of each of the following poems is something that is very familiar. Swift describes morning coming in the city, and Eberhart writes about a rock he holds in his hand. As in the last pair of examples, the contrast lies in the different directions the poets take in developing their subjects. Swift remains specific and objective, accumulating many details, while Eberhart enlarges the scope of his thinking to arrive at a general insight.

A DESCRIPTION OF THE MORNING

JONATHAN SWIFT (1667–1745)

Now hardly here and there a hackney-coach
Appearing, show'd the ruddy morn's approach.
Now Betty from her master's bed had flown,
And softly stole to discompose her own;
The slip-shod 'prentice from his master's door   5
Had par'd the dirt, and sprinkled round the floor.
Now Moll had whirl'd her mop with dextrous airs,
Prepar'd to scrub the entry and the stairs.
The youth with broomy stumps began to trace
The kennel-edge, where wheels had worn the place.   10
The small-coal man was heard with cadence deep,
Till drown'd in shriller notes of chimney-sweep:
Duns at his lordship's gate began to meet;
And brickdust Moll had screamed through half the street.
The turnkey now his flock returning sees,   15
Duly let out a-nights to steal for fees:
The watchful bailiffs take their silent stands,
And schoolboys lag with satchels in their hands.

10 *kennel:* gutter running along the street 13 *duns:* bill collectors 14 *brickdust Moll:* the adjective probably refers to her complexion 17 *bailiffs:* officers set to see that no property is removed from the houses of debtors

QUESTIONS

1) Does Swift regard the actions he has described as exceptional? If not, why has he written about them?

2) Are the details chosen at random? What prevailing impression does the poet seek to achieve?

3) Why have the jailkeepers let the criminals out of prison in line 16? What is the force of "duly"?

4) What is the relation between Betty's behavior in lines 3–4 and the action described in lines 5–10?

5) This poem is not conventionally "poetic." Some readers may feel that it is not poetry at all. How would you defend the point of view that it *is* poetry rather than prose?

RUMINATION

RICHARD EBERHART (1904–   )

When I can hold a stone within my hand
And feel time make it sand and soil, and see
The roots of living things grow in this land,
Pushing between my fingers flower and tree,
Then I shall be as wise as death,   5
For death has done this and he will
Do this to me, and blow his breath
To fire my clay, when I am still.

QUESTIONS

This chapter has made the point that "poetry works at the limits of knowledge, seeking to express the inexpressible." "Rumination" is an exceptionally good example of this.

1) In the first four lines, Eberhart makes a series of statements about the stone that move from the reasonable to the irrational. At what point does the poem go beyond common sense to something else?

2) What is the antecedent of "this" in line 6? Is it the same as "this" in line 7?

3) When the poet is "as wise as death," what will he know?

4) What process or occupation does the expression "fire my clay" in line 8 come from? What does this suggest about death, who is responsible for the firing?

5) Both "A Description of the Morning" and "Rumination" express generalized emotion, though the emotional element in the former is less obvious. Characterize these two different feelings. How do they differ in scope and intensity?

6) The generalized emotion in each of the poems begins with a

specific subject. What part do the actual subjects play in the conclusions reached by the poets? Which poet stays closer to his subject? Which subject provides better evidence for the conclusion that is reached or implied?

Language in Poetry 2

WORDS AND THEIR CONTEXT

The nature of poetry is closely related to that of its raw material, language. Insofar as language is flexible, expressive, or euphonious, it presents the poet with welcome resources. However, like every artistic medium, language has its limitations and its disadvantages. For example, it is comparatively indefinite in meaning, it is not very durable, and it is, in some ways, awkward and intractable. But in poetry, as in every art, the limitations of the medium provide the artist with his most exciting opportunities. Just as a sculptor may shape hard stone into the soft-looking curves of a body, or a painter may produce the effect of depth on a flat canvas, so a poet works with language to overcome its natural deficiencies. He does this not by using a special vocabulary of unusually high-powered words, but by using more or less ordinary words in special ways.

For one thing, he makes the most of the intrinsic expressiveness of words. Since a particularly vivid or colorful word can heighten the effect of a whole passage, the poet will often go to considerable trouble to make sure that he has chosen the word that has the most to contribute to his purpose. A clear example of such an effort occurs in Shelley's description of the ocean bottom as

> The sea-blooms and the *oozy* woods which wear
> The sapless foliage of the ocean.

Obviously, "oozy" is in a class by itself as an expressive adjective; probably no other word that approximates its meaning approaches it in vividness. This does not mean that it is a perfect choice, however. The objection might be made that it calls attention to itself, much as an unusually bright color in a painting would, and thereby detracts somewhat from the effect of the passage as a whole. There is a more natural and less conspicuous example of the skillful choice of words in Coleridge's description of the ghost ship that appears in "The Ancient Mariner":

> Almost upon the western wave
> Rested the broad bright Sun;
> When that strange shape *drove* suddenly
> Betwixt us and the Sun.

It is difficult to account for the effectiveness of "drove" here. Perhaps it has just the right suggestion of swift, but indefinite movement and independent life, or perhaps it contrasts subtly with "rested" in the previous line. The fact that it does operate powerfully can be appreciated if we try other words, such as "moved," "sailed," or "thrust" in its place. None of them makes a satisfactory substitute.

The virtue of "the right word" in poetry is generally recognized, and the reader should have no difficulty in collecting examples of the felicitous choice of words by poets. Emily Dickinson's description of her feeling at seeing a snake as "*zero* at the bone," T. S. Eliot's "I should have been a pair of *ragged* claws / *Scuttling* across the floors of silent seas," W. B. Yeats' ". . . what rough beast, its hour come round at last, / *Slouches* towards Bethlehem to be born?" are good examples of the resourceful and imaginative use of vocabulary in poetry. It is obvious, however, that the merit of a passage cannot depend upon a particular word alone. The "right" word is right only for a certain context. The words that appear in our examples (with the exception of "oozy") are not remarkable in themselves. Attributing the effectiveness of the passages in which they appear to the expressive power of these words is imagining that the rest of the poem was ineffective until the word was added to it. But the reverse is true. The words themselves are most expressive only when they appear in their contexts. The poet's real achievement lies not so much in choosing the right word as in creating a context for which there is some one word that is right. His problem with regard to vocabulary is not merely finding words that are vivid or expressive in themselves, but choosing words that fit in with the purpose of his poem as a whole. It is not the word itself, but the way in which it is used that counts.

For the fact is that any given word is flexible enough to be used in a variety of ways. One of the peculiarities of language that present the poet with both complications and opportunities is the fact that an individual word is likely to have a wide range of meaning. The word "animal," for example, stands for a very large number of possible objects; the possible meanings are narrowed somewhat if the animal is described as a "bird"; and the name of a particular variety of bird, such as "peacock" or "swallow" has a still narrower range, though from the ornithologist's point of view, these terms are still quite indefinite. Practically speaking, the wide area of meaning attached to most words is an advantage, for if we had to have a different word for every possible meaning, we would need tremendous vocabularies, and no one word in them would be used very often. If words are so indefinite in their meanings, how do we manage to communicate efficiently with them? The answer is that, in practice, the comparatively vague dictionary meaning of a word is focused more sharply by its context. The significance of a word depends on its environment. Or, to put it another way, the word is like a relatively shapeless lump of clay which is molded into a more definite form by the pressure of the words around it.

This important fact is easily demonstrated. If someone approached you with the invitation, "Let's play," you would not know what you were being asked to do, or whether you were expected to get a tennis racket or go to the piano. But the speaker, by adding something to this one verb, could make it take on any of a large number of meanings. "Let's play tennis," "Let's play Mozart," "Let's play house," "Let's play dead," or even, in an obsolete use, "Let's play *Othello*" are some of the widely varying possibilities. Ordinary prose writing involves using words in this way to channel each other's meaning in particular directions. One word chops off part of the meaning of another, thus narrowing and focusing it. In poetry this same process is carried to an extreme; the words are whetted against each other, so that their edges of meaning are made far sharper than usual.

Let us observe the operation of these effects in this sonnet by Milton:

WHEN I CONSIDER HOW MY LIGHT IS SPENT

JOHN MILTON (1608–1674)

When I consider how my light is spent
  Ere half my days, in this dark world and wide,
  And that one talent which is death to hide,
  Lodged with me useless, though my soul more bent
To serve therewith my Maker, and present   5
  My true account, lest he returning chide;
  "Doth God exact day-labor, light denied?"
  I fondly ask; but Patience to prevent
That murmur, soon replies, "God doth not need
  Either man's work or his own gifts; who best   10
  Bear his mild yoke, they serve him best. His state
Is kingly. Thousands at his bidding speed
  And post o'er land and ocean without rest:
  They also serve who only stand and wait."

Ordinarily, the word "spend" has a number of loosely related meanings. It can mean to pay out money, to devote time to something, to pass time with someone, to waste something, or to use something up, not necessarily wastefully. In the first line, it is clear that Milton means "spent" in the sense of used up, not necessarily wastefully. It is also clear, however, that this meaning is determined by the word's context. If the line had read "When I consider how my money is spent," or "When I consider how my years are spent," or "When I consider that I have spent my sight on useless work," the word would have different connotations in each case.

Milton has done no more with "spent" than put it into a context that limits it to one of its recognized meanings. With "light," however, he has used the same method to accomplish something a little more adventurous. It is clear from the title of the sonnet and from the poem itself that by "light" Milton means his eyesight. This is, of course, not its usual meaning. The context has, in effect, transformed the word into a *metaphor* (see Glossary) and extended its meaning into a comparatively unfamiliar area for the purposes of the poem.

Another interesting verbal problem is represented by the word "talent" in line 3. It means, of course, Milton's gift for poetry, which he feared his blindness would prevent him from putting to use. But the word, together with the warning that it is "death to hide," is an allusion to the familiar parable in Matthew XV, where the "talent" is a sum of money that the servant is punished for failing to invest. Which of these two meanings did Milton wish the reader to have in mind? The answer is, both. It is hard to avoid the conclusion that he deliberately took advantage of the two meanings of the word, each appropriate to his idea in a different way, to gain the poetic effect called *ambiguity* (see Glossary; for a fuller discussion of ambiguity, see the section later in this chapter).

Context works both ways. Just as the rest of a line is the context of a particular word, and influences its meaning, so an individual word is part of the context of the words around it and has an effect on them. To consider another possible variation, in Milton's line "When I consider how my days are spent," "spent" is used to mean simply "passed the time," and this in turn changes the meaning of the clause as a whole to "When I think about how I occupy my time."

This delicate reciprocal relationship between the individual words and the meaning of a passage as a whole is characteristic of poetry. An example may help to clarify the point. Hardy, in the following poem, describes a depressing, cloudy landscape he saw on the last day of the nineteenth century.

THE DARKLING THRUSH

THOMAS HARDY (1840–1928)

I leant upon a coppice gate
　　When Frost was spectre-gray,
And Winter's dregs made desolate
　　The weakening eye of day.

1 *coppice:* grove of trees

The tangled bine-stems scored the sky   5
    Like strings of broken lyres,
And all mankind that haunted nigh
    Had sought their household fires.

The land's sharp features seemed to be
    The Century's corpse outleant,   10
His crypt the cloudy canopy,
    The wind his death-lament.
The ancient pulse of germ and birth
    Was shrunken hard and dry,
And every spirit upon earth   15
    Seemed fervorless as I.

At once a voice arose among
    The bleak twigs overhead
In a full-hearted evensong
    Of joy illimited;   20
An aged thrush, frail, gaunt and small,
    In blast-beruffled plume,
Had chosen thus to fling his soul
    Upon the growing gloom.

So little cause for carolings   25
    Of such ecstatic sound
Was written on terrestrial things
    Afar or nigh around,
That I could think there trembled through
    His happy good-night air   30
Some blessed Hope, whereof he knew
    And I was unaware.

                              DECEMBER 1900.

    20 *illimited:* unlimited

In this scene, with its "sharp features," Hardy saw the death
of the century that was passing. The words "spectre-gray,"
"corpse," "crypt," and "death-lament" tell us that the land seemed
dead. The people in the area "haunted" it, as if they were ghosts.
So pervasive was Hardy's sense of dissolution that he saw it reflected in every detail. The branches were like broken lyre strings,

and their lines "scored" the sky, as if they were the angry marks of a knife. The weak light was "Winter's dregs." Even the thrush was fragile looking and had been shaken up by the wind. But his song is described with words that have strong suggestions of life and energy, such as "joy," "fling," and "ecstatic." The contrast between the gloom of the landscape and the happy song of the bird forms a *paradox* (see Glossary), and leads the poet to the speculation of the last two lines. Without the idea that the landscape and the vast stretch of time it represents are lifeless, the bird's song would seem neither as anomalous nor as suggestive as it does.

Poets occasionally go to considerable lengths to make the reader aware of the exactness of meaning they intend their language to have. Matthew Arnold, in the famous last line of his "Dover Beach" (p. 291), described the world as a depressing place "Where *ignorant* armies clash by night." Arnold's poem implies that "ignorant," which is certainly odd in its place, is to be understood in an unusually strict sense; Arnold is concerned, not with general ignorance, but with ignorance of the perception the poem as a whole is expressing. Josephine Miles, describing a lady in a doctor's waiting-room, says,

> She was pale but not because she was frightened.
> She was afraid.

thus making "afraid" refer clearly to a profound emotional experience, and not, as it usually does, to something transient and superficial.

EXAMPLES. Shakespeare, "Sonnet 30," p. 173; Donne, "A Hymn to God the Father," p. 179; Shelly, "Lines: When the Lamp Is Shattered," p. 258; Keats, "On Seeing the Elgin Marbles," p. 261; Tennyson, *In Memoriam*, XV, p. 270; Whitman, "The Dalliance of the Eagles," p. 287; Emily Dickinson, "A Certain Slant of Light," p. 295; Hopkins, "Pied Beauty," p. 304; Frost, "Desert Places," p. 311; Stevens, "Anecdote of the Jar," p. 318; Muir, "The Window," p. 334; Roethke, "Epidermal Macabre," p. 367; Shapiro, "Buick," p. 375.

CONNOTATIONS

These sharpenings and intensifications of meaning are possible because each word has, as we have observed, a large number of potential meanings. But words have not merely many meanings, but different *kinds* of meaning as well. For our purposes it will be enough to divide these kinds of meaning into two, denotation and connotation. This familiar division of the semantic properties of words simply means that most words refer to some object or experience and also suggest an emotional attitude toward it on the part of the speaker which he normally intends his hearer to share. For example, the denotation of the word "puppy" is simply a young dog; but the word carries with it the definite suggestion that the speaker's attitude is affectionate and amused. On the other hand, the word "mongrel," which might be applied by the same speaker to the same dog in a different situation, suggests contempt. Connotations are the emotional auras of words. They vary in force, but very few ordinary words are entirely without them. "Mother" and "father" may seem to be matter-of-fact, unemotional terms, but when they are contrasted with the word "parents," they appear to have warm and vivid connotations.

One of the distinguishing characteristics of poetry is its use of the connotative powers of words. Unlike the prose writer, who is mainly concerned with the denotative capacities of language, and occupies himself with the connotations of his words only to the extent necessary to keep them in order, the poet takes the denotations of the words he uses for granted and concentrates on exploiting their connotative qualities. In fact when words are used in poetry they generally undergo a subtle and curious transformation; their connotative meaning tends to dominate the denotation. This sometimes occurs in prose. "Childish" and "childlike" are certainly synonyms if their denotations alone are considered; they have the same meaning, "resembling a child." But "childish" obviously carries with it a connotation of vigorous disapproval and "childlike" is at least mildly favorable or sympathetic. Further, these connotations are so important within the words that they tend to monopolize their meaning and erase their objective or denotative qualities.

The importance of connotation in the language of poetry can best be demonstrated by two examples, one that uses words with very obvious emotional suggestions and one that makes a subtler and quieter use of connotation.

> Bottomless vales and boundless floods,
> And chasms, and caves, and Titan woods, . . .
> Mountains toppling evermore
> Into seas without a shore;
> Seas that restlessly aspire,
> Surging, unto skies of fire.

The effect of this passage from Poe's "Dream Land" is derived not so much from the landscape it portrays as from the emotional impact of such words as "bottomless," "boundless," "evermore," and "surging." The poet is seeking to create an impression of great size and vitality, and he has chosen words that have suitable connotations, nearly disregarding their denotations. In fact, if we insist on interpreting the words strictly according to their denotations, the poem approaches incoherence. Vales cannot actually be 'bottomless" and "floods" cannot be "boundless." It is hard to see how mountains can topple "evermore," even if they are very large, and it is also hard to see how they can topple into seas "without a shore." Poetry that makes elaborate use of connotative language need not become involved in contradictions of this kind; one would say that Poe was using words carelessly and that the result is a poor poem.

The diction of the following poem, on the other hand, is carefully chosen to produce a subtle and highly individual effect.

A LIGHT EXISTS IN SPRING

EMILY DICKINSON (1830–1886)

> A Light exists in Spring
> Not present on the Year
> At any other period—
> When March is scarcely here

A Color stands abroad   5
On Solitary Fields
That Science cannot overtake
But Human Nature feels.

It waits upon the Lawn,
It shows the furthest Tree   10
Upon the furthest Slope you know
It almost speaks to you.

Then as Horizons step
Or Noons report away
Without the Formula of sound   15
It passes and we stay—

A quality of loss
Affecting our Content
As Trade had suddenly encroached
Upon a Sacrament.   20

It is interesting to observe that the denotations, or actual meanings, of some of the words in this poem are less important than
their connotations. The conclusion turns upon the contrasting
connotations of "Trade" in line 19 and "Sacrament" in line 20;
the former is regarded as being materialistic and unworthy of the
spirituality of the latter. But there is a subtler use of connotation
in the words "step," "report away," and "Formula" (that is, a set
phrase) in lines 13–15. These words suggest that the elements of
nature which are being discussed are living people. (See *Personification* in the Glossary.)

But the last two expressions also suggest that the relationship
between nature and the poet is distant and formal. Noons "report
away" as an employee or a pupil might send a note to say he was
going to be absent. The light that is the subject of the poem de-
parts without the equivalent for the polite, impersonal phrase of
farewell that might be expected of it. Through their connotations
the words suggest that the poet and nature are not on very intimate
terms. These connotations are essential to the poem as a whole,
which expresses the feeling, characteristic of Emily Dickinson,
that though nature is a valuable source of comfort, man must not
presume upon his relationship with it.

The poet's responsibilities with respect to connotation are not, as many readers think, merely a matter of picking strongly connotative words. He must be careful, first of all, to avoid words that have unsuitable connotations. Unless he does, he may commit such blunders as the one Keats was guilty of when he addressed the poet Milton as "Chief of *organic* numbers!" (by "numbers" he meant meter, or poetry). By "organic" Keats intended, of course, the meaning "organ-like," but the connotation "resembling an organism," which existed in Keats's day and has become more prominent today, is just plausible enough in the context to cause confusion and unintended amusement. But the words that have the strongest suitable connotations are not always, nor even usually, the best. Writing poetry is not merely a matter of saying "agonizing" instead of "painful," "intoxicating" instead of "sweet," or "ecstatic" instead of "happy." Discriminating poets and readers of poetry are embarrassed by such excesses of connotation. Good poetry is more likely to use connotation to improve the exactness of language, to focus more precisely on the feelings it is expressing than denotative language enables it to do.

For example, the effect of the famous line "Life is a tale told by an idiot" is due in large part to the exactness produced by the connotations of "tale" and especially, "idiot." What equivalent expressions are there for "a tale told by an idiot"? We could say "a confused tale, an incoherent tale, a senseless, garbled, meaningless tale." But it becomes obvious that no collection of adjectives can approach the effect of Shakespeare's phrase. The idiot's recital is not merely a babble of incoherent sounds, but "a tale"; that is, it has some recognizable meaning and consecutiveness. But since it is an idiot's tale, it has only enough sense to be stupid. Its stupidity is offensive, it makes the hearer grit his teeth with irritation, but it is also pitiful. Macbeth is not merely saying that life is senseless, therefore; he is also suggesting that it is senseless in a way that arouses this particularly harrowing mixture of feelings. And Shakespeare's phrase is more than an emphatic way of saying that life is meaningless; it also brings a fairly complicated attitude to bear on that fact. It achieves through connotation a precision that could not be achieved with the same economy and force of effect through denotation.

The poet can make connotations work for him in a number of ways. Probably the commonest and most familiar is that in which the connotative qualities of the words simply emphasize and reinforce the stated meaning. Describing the statues in a chapel, Keats wrote:

> The sculptur'd dead, on each side, seem to freeze.

The connotations of "freeze," which include coldness, stiffness, and motionlessness are eminently appropriate to the subject; they add no new meaning, but instead make the denotation vivid. However, poetry may also use words in such a way as to make them carry connotations they would not ordinarily have. This is poetry's most distinctive and most characteristic use of words. It is one of the ways in which poetry seeks to overcome the natural limitations of language. In a poem about the unnecessary and artificial pains he took with his early writing, "Jordan (II)" (p. 188), George Herbert describes his action as

> Decking the sense as if it were to sell.

The usually innocent word "sell" here suggests the vanity and superficiality of the young poet's attempts at ornamentation and the experienced poet's gentle amusement at it. Richard Eberhart, in "The Groundhog" (p. 355), describes how, in the processes of decay going on in the body of a dead groundhog, he perceives the great power of nature at work.

> His form began its senseless change,
> And made my senses waver dim
> Seeing nature ferocious in him.
> Inspecting close his maggots' might
> And seething cauldron of his being,

"Might" generally means obvious, arbitrary strength. By using it for the slow, insistent sort of strength the maggots possess, Eberhart brings their destructive power sharply before us, making us realize that in spite of their apparent insignificance, they represent a great force. Wallace Stevens, in "Peter Quince at the Clavier" (p. 320), uses what may be described as a built-in device for extending the ordinary meanings of words. The speaker of the poem, commenting upon the fact that musical sounds have their counterparts in the spirit, presents the reader with the equation "Music is feeling, then, not sound." He then follows this principle in narrating some of the episodes in the tale of Susanna and the Elders, describing the feelings the people experience in terms of musical equivalents. Thus, the old men who see the beautiful girl in her bath feel "the basses of their being throb" and their blood "pulse pizzicati." For the purposes of the poem, the musical terms are successfully made to suggest emotions.

Another way in which a poet may use connotation to augment the ordinary resources of language is by making his words carry an undertone that expresses a feeling contradictory to their denotation. Hence, by saying two contradictory things at once, the poem really expresses, through irony, a third meaning. A subtle, though clear, example occurs in Keats's "Hyperion," where the poet, describing the decline of the Titan Hyperion says that when he smelled sacrificial incense, instead of finding it sweet, he

> . . . took
> Savour of poisonous brass and metal sick.

"Savour" usually connotes something tasty and delicious; in using it, Keats is recalling the odor Hyperion expects in the incense; this expectation, combined with what he actually does smell, effectively conveys the sharp edge of his disappointment.

Good examples of ironic connotation occur in the following poem:

THE MALDIVE SHARK

HERMAN MELVILLE (1819–1891)

About the Shark, phlegmatical one,
Pale sot of the Maldive sea,
The sleek little pilot fish, azure and slim,
How alert in attendance be.
From his saw-pit of mouth, from his charnel of maw   5
They have nothing of harm to dread,
But liquidly glide on his ghastly flank

Or before his Gorgonian head;
Or lurk in the port of serrated teeth
In white triple tiers of glittering gates,   10
And there find a haven when peril's abroad,
An asylum in jaws of the Fates!
They are friends; and friendly they guide him to prey,
Yet never partake of the treat—
Eyes and brains of the dotard lethargic and dull,   15
Pale ravener of horrible meat.

8 *Gorgonian:* the Gorgons were legendary women whose terrible faces turned those who saw them into stone

In "ravener" and "horrible" (line 16), Melville is simply using words with strong connotations which harmonize with their denotations. But there are ironies in such words as "phlegmatical" (line 1), "sot" (line 2), and "haven" (line 11). Perhaps the most interesting of the many interesting words in this poem is "treat" (line 14). At first it simply seems to be an inappropriate way of referring to the shark's "horrible meat." But what Melville is doing is adopting the condescending language which the intelligent pilot fish can be imagined as using in talking to the dull shark. By bringing together the patronizing, pretended naïveté of "treat" and the later description of the shark's food, Melville effects a powerful condemnation of the simpering, detached cruelty of the pilot fish.

EXAMPLES. Shakespeare, Sonnet 71 ("No longer mourn for me when I am dead"), p. 173; Wordsworth, "Composed Upon Westminster Bridge," p. 239; Tennyson, *In Memoriam*, LXXXVI ("Sweet after showers, ambrosial air"), p. 271; Poe, "Israfel," p. 268; Whitman, "To a Locomotive in Winter," p. 287; Emily Dickinson, "After great pain a formal feeling comes," p. 294; Owen, "Anthem for Doomed Youth," p. 347; Shapiro, "Buick," p. 375.

AMBIGUITY

We have been saying that the poet uses context and connotation to sharpen or narrow the meaning of his words. However, in the examples involving "talent" and "treat" it is hard to say which of two possible meanings is the "real" one. In these cases the poet has not reduced the word to a single meaning, but has exploited or stressed two distinct parts of the word's range of meaning. In his *Poetics*, Aristotle, discussing the problems of interpretation that sometimes arise in poetry, advised "when a word seems to involve some inconsistency of meaning, we should consider how many senses it may bear in the particular passage." But the modern critic, William Empson, has shown that this question may be appropriate even when there is no difficulty of interpretation. Occasionally a word or expression *may* logically have more than one meaning. This is the interesting effect known technically as *ambiguity*. In prose, ambiguity of language is generally both a symptom and a cause of confusion; but in poetry it is a particularly subtle device for enriching the expressive power of language, a way of saying two things at once.

Our first example, though it occurs in a prose passage, is an excellent illustration of the poetic use of ambiguity. In Shakespeare's *Hamlet*, the Prince, toward the end of his famous speech about the double nature of man, declares "Man delights not me." When the two courtiers to whom he is speaking smile at each other, Hamlet hastily adds, "No, nor woman neither, though by your smiling you seem to say so." Here Hamlet is attributing two different, though overlapping senses to his one use of the word "man." It is obvious from his speech that originally he meant "mankind," the human race in general, including women. After he has seen the smiles of his friends, he tries to guess the joke by adding "woman" to "man" thus indicating that he originally used the word to mean "males" only.

Two interesting examples of ambiguity are to be found in the following poem.

THE GIFT OUTRIGHT

ROBERT FROST (1875–1964)

The land was ours before we were the land's.
She was our land more than a hundred years
Before we were her people. She was ours
In Massachusetts, in Virginia,

But we were England's, still colonials, 5
Possessing what we still were unpossessed by,
Possessed by what we now no more possessed.
Something we were withholding made us weak
Until we found out that it was ourselves
We were witholding from our land of living, 10
And forthwith found salvation in surrender.
Such as we were we gave ourselves outright
(The deed of gift was many deeds of war)
To the land vaguely realizing westward,
But still unstoried, artless, unenhanced, 15
Such as she was, such as she would become.

In line 13, the one in parentheses, the first "deed" is (as the second "deed" shows) a pun, meaning both "an action" and "a proof of ownership." Frost intends both meanings to operate, as a way of showing that fighting for the land gave the right to own it. In lines 6 and 7 he also exploits the dual meaning of the word "possess," though here he is more concerned with keeping the two meanings separate than with having the word mean both at once. The two meanings are, of course, "to own something" and "to be dominated by a passion." An understanding of the two lines, with their repetition of the same word, involves a clear awareness of how Frost shuttles back and forth between these two meanings.

Some highly sophisticated examples of ambiguity, involving well-controlled *irony* (see Glossary) are offered in the following poem.

THE HABIT OF PERFECTION

GERARD MANLEY HOPKINS (1845–1889)

Elected Silence, sing to me
And beat upon my whorlèd ear,
Pipe me to pastures still and be
The music that I care to hear.

Shape nothing, lips; be lovely-dumb: 5
It is the shut, the curfew sent

From there where all surrenders come
Which only makes you eloquent.

Be shellèd, eyes, with double dark
And find the uncreated light: 10
This ruck and reel which you remark
Coils, keeps, and teases simple sight.

Palate, the hutch of tasty lust,
Desire not to be rinsed with wine:
The can must be so sweet, the crust   15
So fresh that come in fasts divine!

Nostrils, your careless breath that spend
Upon the stir and keep of pride,
What relish shall the censers send
Along the sanctuary side!   20

O feel-of-primrose hands, O feet
That want the yield of plushy sward,
But you shall walk the golden street
And you unhouse and house the Lord.

And, Poverty, be thou the bride   25
And now the marriage feast begun,
And lily-coloured clothes provide
Your spouse not laboured-at nor spun.

11 *ruck:* crowd *reel:* a reeling motion 12
coils: encircles 18 *keep:* maintenance 24 *unhouse and house the Lord:* that is, take out
and put back the implements of the mass.

This poem expresses the ascetic doctrine that the self-denial of
a priest is superior to sensuous experience. But in explaining the
beauty of renouncing pleasure, Hopkins uses the language of
pleasure. Silence, muteness, darkness, and so on, he is saying, are
(or should be) more pleasing than music, speech, and light. The
question of ambiguity arises in connection with such words as
"music" and "hear" in line 4. In one sense, they have their ordinary meanings, but it is startling to realize that, in Hopkins' poem,

they *also* mean, respectively, "silence" and "not hear." The same ambiguity of contraries is found in "eloquent" in line 8, "light" in line 10, and in the diction of the fourth stanza.

EXAMPLES. Shakespeare, Sonnet 146 ("Poor soul, the centre of my sinful earth"), p. 174; Donne, "Batter my heart," p. 181; Herbert, "The Pulley," p. 188; Lovelace, "To Lucasta, Going to the Wars," p. 201; Robinson, "The Sheaves," p. 317; Miles, "Monkey," p. 374; Thomas, "A Refusal to Mourn the Death, By Fire, of a Child in London," p. 382.

TONE AND LEVELS OF LANGUAGE

Another aspect of language that has some importance in poetry is the fact that words have varying degrees of formality; they belong to different levels of usage, such as slang, colloquial, formal, and the like. These levels are not very clearly defined, for most words can belong to any of them. Such words as "man," "tree," "bridge," "hand," are appropriate on almost any level of usage. However, there are words which always create an informal atmosphere because they are peculiar to slang, dialect, or highly informal language; examples would be "whippersnapper," "nag," "pup," "two bits." On the other hand, certain words are appropriate only to the language of formal relationships; such words as "matrimony," "monograph," "scrutinize," "iconoclast" would be out of place in any speech or writing that was not fairly serious and formal. The atmosphere that words create in this way can be an important element of the poet's feeling about his subject and can play an important part in his poem.

Throughout the history of English literature, and in the literature of most modern languages as well, there has been considerable difference of opinion about the level of usage appropriate for poetry. It used to be felt that the language of ordinary speech was inappropriate, and that poetry should avoid undignified language and confine itself to noble and exalted diction. Milton and certain eighteenth-century poets carried this policy so far that they produced, through the use of archaisms, circumlocutions, and Latinate grammatical constructions, an artificial poetic language that

had little to do with other kinds of English. Milton's description
of Adam and Eve going to bed

> . . . into their inmost bower
> Handed they went; and, eased the putting off
> These troublesome disguises which we wear,
> Straight side by side were laid; nor turned, I ween,
> Adam from his fair spouse; nor Eve the rites
> Mysterious of connubial love refused . . .

was indirect and old-fashioned in its language, even in Milton's
day, but it did have the loftiness and dignity necessary for an epic
poem like *Paradise Lost*.

At the end of the eighteenth century, Wordsworth rebelled
against artificiality of language in poetry and argued that its
vocabulary should resemble the simple, straightforward language
of country people. Actually, poets had been trying to achieve
more naturalness in their language for a long time before Wordsworth stated his arguments for it. As a result of this development,
Wordsworth could write in words and constructions so simple
that a hundred years before his time they would have seemed a
threat to the dignity of poetry.

> I wandered lonely as a cloud
> That floats on high o'er vales and hills,
> When all at once I saw a crowd,
> A host, of golden daffodils;
> Beside the lake, beneath the trees,
> Fluttering and dancing in the breeze.

Wordsworth's doctrine became increasingly influential, but
neither he nor most of the poets who were influenced by it limited
themselves to natural language of this kind. It is certainly true
that extreme simplicity of language is no longer felt to be unsuitable for poetry, as these lines by Robert Frost show.

> Whose woods these are I think I know.
> His house is in the village though;
> He will not see me stopping here
> To watch his woods fill up with snow.

But another, and perhaps even more important, result of Words-worth's teaching was the feeling that poetry need not be limited either to the very natural or the very artificial level of language, but can vary its level according to its subject, and even make use of the differing formality of words, in much the same way as it makes use of connotations, to improve and reinforce its power of expression. For example, Archibald MacLeish in his poem "Ein-stein" subtly criticizes science as an interpreter of life by describ-ing simple facts in inappropriately formal language.

> And he terminates
> In shoes which bearing up against the sphere
> Attract his concentration. . . .

On the other hand, it is extremely common for modern poetry to deal with serious matters in the casual, almost offhand style of conversation. The conversational tone seems to say that the poet assumes no particular prophetic role, does not set himself apart from his reader, but instead adopts an attitude of communicating something ordinary and familiar. When the idea of the poem turns out to be extraordinary, novel, or charged with emotion, its effect is subtly increased by contrast with the manner in which it is ex-pressed. For example, W. H. Auden points out in "Musée des Beaux Arts" (p. 361) that the suffering of one man is always ac-companied by indifference somewhere nearby, and he cites a painting that illustrates the situation, introducing it in language that imitates ordinary conversation:

> In Brueghel's *Icarus*, for instance: how everything turns away
> Quite leisurely from the disaster; the ploughman may
> Have heard the splash, the forsaken cry,
> But for him it was not an important failure; . . .

Linguistic elements that mold or refine literal meaning, such as connotations and levels of usage, establish the general quality of a poem that is called *tone*. The tone may be described as the mood dominating the poem or the attitude toward both the subject and the audience that the poem adopts. Often it is an important, or even an essential, part of the meaning of the poem as a whole. The reader who fails to grasp the irony of the lines from MacLeish's "Einstein" quoted above or the understatement of Auden's "Museé des Beaux Arts" would misunderstand these poems. Similarly, the first part of Marvell's "To His Coy Mistress" (p. 204), which expands the idea of "This coyness, lady, were no crime," is not meant literally, but is really a preparation for a statement of the opposite point of view.

A wide variety of tones and combinations of tones is possible in poetry. Irony, jocularity, bitterness, ardor, indignation, and speculativeness are among the most common. Since they may sometimes be found in incongruous or inconsistent combinations, good reading requires an alertness to possible shifts of mood or tone. These changes, like the tone itself, are projected through the words and their connotations.

A special handling of tone is found in the form called *dramatic monologue*. In poems of this class, the poet speaks through a character, and the whole poem is the speech of the character. Usually the main aims of this form are characterization of the speaker, and the expression of a point of view. When the poet simply uses the speaker as a medium for expressing his own ideas, the dramatic monologue is not radically different from other poems. But in most dramatic monologues, the point of view expressed is that of the character, not that of the poet at all, and it is presented in such a way that the reader is called upon to take a critical attitude toward it. This introduces a fairly complex situation. We cannot accept what the character tells us at face value—apart, that is, from ordinary facts—but must understand that the poet's real meaning is something that lurks behind what is being said. Thus, when Browning's Bishop quotes the Bible in the first line of his dramatic monologue, saying, "Vanity, saith the preacher, vanity!" we cannot accept this simply as evidence of his piety, but must wait until we can consider the dramatic situation as a whole (see "The Bishop Orders His Tomb," p. 282). In the course of the monologue, the Bishop reveals, through his own speech, that he has never freed himself from vanity, and that even on his deathbed he remains one of the greediest and most sensuous of men; within this context, the virtuous remarks he occasionally makes reveal not virtue but hypocrisy. Thus, we may find that in a dramatic monologue not a single word or idea is to be accepted directly, but must be carefully interpreted as the expression of the character who speaks the monologue.

We have been seeing that poetry's way of taking advantage of the various kinds of meaning language may have makes it difficult to do justice to its full significance. Certain linguistic facts complicate the task of reading poetry even further. The meanings of words do not remain constant, but are continually changing. Hence, while it is often difficult enough to gauge the exact shade of meaning and connotation of a particular word in contemporary poetry, the problem is intensified in poetry of the past. Every reader of Shakespeare has encountered words or expressions whose meanings have shifted, or which are no longer in use. The older a poem is, the more likely is it to present vocabulary difficulties of this kind. This does not mean that such poetry is indecipherable; but it does mean that it cannot be read intelligently unless allowances are made for changes in the use of words. Edmund Waller discusses this subject in his poem, "Of English Verse" (p. 192).

Often a word will survive in the same or nearly the same spelling into modern English, but with a changed meaning. This confronts the reader with a deceptive situation, for the word seems familiar to him, and he may not see why he is unable to understand the passage as a whole. A good example of this phenomenon occurs in one of Spenser's sonnets where the poet says, after expressing a hope that his loved one will some day pay some attention to him, "Till then I wander, *carefull*, comfortless. . . ." Obviously, Spenser means "careful" in an older sense which has now died out, "full of sorrow." Similarly, in the first book of *Paradise Lost*, Satan asks his army

> . . . have ye chos'n this place
> After the toil of battle to repose
> Your wearied *virtue*. . .

One of the usual meanings of "virtue" in Milton's day was "strength," but it is hard to recognize that meaning in it today. Change of meaning is commonplace in language, and constitutes a problem in prose as well as poetry. Very few words keep the same meaning after hundreds of years of use; as it happens, some of the words commonest in poetry of the past, such as *wit, art, dear, nature, humor, spleen, awful,* and *meat* are very old today, and hence have undergone the inevitable changes of meaning.

These meaning shifts and other linguistic phenomena are the subject of careful study by scholars. The results of their work are presented as aids to the reader in footnotes and glossaries that often accompany poetry published in scholarly editions, and they also appear in special dictionaries. The reader need not conclude that the poetry of such writers as Milton and Shakespeare will always be as difficult as it seems at first. One quickly becomes accustomed to slight departures from present-day English. In addition, the excitement of entering into the thoughts of great men of another time usually stimulates the reader's imagination, so that he can make excellent guesses about the meaning of unfamiliar words and expressions.

EXAMPLES. Differences in language level are illustrated in: "Edward," p. 163; Browning, "Soliloquy of the Spanish Cloister," p. 277; Swinburne, "A Lyke-Wake Song," p. 296; Williams, "The Poor," p. 323; Pound, from *Canto LXXXI*, p. 326. Examples of dramatic monologues: Tennyson, "Tithonus," p. 274; Browning, "The Bishop Orders His Tomb," p. 282; Eliot, "The Love Song of J. Alfred Prufrock," p. 339; Betjeman, "In Westminster Abbey," p. 387.

FURTHER READING

R. P. Blackmur, *Language as Gesture,* New York, 1952, pp. 3–23.

Robert Langbaum, *The Poetry of Experience,* New York, 1957, pp. 75–108 ("The Dramatic Monologue").

I. A. Richards, *The Philosophy of Rhetoric,* New York, 1936, pp. 47–57 ("The Interinanimation of Words").

Allen Tate, *Reason in Madness,* New York, 1941, pp. 62–81 ("Tension in Poetry").

Examples

FROM AMORETTI

Sonnet 79

EDMUND SPENSER (1522–1599)

Men call you fair, and you do credit it,
For that yourself ye daily such do see;
But the true fair, that is the gentle wit,
And virtuous mind, is much more praised of me.
For all the rest, however fair it be,   5
Shall turn to nought, and lose that glorious hue;
But only that is permanent and free
From frail corruption that doth flesh ensue.
That is true beauty; that doth argue you
To be divine and born of heavenly seed,   10
Derived from that fair Spirit, from whom all true
And perfect beauty did at first proceed.
He only fair, and what he fair hath made;
All other fair, like flowers, untimely fade.

1 *credit:* believe 8 *ensue:* outlast

Questions

1) This sonnet is based upon the two different meanings the poet attaches to the word "fair." It illustrates both ambiguity and the power of context to shift the meanings of words. Distinguish clearly between these two meanings, and identify the sense intended with each occurrence of the word "fair."

2) The thought of this sonnet proceeds by a number of logical steps. Each of the steps occupies two lines. Trace the development of the thought by stating the idea expressed in each pair of lines, then determining the relation of each to the one before. Does it amplify, contradict, or simply add something new? What effect does this orderly arrangement have?

3) Compare this sonnet with Milton's "When I Consider How My Light Is Spent" (p. 25). How does the method of introducing new thoughts differ? What conclusions can you draw from this?

4) How do the thought and feeling of this sonnet differ from those of Shakespeare's Sonnet 138, "When my love swears that she is made of truth" (p. 12)? What different notion of womanhood is suggested by each?

ODE TO A NIGHTINGALE

JOHN KEATS (1795–1821)

1

My heart aches, and a drowsy numbness pains
  My sense, as though of hemlock I had drunk,
Or emptied some dull opiate to the drains
  One minute past, and Lethe-wards had sunk:
'Tis not through envy of thy happy lot,   5
  But being too happy in thine happiness—
    That thou, light-wingéd Dryad of the trees,
      In some melodious plot
  Of beechen green, and shadows numberless,
    Singest of summer in full-throated ease.   10

2

O, for a draught of vintage! that hath been
  Cooled a long age in the deep-delvéd earth,
Tasting of Flora and the country green,
  Dance, and Provençal song, and sunburnt mirth!
O for a beaker full of the warm South,   15
  Full of the true, the blushful Hippocrene,
    With beaded bubbles winking at the brim,
      And purple-stainéd mouth;
  That I might drink, and leave the world unseen,
    And with thee fade away into the forest dim: 20

3

Fade far away, dissolve, and quite forget
  What thou among the leaves hast never known,

2 *hemlock:* the drink (brewed from an herb) used as a poison in antiquity 4 *Lethe-wards:* Lethe was the river of Hades whose waters brought forgetfulness 7 *Dryad:* a wood nymph 13 *Flora:* the goddess of flowers 14 *Provençal:* referring to Provence, in the south of France 16 *Hippocrene:* the fountain of the Muses

The weariness, the fever, and the fret
  Here, where men sit and hear each other groan;
Where palsy shakes a few, sad, last gray hairs,   25
    Where youth grows pale, and specter-thin, and dies;
      Where but to think is to be full of sorrow
        And leaden-eyed despairs,
  Where Beauty cannot keep her lustrous eyes,
    Or new Love pine at them beyond tomorrow.   30

4

Away! away! for I will fly to thee,
  Not charioted by Bacchus and his pards,
But on the viewless wings of Poesy,
  Though the dull brain perplexes and retards:
Already with thee! tender is the night,   35
  And haply the Queen-Moon is on her throne,
    Clustered around by all her starry Fays;
      But here there is no light,
  Save what from heaven is with the breezes blown
    Through verdurous glooms and winding mossy ways.   40

5

I cannot see what flowers are at my feet,
  Nor what soft incense hangs upon the boughs,
But, in embalmèd darkness, guess each sweet
  Wherewith the seasonable month endows
The grass, the thicket, and the fruit-tree wild;   45
  White hawthorn, and the pastoral eglantine;
    Fast fading violets covered up in leaves;
      And mid-May's eldest child,
  The coming musk-rose, full of dewy wine,
    The murmurous haunt of flies on summer eves.   50

6

Darkling I listen; and for many a time
  I have been half in love with easeful Death,
Called him soft names in many a musèd rhyme,
  To take into the air my quiet breath;

32 *Bacchus:* the god of wine; *pards:* his cart was sometimes depicted as drawn by leopards 33 *viewless:* invisible 37 *Fays:* fairies 51 *Darkling:* in the dark

Now more than ever seems it rich to die,   55
  To cease upon the midnight with no pain,
    While thou art pouring forth thy soul abroad
      In such an ecstasy!
  Still wouldst thou sing, and I have ears in vain—
    To thy high requiem become a sod.   60

7

Thou wast not born for death, immortal Bird!
  No hungry generations tread thee down;
The voice I hear this passing night was heard
  In ancient days by emperor and clown:
Perhaps the selfsame song that found a path   65
  Through the sad heart of Ruth, when, sick for home,
    She stood in tears amid the alien corn;
      The same that oft-times hath
  Charmed magic casements, opening on the foam
    Of perilous seas, in faery lands forlorn.   70

8

Forlorn! the very word is like a bell
  To toll me back from thee to my sole self!
Adieu! the fancy cannot cheat so well
  As she is famed to do, deceiving elf.
Adieu! adieu! thy plaintive anthem fades   75
  Past the near meadows, over the still stream,
    Up the hill-side; and now 'tis buried deep
      In the next valley-glades:
  Was it a vision, or a waking dream?
    Fled is that music:—Do I wake or sleep?   80

66 *Ruth:* the Biblical character

Questions

1) In general, Keats employs the connotations of words to reinforce and augment their denotations. Also, in accordance with the
usual practice of Romantic poets, he often favors words with exceptionally strong connotations. Sometimes his search for words of this
kind leads him to use terms that are rare, or even invented. Point out
some of the unusual words—such as "blushful" in line 16—which seem
to be chosen for the sake of their strong connotations.

2) What effect does Keats achieve by the use of words that are

no longer common (and were not in his own time), such as "beechen," line 9, "pards," line 32, "haply," line 36, and "Fays," line 37?

3) In spite of the strongly connotative words Keats generally uses, there are some passages in the poem where a certain neutrality emerges. Consider line 54, "To take into the air my quiet breath." Why should there be an apparent discrepancy between the meaning of this and the emotive quality of the language? Are there any other "neutral" or comparatively unemotional passages in the poem?

4) One of the characteristics of this poem is the generous use of adjectives. This is generally considered poor practice, but Keats has carried it off very well. Some idea of the contribution made by the adjectives can be gained if they are isolated from their contexts and examined separately. For example, the adjectives in the last two lines of stanza 5 are "coming . . . dewy . . . murmurous . . . summer." Consider the adjective sequences in lines 51–54, 66–70, 75–78.

5) Are "fade far away" and "dissolve" in line 21 synonymous? Why does Keats use both of them?

6) What is the difference between a "requiem," line 60, and an "anthem," line 75? Why does Keats choose these words for the nightingale's song? Do their modifiers play an important role?

7) What is the difference between a "vision" and a "waking dream" (line 79)? Why is the distinction of importance?

8) It is particularly interesting to readers concerned for the moment with the subject of this chapter—the properties peculiar to the language of poetry—that a vital part in the thought and action of this poem should be played by a word considered as a word, "forlorn," in lines 70 and 71. What effect exactly does the word have on the poet? What properties of the word influence him? In what way is the word an appropriate bridge between the mood dominated by the nightingale and the waking mood to which the poet returns at the end of the poem?

THE CONVERGENCE OF THE TWAIN

(*Lines on the loss of the* Titanic)

THOMAS HARDY (1840–1928)

I

In a solitude of the sea
Deep from human vanity,
And the Pride of Life that planned her, stilly couches she.

II

Steel chambers, late the pyres
Of her salamandrine fires,   5
Cold currents thrid, and turn to rhythmic tidal lyres.

III

Over the mirrors meant
To glass the opulent
The sea-worm crawls—grotesque, slimed, dumb, indifferent.

IV

Jewels in joy designed   10
To ravish the sensuous mind
Lie lightless, all their sparkles bleared and black and blind.

V

Dim moon-eyed fishes near
Gaze at the gilded gear
And query: "What does this vaingloriousness down here?" . . .   15

VI

Well: while was fashioning
This creature of cleaving wing,
The Immanent Will that stirs and urges everything

VII

Prepared a sinister mate
For her—so gaily great—   20
A Shape of Ice, for the time far and dissociate.

VIII

And as the smart ship grew
In stature, grace, and hue,
In shadowy silent distance grew the Iceberg too.

5 *salamandrine:* there is a belief that fire is the salamander's natural element 6 *thrid:* penetrate 18 *Immanent Will:* a term for the supreme power that Hardy often used

IX

Alien they seemed to be: 25
No mortal eye could see
The intimate welding of their later history.

X

Or sign that they were bent
By paths coincident
On being anon twin halves of one august event,   30

XI

Till the Spinner of the Years
Said "Now!" And each one hears,
And consummation comes, and jars two hemispheres.

QUESTIONS

1) Hardy exploits the connotative properties of words in two different ways in this poem. At first he simply seeks terms with strong connotations, such as "opulent" (line 8), "ravish" (line 11), and "bleared" (line 12). In what way do the strained words, "stilly" (line 3) and "vaingloriousness" (line 15) reflect similar intentions?

2) But as he turns to placing emphasis on the irony of the catastrophe, Hardy manipulates his vocabulary in such a way that connotation and denotation contrast ironically with each other. Comment upon "mate" (line 19), "welding" (line 27), and "consummation" (line 33).

3) What is the literal meaning of "consummation" in line 33? What secondary meaning or connotation does it have in this context? What is the relation between these two?

4) Explain (after looking them up in the dictionary, if necessary) the presence of such words as "thrid" and "anon."

5) What is the effect of "gear" in line 14?

6) What is the effect of "august" in line 30?

JABBERWOCKY

LEWIS CARROLL (1832–1898)

'Twas brillig, and the slithy toves
    Did gyre and gimble in the wabe;
All mimsy were the borogoves,
    And the mome raths outgrabe.

"Beware the Jabberwock, my son!   5
    The jaws that bite, the claws that catch!
Beware the Jubjub bird, and shun
    The frumious Bandersnatch!"

He took his vorpal sword in hand:
    Long time the manxome foe he sought,—   10
So rested he by the Tumtum tree,
    And stood awhile in thought.

And as in uffish thought he stood,
    The Jabberwock, with eyes of flame,
Came whiffling through the tulgey wood,   15
    And burbled as it came!

One two! One two! And through and through
    The vorpal blade went snicker-snack!
He left it dead, and with its head
    He went galumphing back.   20

"And hast thou slain the Jabberwock?
    Come to my arms, my beamish boy!
O frabjous day! Callooh! Callay!"
    He chortled in his joy.

'Twas brillig, and the slithy toves   25
    Did gyre and gimble in the wabe;
All mimsy were the borogoves,
    And the mome raths outgrabe.

QUESTIONS

1) This remarkable poem illustrates a number of things about the use of language in poetry. According to the explanation given by Humpty Dumpty in Chapter 6 of Lewis Carroll's *Through the Look-*

ing Glass, some of the words are "portmanteau" words, that is, combinations of two other words. "Slithy" in line 1, for example, is a combination of "lithe" and "slimy." What poetic use of language does this device approximate?

2) Many of the words, such as "toves," in line 1, are not derivations, but are fresh coinings. What prevents such coined words as "Jabberwock," "vorpal" (line 9), and "manxome" (line 10) from being meaningless?

3) Some of the coinings seem immediately and independently expressive. How would you define "uffish" (line 13), "whiffling" (line 15), and "galumphing" (line 20)?

4) In spite of all the clues available, it is probably impossible to be definite about the meaning of most of the new words. In what way is this an advantage?

5) This poem has, in spite of all difficulties, been translated into French, German, and Latin. State the problems that would be encountered in translating it, and tell how they might be met.

6) "Chortled" in line 24 was invented by Lewis Carroll for this poem, but it has become a part of the language and is now listed in standard dictionaries. What conditions made this possible?

7) Are there any other words in the poem that would be useful in the general vocabulary? What are their special qualities?

FOR A' THAT AND A' THAT

ROBERT BURNS (1759–1796)

Is there, for honest poverty,
 That hangs his head, and a' that?
The coward slave, we pass him by,
 We dare be poor for a' that!
  For a' that, and a' that,   5
   Our toils obscure, and a' that;
  The rank is but the guinea's stamp,
  The man's the gowd for a' that.

What though on hamely fare we dine,
 Wear hodden-gray, and a' that;   10

For A' That and A' That: this means approximately "In spite of all that." 7 *the guinea's stamp:* the design on the coin 8 *gowd:* gold 10 *hodden-gray:* coarse cloth

Gie fools their silks, and knaves their wine,
    A man's a man for a' that.
        For a' that, and a' that,
            Their tinsel show, and a' that;
            The honest man, though e'er sae poor,   15
            Is king o' men for a' that.

Ye see yon birkie, ca'd a lord,
    Wha struts, and stares, and a' that;
Though hundreds worship at his word,
    He's but a coof for a' that: 20
        For a' that, and a' that,
            His riband, star, and a' that,
            The man of independent mind,
            He looks and laughs at a' that.

A prince can mak a belted knight,   25
    A marquis, duke, and a' that;
But an honest man's aboon his might,
    Guid faith he mauna fa' that!
        For a' that, and a' that,
            Their dignities, and a' that,   30
            The pith o' sense, and pride o' worth,
            Are higher rank than a' that.

Then let us pray that come it may,
    As come it will for a' that,
That sense and worth, o'er a' the earth,   35
    May bear the gree, and a' that!
        For a' that, and a' that,
            It's coming yet, for a' that,
            That man to man the warld o'er
            Shall brothers be for a' that.   40

11 *Gie:* give 16 *birkie:* young man 20 *coof:* fool
27 *aboon:* above 28 *he mauna fa':* he must not
claim 36 *gree:* prize

QUESTIONS

1) The language of this poem is the dialect of the peasants in the
Scottish countryside where Burns was born and brought up. In what
way is the dialect appropriate to the poem? What elements does it

contribute that would not be there if the poem were written in standard English?

2) What are the connotations of the unfamiliar words, "birkie,"
line 17, and "coof," line 20?

3) For what sort of audience is the poem intended?

4) Would the poem be improved if the vague "a' that" were
made more specific in at least some cases? What does this indefinite
expression contribute to the poem?

FROM AN ESSAY ON CRITICISM

ALEXANDER POPE (1688–1744)

Some have at first for wits, then poets pass'd,
Turn'd critics next, and proved plain fools at last.
Some neither can for wits nor critics pass,
As heavy mules are neither horse nor ass.
Those half-learn'd witlings, numerous in our isle,   5
As half-form'd insects on the banks of Nile;
Unfinish'd things, one knows not what to call,
Their generation's so equivocal:
To tell them would a hundred tongues require,
Or one vain wit's, that might a hundred tire.   10
  But you who seek to give and merit fame,
And justly bear a critic's noble name,
Be sure yourself and your own reach to know,
How far your genius, taste, and learning go;
Launch not beyond your depth, but be discreet,   15
And mark that point where sense and dulness meet.
  Nature to all things fix'd the limits fit,
And wisely curb'd proud man's pretending wit.
As on the land while here the ocean gains,
In other parts it leaves wide sandy plains;   20
Thus in the soul while memory prevails,
The solid power of understanding fails;
Where beams of warm imagination play,
The memory's soft figures melt away.
One science only will one genius fit: 25
So vast is art, so narrow human wit:
Not only bounded to peculiar arts,

8 *generation:* origin

But oft in those confined to single parts.
Like kings we lose the conquests gain'd before,
By vain ambition still to make them more: 30
Each might his sev'ral province well command,
Would all but stoop to what they understand.
    First follow Nature, and your judgment frame
By her just standard, which is still the same:
Unerring Nature, still divinely bright,   35
One clear, unchanged, and universal light,
Life, force, and beauty, must to all impart,
At once the source, and end, and test of Art.
Art from that fund each just supply provides;
Works without show, and without pomp presides: 40
In some fair body thus th' informing soul
With spirits feeds, with vigour fills the whole,
Each motion guides, and every nerve sustains;
Itself unseen, but in th' effects remains.
Some, to whom Heaven in wit has been profuse,   45
Want as much more to turn it to its use;
For wit and judgment often are at strife,
Though meant each other's aid, like man and wife.
'Tis more to guide, than spur the Muse's steed;
Restrain his fury, than provoke his speed: 50
The winged courser, like a generous horse,
Shows most true mettle when you check his· course.

Questions

1) The frequent use of the word "wit" is typical of Pope's time, for the word embodied a number of qualities important to Pope and his contemporaries. What different meanings for the word can be inferred from this passage?

2) What is the difference between a "wit" and a "witling," as in line 5?

3) What is the older sense in which Pope uses "science" in line 25?

4) What is the older sense in which he uses "peculiar" in line 27?

5) What is the modern term for "genius" in line 14?

6) What old meaning of "informing" is intended in line 41?

7) Up to this point, we have been considering words whose meanings have shifted in an obvious manner. But "Nature" raises another and larger question; there the shift has been more subtle, yet more fundamental, for the concept of "nature" is a basic one in all thinking.

Pope's ideas about nature, as they are expressed in lines 36 and 37—that it is clear, unchanging, beautiful—are strongly influenced by Newton's discoveries. Since his time, of course, our concept of nature has undergone many changes, not only under the influence of such scientific developments as evolution and nuclear physics but also as a result of romantic attitudes. To what extent does Pope's advice to "follow Nature" still make sense? What might it mean today that it did not mean in his own time? Is it possible *not* to follow nature?

Imagery 3

SIMILE AND METAPHOR

Since poetry's function is that of extending our ordinary powers of expression, it is obvious that it must have special methods for doing that. Probably the most important of these special methods are carefully chosen comparisons which are called *figures of speech* or *images*. Expressive comparisons are not, of course, limited to poetry. They are often found in prose and they occur in ordinary conversation at moments when people feel the need to express themselves with special force. Examples are: "pretty as a picture," "his back was straight as a ramrod," "the boy was quiet as a mouse." Poetic figures of speech are not essentially different from familiar, vivid comparisons like these, but they are more original and are usually far more complicated.

Figures of speech, it will be noticed, contain two parts or "terms": a subject that is the center of attention and some other element that is brought in for the sake of pointing out some quality in the subject. "He ran like a scared rabbit" mentions the rabbit as a particularly vivid way of describing how fast the subject ran. The figures of speech found in conversation or in ordinary prose usually concentrate on some familiar quality of the subject and are not difficult to understand. But in poetry figures of speech are generally used to focus on unfamiliar qualities or to give familiar qualities unusual vividness and stress. The important point is not that the two things being compared resemble each other closely, but that the feeling that is normally associated with one can be transferred to the other. Hence, the comparison will generally seem strange and thought provoking; often enough, it is a result of the poet's ingenuity and a test of the reader's.

Though figures of speech can be divided into an indefinite number of classes, they will be discussed here in terms of three categories which have much in common with each other: simile, metaphor, and symbol. A *simile* is a figure of speech which uses some such word as "as" or "like" to show that a comparison is being made. For example:

> It is a beauteous evening, calm and free,
> The holy time is quiet as a Nun
> Breathless with adoration; . . .

By comparing the evening with the praying nun, Wordsworth, the author of these lines, brings forward certain obvious resemblances that justify the comparison: the nun and the evening are both calm; the nun's dark habit resembles the darkness of the evening. But the real purpose of the simile is to relate the feelings appropriate to the nun to the "beauteous evening," thus conveying a sense of the sacred mystery the poet feels in it. (See Wordsworth's "It is a beauteous evening, calm and free," page 240.)

A second example of simile is drawn from a poem that describes an expedition into a polar region.

> As clerks in whited banks
> With bird-claw pens column virgin paper,
> To snow we added foot-prints.
> —STEPHEN SPENDER, "Polar Exploration"

Here two points of resemblance are working. There is a striking, if superficial, resemblance between the appearance of the foot-prints in the snow and the figures the bank clerks are writing on the clean paper. More significantly, the poet wants to suggest that, because the polar explorers have been traveling for a long time and are too tired to think of anything but their journey, their steps have become unthinking and automatic like the monotonous task being performed by the clerks.

The figure of speech called *metaphor* differs from simile only in omitting the comparative word. Thus, instead of saying "Her eyes are like stars," the metaphor says "Her eyes *are* stars." This distinction may seem trivial, but in practice it makes a great deal of difference. The stated comparison involving "as" or "like" seems to mean that the poet still has his eyes firmly on the object he is describing. But a metaphor, which actually identifies the two things being compared, is obviously a departure from the facts, and must therefore justify itself. The point of the metaphor usually lies within this process of justification. Perhaps the resemblance between the two things being compared is rich and complicated. Perhaps it is part of a larger whole, a general view which the comparison exemplifies. In any case, metaphors appear more frequently than similes. They seem to have more expressive power, and they are more flexible and economical than similes.

In one of its commonest uses, metaphor compares two things which are dissimilar for the sake of stressing a single quality that they have in common.

> . . . the broad cloud-driving moon in the clear sky
> Lifts o'er the firs her shining shield. . . .
>
> —ROBERT BRIDGES, "The Storm Is Over"

The comparison with the shield here simply brings out the roundness, and possibly the hard, bright appearance of the moon. All that is intended or gained is a touch of vividness that probably could not have been achieved in any other way.

One of the great advantages of metaphor, and a characteristic that helps to give poetry its special depth, is its way of establishing numerous relationships between the two things that are compared. Here is an example from W. B. Yeats's "Sailing to Byzantium" (see p. 309 for the whole poem):

> An aged man is but a paltry thing,
> A tattered coat upon a stick, . . .

Why is an old man like a ragged coat upon a stick? No specific reason is given; instead, the reader is left to find the similarities himself. As it turns out, the imagination easily supplies many points of resemblance. The two have in common certain qualities of thinness, limpness, and emptiness. There are also some abstract meanings that arise, such as futility, lifelessness, and pathetic pretense. It becomes clear, then, that the metaphor can act as a kind of shorthand, condensing many bits of information into a single comparison. But metaphors are not merely collections of details;

on the contrary, their power lies in their capacity for making telling general impressions. Yeats's comparison is effective, in the final analysis, because it presents a single, vivid, scarecrow image that could not be made clearer by further explanation. Let us compare it with a simile on the same subject from another poem:

> I, an old woman whose heart is like the Sun
> That has seen too much, looked on too many sorrows
> Yet is not weary of shining. . . .
>
> —EDITH SITWELL, "An Old Woman"

Note that, in contrast to the metaphor, the simile controls the comparison narrowly. The old woman's heart is like the sun in two ways and two ways only: it has seen too much, and it is still shining. The cleverness of the comparison is pleasing and impressive; but its clarity and exactness constitute a barrier to any additions of meaning by the reader's imagination. He is not encouraged to look for any further resemblance between the two terms, and the ultimate effect seems somewhat shallow in comparison with the metaphor about the old man.

Metaphor can, of course, be controlled in a similar way. It is possible for a poet to gain a special effect by comparing his subject with something else at length, enumerating the many points of resemblance instead of leaving them to the reader's imagination. Such an effect is called an *extended metaphor*. In an elegy written in memory of a young woman who had learned painting after she had mastered the art of poetry, John Dryden wrote of her as a conqueror who took over painting as though it were a new country.

> Born to the spacious empire of the Nine,
>> One would have thought she should have been content
>> To manage well that mighty government;
> But what can young ambitious souls confine?
>> To the next realm she stretched her sway,
>> For Painture near adjoining lay,
> A plenteous province and alluring prey.
> A chamber of dependences was framed
>> (As conquerors will never want pretense,
>>> When armed, to justify the offense),

And the whole fief in right of Poetry she claimed.
The country open lay without defense,
For poets frequent inroads there had made,
    And perfectly could represent
The shape, the face, with every lineament;
And all the large demesnes which the dumb sister swayed;
    All bowed beneath her government,
Received in triumph wheresoe'er she went.

> —JOHN DRYDEN, "To the Pious Memory of
> Mrs. Anne Killigrew"

In this elaborate and playful metaphor, Dryden sees a number of resemblances between the actual situation and its metaphoric equivalent. Mrs. Killigrew is born heir to the country of the Muses, which includes poetry, but is too ambitious to be satisfied even with this large realm. Painting, since it resembles poetry, is a neighboring country. Mrs. Killigrew argues that painting is really a part of poetry, just as an aggressor is likely to argue that he has a natural right to the territory he is invading. The new territory is not well fortified, for many earlier poets have invaded it, that is to say, they have turned from poetry to painting. Consequently Mrs. Killigrew easily gains absolute control—she becomes a skillful painter—and is "received in triumph wheresoe'er she went,"—she excels in the various branches of the art.

Sometimes an entire poem is devoted to an extended metaphor. The following poem is an example. In comparison with Dryden's metaphor it is less complicated, but more visual and more openly emotional.

TO MARGUERITE, CONTINUED

MATTHEW ARNOLD (1822–1888)

Yes: in the sea of life enisl'd,
With echoing straits between us thrown,
Dotting the shoreless watery wild,
We mortal millions live *alone*.
The islands feel the enclasping flow,
And then their endless bounds they know.

5

But when the moon their hollows lights,
And they are swept by balms of spring,
And in their glens, on starry nights,
The nightingales divinely sing;   10
And lovely notes, from shore to shore,
Across the sounds and channels pour;

Oh then a longing like despair
Is to their farthest caverns sent;
For surely once, they feel, we were   15
Parts of a single continent.
Now round us spreads the watery plain—
Oh might our marges meet again!

Who order'd, that their longing's fire
Should be, as soon as kindled, cool'd?   20
Who renders vain their deep desire?—
A God, a God their severance ruled;
And bade betwixt their shores to be
The unplumb'd, salt, estranging sea.

The poet, painfully conscious of his separation from the woman he loves, is impressed with the idea that individual persons are like islands separated by the sea. On particularly beautiful evenings the islands, recalling the geologic fact that they were once parts of a single tract of land, long to be joined again; the intended parallel with the feelings of lovers is obvious. Nevertheless, Arnold reflects in the last stanza, the separation of the islands (and of the lovers) is the decree of a divine authority.

These examples demonstrate the strengths and weaknesses of the extended metaphor. Long explanation tends to spoil the singleness of effect, and the ingenuity that is required in working out parallels tends to interfere with the feelings that are expressed. On the other hand, the extended metaphor is a way of gathering a scattering of details into a single elegant group, and of achieving a particularly satisfying balance and unity.

In the examples of metaphor we have had so far, the two things being compared, and the reasons for the comparisons, have been fairly clear. Sometimes, however, a poet will make use of a metaphor without openly stating what his subject is being compared to. Take, for example, the first lines of this sonnet by Sir Philip Sidney (see p. 169 for the whole sonnet):

> With how sad steps, Oh Moon, thou climb'st the skies!
> How silently, and with how wan a face!

The poet does not say that he is comparing the moon to a person, though it is, of course, perfectly clear. This is a *submerged* or *implied metaphor*. One term of the comparison is clear, but the other is unstated. Later in his sonnet, Sidney shows that he is thinking of the moon as another lover, like himself, whose sadness and paleness are due to the indifference of his mistress.

The following poem also illustrates submerged metaphor:

BECAUSE I COULD NOT STOP FOR DEATH

EMILY DICKINSON (1830–1886)

> Because I could not stop for Death,
> He kindly stopped for me;
> The carriage held but just ourselves
> And Immortality.
>
> We slowly drove, he knew no haste,   5
> And I had put away
> My labor, and my leisure too,
> For his civility.
>
> We passed the school, where children strove
> At recess, in the ring;   10
> We passed the fields of gazing grain,
> We passed the setting sun.
>
> Or rather, he passed us;
> The dews grew quivering and chill,
> For only gossamer my gown,   15
> My tippet only tulle.

15 *gossamer:* thin, cobweb-like fabric 16 *tippet:* scarf or cape *tulle:* a thin fabric

We paused before a house that seemed
A swelling of the ground;
The roof was scarcely visible,
The cornice in the ground.   20

Since then 'tis centuries, and yet
Feels shorter than the day
I first surmised the horses' heads
Were toward eternity.

This poem is far from being as simple as it seems. It does its work
by using a set of innocuous images to convey an idea about death.
The leisurely carriage ride is a submerged metaphor for dying, or
it would be if its meaning were not revealed by the names of the
gentleman who drives the poet to her visit and the other passenger.
The "house" that appears in the fifth stanza may attract little attention on a first reading; but when we consider that it is a "swelling"
and is "in the ground," and connect it with the name of the gentleman, we see that it is another submerged metaphor. The thing for
which it stands, the grave, is never mentioned. Not until the poem
has been studied with some care do the ironic effect of "civility"
in line 8 and the significance of the odd remark about the sun in
line 13 become clear.

But there are wheels within wheels. The final stanza is cryptic
only if we cling to the expectation (which is only natural) that
Emily Dickinson is expressing fear of death; actually, she is saying
that the existence she is in now is pleasanter than life was. And it
follows that the pleasant and familiar imagery with which she
describes her entrance into the grave is fully justified as a means
of expressing her feeling that death is to be welcomed rather than
feared.

The image of the grave in Emily Dickinson's poem illustrates
one way of using a submerged metaphor; the poet does not explain
the comparison he has in mind, so that the metaphor remains submerged. Unless the comparison is obvious (and in modern poetry
it seldom is), difficulties arise. The language that confronts the
reader, if it is taken literally, makes no sense; it is up to him to
exhume the comparison that lies below the surface. For example,
in his poem "In the Dock" (p. 311), Walter de la Mare describes

a poor and ignorant criminal on trial in a courtroom filled with officials. He sums up the situation in the single line:

> Justice for carrion pants; and these the flies.

It takes a moment's thought to fill in the complete picture suggested by this powerful submerged metaphor. De la Mare is saying that the legal system is a scavenger eager for dead flesh, for the conviction of the defenseless criminal, and that the judges and lawyers who earn their living from these proceedings are parasites feeding on the corpse.

Sometimes the clues to a submerged metaphor may be very slight; in fact, they are often limited to a single word or phrase. Here is an example from W. H. Auden's "In Memory of W. B. Yeats":

> For poetry makes nothing happen: it survives
> In the valley of its saying where executives
> Would never want to tamper; it flows south
> From ranches of isolation and the busy griefs,
> Raw towns that we believe and die in; . . .

It is hard to see what poetry has to do with a valley, with ranches and towns. But a clue to the metaphor is given by "flowing south." If the reader works back from this indication, he sees that poetry is being compared to a river. Like a river, it remains in the remote valley where it flows, it "makes nothing happen." Its connection is with obscure lives, like the ones in the lonely ranches and "raw towns" past which the river flows. Note that this rich and complicated metaphor is only hinted at in two words, "flowing south," and without attentive reading the idea of the river and the meaning of the passage would be lost.

The name of *personification* has been given to the special type of metaphor which compares its subject to a human figure. The subject itself may be a quality, an idea or an object; it is compared to a person, usually through an implied metaphor which leaves one of the terms unstated. Sir Philip Sidney's lines to the moon quoted earlier (p. 64) illustrate the common type of personification which establishes the image by speaking to the subject, as if it were a person. A fine example from the beginning of Samuel Daniel's "To the Lady Lucy, Countess of Bedford," shows some of the possibilities of this variety of metaphor. It makes use of an elaborate personification of "virtue."

> Though virtue be the same when low she stands
>   In th' humble shadows of obscurity,
>   As when she either seats in martial bands
>   Or sits in court clad with authority

Having imagined virtue in these lines as an obscure person, a soldier, and a judge, Daniel goes on to cast her as a recluse and a lady of the manor, all in the course of arguing that she should occupy a high position if she is to be most effective.

Personification is useful because our knowledge of people is more detailed and elaborate than any other kind of knowledge. Hence, the poet draws upon a ready-made fund of common information that every reader is sure to have, and can proceed with economy and vividness. To speak of love as a dying man (see Drayton's "Since There's No Help," (p. 15), of the spring as a woman blowing a trumpet (see Shelley's "Ode to the West Wind," p. 80), or to write about frogs and tortoises as if they were human, as Aesop does, saves much explanation and may be highly suggestive. But there is the danger that personification may become careless and unimaginative and may be used because it is readily understandable rather than because it is vivid.

EXAMPLES. Shakespeare, "Sonnet 146," p. 174; King, "Sic Vita," p. 185; Herbert, "Redemption," p. 186; Marvell, "On a Drop of Dew," p. 202; Browning, "Memorabilia," p. 276; Arnold, "Dover Beach," p. 291; Emily Dickinson, "After Great Pain a Formal Feeling Comes," p. 294; Robinson, "The Sheaves," p. 317; Jeffers, "Hurt Hawks," p. 328; Auden, "Herman Melville," p. 363; Wilbur, "Mind," p. 391. Examples of personification: Keats, "Ode on a Grecian Urn," p. 263; De la Mare, "In the Dock," p. 311; Masefield, "The Downland," p. 330.

SYMBOLS

A third figure of speech that appears in poetry is the *symbol*. Symbols are not distinctively poetic devices, but are found in every sphere of intellectual activity, from the simplest to the most complicated. At its simplest, a symbol is a concrete object to which some abstract and usually emotive significance is attached. National flags, military uniforms, and crosses are symbols. Words are symbols, for though they may ultimately refer to material things, their primary reference is to something abstract, meaning. Paradoxically, symbols embody and conceal meaning at once. A crown, for example, is the symbol of a king's authority, but there is nothing about it to relate it to its meaning. With the crown, as with symbols in general, the relationship between the symbolic object and its significance is more or less arbitrary, dependent upon something other than the qualities of the symbolizing object.

In this respect, the symbol is unlike the metaphor. The two terms of a metaphor must resemble each other, even if only incidentally, but a symbol usually has no physical characteristics at all to justify its abstract meaning. Metaphor is a matter of identifying two things with each other. In symbolism, however, the symbolic object and its significance are thought of as clearly separate things, the one concrete, the other abstract. Further, symbolism tends to remain fixed; once a symbol has acquired a certain value, it tends to keep it. This characteristic makes symbols particularly useful in extended works of literature like novels or plays.

Symbols communicate abstract conceptions that would be difficult, if not impossible, to communicate in any other way. Further, as visible and expressive objects in their own right, they are capable of evoking strong feelings associated with the concepts they represent. Though patriotism is a feeling connected with a country or group of people, neither of these can normally be presented in such a way as to arouse patriotism. One does not usually feel patriotism when seeing an actual part of America, such as a landscape, or a crowd of Americans. Yet the flag of a country, or a national anthem, whose connection with the country is merely arbitrary and symbolic, can be very effective in directly stimulating patriotic feeling.

This capacity for evoking emotional responses makes symbols useful and important in poetry and in art generally. Because they are actual objects with sensuous characteristics of their own, they can engage the imagination strongly; and they may carry a complex of feelings and ideas without sacrificing their effectiveness. A typical instance of poetic symbolism occurs in Shakespeare's *Antony and Cleopatra*, when Cleopatra, having decided to kill herself, declares that she will remain firm in her intention:

> Now from head to foot
> I am marble-constant. Now the fleeting moon
> No planet is of mine.

Because of its changing phases, the moon is used here, as it often is in Shakespeare, as a symbol of unfaithfulness or indecision. Cleopatra is saying that it is inappropriate to her mood of determination.

Though it is often used in poetry, symbolism is not as much at home in it as are the other figures of speech, for it takes more space to develop than most poems can afford. Bad poems often abound in easily recognized symbols which do not tax the reader's imagination, but do not create any new awareness either. In such poems we are sure to find that the moon is a symbol of love, the rose is a symbol of beauty, and clouds are symbols of trouble. On the other hand, it is perfectly possible for poets to exploit symbols to good effect by using them in new ways or by inventing their own. For example:

THE CLOD AND THE PEBBLE

WILLIAM BLAKE (1757–1827)

"Love seeketh not Itself to please,
    Nor for itself hath any care,
    But for another gives its ease,
    And builds a Heaven in Hell's despair."

So sung a little Clod of Clay   5
    Trodden with the cattle's feet,
    But a Pebble of the brook
    Warbled out these metres meet:

"Love seeketh only Self to please,
    To bind another to Its delight,   10
    Joys in another's loss of ease,
    And builds a Hell in Heaven's despite."

Here the clod and the pebble are symbolic objects which represent, respectively, altruism and selfishness. The symbolism is effective as poetry because it is clear and appropriate without being trite.

Since poets sometimes use symbols with private or peculiar meanings, symbolism can become a cause of obscurity. Robert Browning gave the title *Bells and Pomegranates* to a series of pamphlets containing his poetry and was surprised to find that his readers did not seem to understand its significance. He was making use of symbols drawn from obscure rabbinical traditions unfamiliar to his public. Browning had to explain that bells were a symbol of sound or music, and that pomegranates represented sense or thought, and that he meant his poetry to have both of these qualities. Enigmatic symbols of this kind tend to occur most often in the work of poets who have developed elaborate philosophical systems of their own. To a reader unfamiliar with W. B. Yeats's philosophy, the last two lines of this stanza about a woman who is loved by an old man, "the wandering Aengus," seem neither particularly obscure nor particularly meaningful.

> I will find out where she has gone,
> And kiss her lips and take her hands;
> And walk among long dappled grass,
> And pluck till time and times are done,
> The silver apples of the moon,
> The golden apples of the sun.

However, when we learn from Yeats's *Autobiographies* that he associated the sun with elaborateness and artificiality and the moon with simplicity and directness, the two lines tell us something significant.

EXAMPLES. Southwell, "The Burning Babe," p. 170; Blake, "The Tyger," p. 238, "A Poison Tree," p. 238; Wordsworth, "The Solitary Reaper," p. 241; Hopkins, "The Windhover," p. 303; Nemerov, "The Snow Globe," p. 390.

IMAGES WORKING TOGETHER

Symbols, metaphors, and similes can, of course, be used together in a single poem. Generally, a poet will prefer to use figures of speech one at a time, but it is not at all unusual to find them occurring simultaneously and overlapping each other. The following poem is a good example of the fairly complicated use of imagery by a modern poet.

REVEILLE

A. E. HOUSMAN (1859–1936)

Wake: the silver dusk returning
   Up the beach of darkness brims,
And the ship of sunrise burning
   Strands upon the eastern rims.

Wake: the vaulted shadow shatters,   5
   Trampled to the floor it spanned,
And the tent of night in tatters
   Straws the sky-pavilioned land.

Up, lad, up, 'tis late for lying,
   Hear the drums of morning play;   10
Hark, the empty highways crying,
   "Who'll beyond the hills away?"

Towns and countries woo together,
   Forelands beacon, belfries call;
Never lad that trod on leather   15
   Lived to feast his heart with all.

Up, lad: thews that lie and cumber
   Sunlit pallets never thrive;
Morns abed and daylight slumber
   Were not meant for man alive.   20

Clay lies still, but blood's a rover;
   Breath's a ware that will not keep.
Up, lad: when the journey's over
   There'll be time enough to sleep.

The description of the dawn in the first two stanzas of this poem consists of four rather elaborate metaphors. In the first two lines, as the word "beach" shows, there is a submerged metaphor which implies a comparison between the returning light of the morning—"the silver dusk"—and an ocean tide. The next two lines contain a metaphor comparing the patch of color seen at the horizon at dawn to a burning ship that has run aground. The two metaphors in the second stanza suggest active movement and seem to imply that the coming of the day is something destructive. The submerged metaphor in the first two lines here compares the disappearing night to an arch which someone has broken down and "trampled." The second metaphor compares it to a tent which has been torn up, and whose pieces now lie over the countryside in the form of long morning shadows.

The figures of speech in the third and fourth stanzas are comparatively trite and uncommunicative, not because Housman's imagination failed here, but because they are appropriate to the language of the poem, which leans toward the dialect of the country "lad" to whom it is addressed. When Housman treats the highways, towns, countries, and belfries as if they can speak, he is using personification, which, as we have seen, gives inanimate objects the attributes of persons. These figures of speech, like the phrase "feast his heart," are so commonplace that they seem intended to create local color rather than to function as expressive images.

Two symbols make their appearance in the first line of the last stanza. "Clay" stands for the passive principle in man, "blood" for the active one. The metaphor "breath's a ware" belongs to the category of trite images drawn from country speech. In the last two lines of the poem, the careful statement of obvious fact draws attention to the metaphorical use of "journey" and "sleep." It becomes clear that Housman is not merely urging his country boy to travel and see the world, but that he is using "journey" and "sleep" as metaphoric equivalents for "life" and "death." Hence, the morning described in the first two stanzas is not merely the beginning of a day, but youth, the beginning of life. The last two lines contain the reminder that life will be followed by death. This explains the undercurrent of pessimism in the metaphor of the stranded ship and the violence in the images of daybreak, for the dawn delivers man to a life which can only end in sorrow. Thus, the metaphor of the last two lines interacts with the other metaphors and with everything else that has gone before to widen the significance of the poem.

EXAMPLES. Shakespeare, "Sonnet 73," p. 174; Donne, "The Ecstasy," p. 177; Herbert, "Virtue," p. 186; Marvell, "The Definition of Love," p. 203; Keats, "Ode on a Grecian Urn," p. 263; Hopkins, "No Worst, There Is None," p. 305; "The Big Rock Candy Mountains," p. 315; Owen, "Arms and the Boy," p. 347; Crane, "The Air Plant," p. 353; Spender, "Port Bou," p. 371; Thomas, "Poem in October," p. 383; Hall, "The Morning Porches," p. 395.

IMAGES AS TOOLS OF THOUGHT

We have been discussing imaginative comparisons as means of expression, but it should be made clear that they are also methods of arriving at the ideas that are to be expressed. They are tools of thought, just as language itself is. When we want to think about subjects that do not lend themselves to verbal manipulation, we have to devise new languages for them, such as mathematics and chemical formulas. Poetry is a way of meeting a somewhat similar situation. As we have seen in Chapter 1, it deals with experiences that cannot be formulated in ordinary language; in thinking about such subject matter the poet must employ special methods of thought. These methods are as characteristic of poetry as addition, multiplication, and so on are of mathematics, and they have the same function: that of putting experience into an orderly arrangement, so that a meaningful conclusion about it may be reached.

The most usual processes of poetic thought are the imaginative comparisons which similes, metaphors, and symbols are used to express. These images explain an aspect of reality by means of an illuminating parallel with some other and more familiar reality. It is natural to try to understand a puzzling situation by recalling some similar situation. Most learning is carried on in this way; it is basically a process of comparing the new thing that is being learned with past experience in order to grasp the differences and resemblances between the two. But ordinary practical thinking compares similar things, while poetic thinking achieves its insights by working out relationships between things that may seem to have little or nothing to do with each other. The poet is ready to go very far in seeking parallels. He is ready to depart from the usual ways of relating things and to bring in resources from areas very distant from the immediate field of thought. In this way, he can explain situations that would otherwise remain incomprehensible.

In the following, for example, the poet uses a scene from nature to overcome the emotional resistance one normally feels toward accepting the fact of death.

A DIRGE IN THE WOODS

GEORGE MEREDITH (1828–1909)

A wind sways the pines,
    And below
Not a breath of wild air—
Still as the mosses that glow
On the flooring and over the lines   5
Of the roots here and there.
The pine-tree drops its dead;
They are quiet, as under the sea.
Overhead, overhead
Rushes life in a race,   10
As the clouds, the clouds chase;
    And we go,
And we drop like the fruits of the tree,
    Even we,
    Even so.   15

The last four lines transform the scene into a metaphor for the human situation, arguing that just as the fallen pine needles lie quiet in spite of the vigorous wind that moves the clouds and trees, so death awaits even those who are full of vitality. In spite of what we know intellectually, future death seems inconsistent with present life. By pointing out that in another, parallel situation such apparent inconsistencies do exist, Meredith offers the reader a way of accepting them.

In a more complicated example, "The Dissolution" (p. 175), John Donne examines the puzzling combination of feelings he experienced after the death of the woman he loved, conducting his analysis by means of metaphors. The surviving poet reasons that since the two lovers had in common "mutual elements," and the woman is dead, he must now contain inert materials associated with her. Yet, surprisingly, he feels more vital than ever since her death. How can dead weight give more energy? The situation is so paradoxical (see Glossary) that Donne might have distrusted his feelings if he had not been able to think of metaphoric situations that resembled his own. First, it seems to him that his "fire of passion" burns more brightly, now that it is fed by the fuel of the elements his mistress left behind. Second, he compares himself to the sort of king whose gains depend on conquest and the sacrifices involved in it. Finally, there is the ingenious parallel of the bullets, which argues that a bullet may overtake others fired before it if it has a larger charge of powder.

> And so my soul more earnestly released
> Will outstrip hers; as bullets flown before
> A latter bullet may o'ertake, the powder being more.

Similarly, C. Day Lewis in "As One Who Wanders . . ." (p. 352) offers an explanation for the persistence men sometimes display in working through obscure difficulties for purposes they do not really understand. In doing this, says the poet, men are like a train going through a tunnel:

> As a train that travels underground track
> Feels current flashed from far-off dynamos,
> Our wheels whirling with impetus elsewhere
> Generated we run, are ruled by rails.

The comparison accounts for the mysterious and powerful motivation (the current coming from distant powerhouses) and for the discipline (the guiding tracks) that are manifested in this sort of behavior. Eventually, says the poem, "the pioneer" comes to see what his goal is, just as the train emerges from the tunnel into daylight. Thus, it is not as illogical as it may seem to work in the dark toward a vague goal.

EXAMPLES. Donne, "A Valediction: Forbidding Mourning," p. 176; Tennyson, *In Memoriam*, CXVIII, p. 272; Whitman, "I Saw in Louisiana a Live-Oak Growing," p. 288; Bridges, "Low Barometer," p. 302; Stevens, "Thirteen Ways of Looking at a Blackbird," p. 318; Moore, "Critics and Connoisseurs," p. 331; Eberhart, "The Groundhog," p. 355; Nemerov, "Writing," p. 390.

FURTHER READING

M. H. Abrams, *The Mirror and the Lamp*, New York (Norton), 1958, pp. 290–297 ("Wordsworth and Coleridge on Personification and Myth").

Christine Brook-Rose, *A Grammar of Metaphor*, London, 1958.

I. A. Richards, *The Philosophy of Rhetoric*, New York, 1936, pp. 115–138 ("The Command of Metaphor").

Susanne K. Langer, *Philosophy in a New Key*, Mentor Books, 1948, pp. 103–116.

Wallace Stevens, *The Necessary Angel*, New York, 1951, pp. 71–82 ("Three Academic Pieces").

Eliseo Vivas, *Creation and Discovery*, New York, 1955, pp. 101–127 ("Literature and Knowledge").

EXAMPLES

MY GALLEY CHARGÉD WITH FORGETFULNESS

SIR THOMAS WYATT (1503–1542)

My galley chargéd with forgetfulness
Thorough sharp seas, in winter nights doth pass
'Tween rock and rock; and eke mine enemy, alas,
That is my lord, steereth with cruelness.
And every oar a thought in readiness,   5
As though that death were light in such a case.

1 *forgetfulness:* neglect 5-6 *And every oar . . .:* These two lines are a paraphrase of a passage in the sonnet by Petrarch on which Wyatt's sonnet is based. Petrarch's lines read: "At each oar a ready and guilty thought which has contempt for both the storm and the destination."

And endless wind doth tear the sail apace
Of forcéd sighs and trusty fearfulness.
A rain of tears, a cloud of dark disdain,
Hath done the wearied cords great hindrance,   10
Wreathéd with error and eke with ignorance.
The stars be hid that led me to this pain,
Drownéd is reason that should me consort,
And I remain despairing of the port.

13 *consort:* accompany

QUESTIONS

1) This sonnet is devoted to the elaboration of an extended metaphor whose second term is not revealed until the last line, though it is made fairly clear by suggestion throughout the poem. Explain this metaphor.

2) The description of the ship's situation involves a number of subsidiary metaphors. Some of these are clearly explained—"A rain of tears, a cloud of dark disdain,"—but some are less easily justified. Why are the oars compared to thoughts? Why is the wind associated with "trusty fearfulness"?

3) There are many submerged metaphors among the details of this scene. What are the metaphoric values of "seas," "nights," the rocks, and so on? Do you think any of these details are simply descriptive and have no metaphoric value? If so, distinguish between the descriptive and the metaphoric details.

4) The stars mentioned in line 12 have a place in the main metaphor, but they also have a symbolic meaning. Explain.

5) The two lines (11–12) about the "cords" that control the sails involve a significant metaphor. Explain it.

6) Does the elaboration of the metaphor help to convince the reader of the sincerity of the poet's love? What effect does it have?

THE SOUL SELECTS HER OWN SOCIETY

EMILY DICKINSON (1830–1886)

The soul selects her own society,
Then shuts the door;
To her divine majority
Present no more.

Unmoved, she notes the chariots pausing   5
At her low gate;
Unmoved, an emperor be kneeling
Upon her mat.

I've known her from an ample nation
Choose one;   10
Then close the valves of her attention
Like stone.

QUESTIONS

1) Explain the personification involved in "soul" and "emperor."

2) What submerged metaphor is suggested by "valves" in line 11?
Is there a problem of ambiguity here?

3) Though it comes in as a simile, does "stone" in line 12 have
any force as an image?

4) This poem contains some particularly effective and well-
chosen words, illustrating some of the points made in Chapter 2.
What, for example, is the special quality of "mat" in line 8? What
does it suggest about the soul and her house?

5) Is "majority" in line 3 a good word choice or a poor one? As
is often the case, a dictionary may be useful in deciding this question.

FIRE AND ICE

ROBERT FROST (1875–1964)

Some say the world will end in fire,
Some say in ice.
From what I've tasted of desire
I hold with those who favor fire.
But if it had to perish twice,   5
I think I know enough of hate
To say that for destruction ice
Is also great
And would suffice.

QUESTIONS

1) Is Frost's imagery in this poem symbolism or metaphor? Explain why.

2) What is the difference between the meaning of the words "fire" and "ice" in their first and second uses?

3) Are there any other images in this poem besides the two involving fire and ice? What do you conclude from this?

4) Is Frost's meaning clear? Why do you think his poem is more effective than a prose statement of it would be?

THE EYE

ROBINSON JEFFERS (1887–   )

The Atlantic is a stormy moat; and the Mediterranean,
The blue pool in the old garden,
More than five thousand years has drunk sacrifice
Of ships and blood, and shines in the sun; but here the Pacific—
Our ships, planes, wars are perfectly irrelevant.   5
Neither our present blood-feud with the brave dwarfs
Nor any future world-quarrel of westering
And eastering man, the bloody migrations, greed of power, clash of faiths—
Is a speck of dust on the great scale-pan.
Here from this mountain shore, headland beyond stormy headland
           plunging like dolphins through the blue sea-smoke   10
Into pale sea—look west at the hill of water: it is half the planet: this
           dome, this half-globe, this bulging
Eyeball of water, arched over to Asia,
Australia and white Antarctica: those are the eyelids that never close;
           this is the staring unsleeping
Eye of the earth; and what it watches is not our wars.

6 *the brave dwarfs:* refers to the conflict with Japan in World War II

QUESTIONS

1) Jeffers' comparison of the ocean to a great eye is not strictly unprecedented. (Hart Crane, for example, speaks of the sea as "this great wink of eternity.") But it is sufficiently different from ordinary feelings about oceans and eyes to be startling. Jeffers' purpose seems to be that of *shocking* us into realizing something. What would this be?

2) The Atlantic and the Mediterranean are characterized through metaphors, as the Pacific is. But the metaphors for the first two are

quite conventional. What qualities does Jeffers emphasize by calling the Atlantic a "moat" and the Mediterranean a "blue pool"?

3) What qualities are suggested by the metaphor of the eye?

4) In the final line, Jeffers says that the eye of the Pacific does not watch "our wars." What does it watch?

5) What is the "great scale-pan" (line 9)? What does this metaphor suggest?

6) What attitude toward man is suggested by the poem? What attitude about man's place in nature and in the universe as a whole?

7) What is the effect of the simile in line 10 in which the mountains are compared to dolphins? Why is it appropriate? How does it harmonize with the poem as a whole?

ODE TO THE WEST WIND

PERCY BYSSHE SHELLEY (1792–1822)

I

O wild West Wind, thou breath of Autumn's being,
Thou, from whose unseen presence the leaves dead
Are driven, like ghosts from an enchanter fleeing,

Yellow, and black, and pale, and hectic red,
Pestilence-stricken multitudes: O thou,   5
Who chariotest to their dark wintry bed

The wingèd seeds, where they lie cold and low,
Each like a corpse within its grave, until
Thine azure sister of the Spring shall blow

Her clarion o'er the dreaming earth, and fill   10
(Driving sweet buds like flocks to feed in air)
With living hues and odors plain and hill:

Wild Spirit, which art moving everywhere;
Destroyer and preserver, hear, oh, hear!

2

Thou on whose stream, 'mid the steep sky's commotion,   15
Loose clouds like earth's decaying leaves are shed,
Shook from the tangled boughs of Heaven and Ocean,

10 *clarion:* trumpet

Angels of rain and lightning: there are spread
On the blue surface of thine aery surge,
Like the bright hair uplifted from the head   20

Of some fierce Maenad, even from the dim verge
Of the horizon to the zenith's height,
The locks of the approaching storm. Thou dirge

Of the dying year, to which this closing night
Will be the dome of a vast sepulchre   25
Vaulted with all thy congregated might

Of vapors, from whose solid atmosphere
Black rain, and fire, and hail will burst: oh, hear!

3

Thou who didst waken from his summer dreams
The blue Mediterranean, where he lay,   30
Lulled by the coil of his crystàlline streams,

Beside a pumice isle in Baiae's bay,
And saw in sleep old palaces and towers
Quivering within the wave's intenser day,

All overgrown with azure moss and flowers   35
So sweet, the sense faints picturing them! Thou
For whose path the Atlantic's level powers

Cleave themselves into chasms, while far below
The sea-blooms and the oozy woods which wear
The sapless foliage of the ocean, know   40

Thy voice, and suddenly grow gray with fear,
And tremble and despoil themselves: oh, hear!

4

If I were a dead leaf thou mightest bear;
If I were a swift cloud to fly with thee;
A wave to pant beneath thy power, and share   45

21 *Maenad:* a female attendant of Dionysos, Greek god of wine
and orgies 32 *Baiae's bay:* modern Baja, near Naples

The impulse of thy strength, only less free
Than thou, O uncontrollable! If even
I were as in my boyhood, and could be

The comrade of thy wanderings over Heaven,
As then, when to outstrip thy skiey speed   50
Scarce seemed a vision; I would ne'er have striven

As thus with thee in prayer in my sore need.
Oh, lift me as a wave, a leaf, a cloud!
I fall upon the thorns of life! I bleed!

A heavy weight of hours has chained and bowed   55
One too like thee: tameless, and swift, and proud.

5

Make me thy lyre, even as the forest is:
What if my leaves are falling like its own!
The tumult of thy mighty harmonies

Will take from both a deep, autumnal tone,   60
Sweet though in sadness. Be thou, Spirit fierce,
My spirit! Be thou me, impetuous one!

Drive my dead thoughts over the universe
Like withered leaves to quicken a new birth!
And, by the incantation of this verse,   65

Scatter, as from an unextinguished hearth
Ashes and sparks, my words among mankind!
Be through my lips to unawakened earth

The trumpet of a prophecy! O, Wind,
If Winter comes, can Spring be far behind?   70

QUESTIONS

1) This poem is exceptionally rich in imagery of all kinds and uses its images as principles of structure. In section 4, line 53, the poet compares himself to "a wave, a leaf, a cloud." First, determine the appropriateness of these comparisons. Then notice that each of the three preceding sections is devoted to one of these elements of nature.

2) In this ode, Shelley sees nature as a whole, which includes both the sterility of winter and the fertility of spring. Point out how the language of section 1 refers to both of these aspects of nature.

3) What suggestions are contained in the metaphor that speaks of the West Wind as an "enchanter" (line 3)?

4) What metaphor is implied by "stream," line 15? by "surge," line 19?

5) What is the effect achieved by the simile in lines 20–21 which compares the clouds to a Maenad's hair?

6) Explain the submerged metaphor, "vast sepulchre," in line 25.

7) Section 3 is devoted to describing two contrasting moods of the wind. Point out the metaphors that indirectly reflect these moods.

8) Why does the poet ask (in section 4) to be treated as "a wave, a leaf, a cloud"? What does he mean by "a heavy weight of hours" in line 55? How does this image differ from most of the others in this poem?

9) Explain the submerged image of the lyre in line 57.

10) In section 5, the poet asks the West Wind to spread his ideas over the world, using as similes "withered leaves" and "ashes and sparks." What quality is emphasized in these two images?

11) The extended image of the West Wind is a complicated one, undergoing several transformations as the poem proceeds. What does the wind represent? Would you call the image as a whole a metaphor or a symbol?

THE HEAVY BEAR

DELMORE SCHWARTZ (1913–   )

"the withness of the body"

The heavy bear who goes with me,
A manifold honey to smear his face,
Clumsy and lumbering here and there,
The central ton of every place,
The hungry beating brutish one   5
In love with candy, anger, and sleep,
Crazy factotum, dishevelling all,
Climbs the building, kicks the football,
Boxes his brother in the hate-ridden city.

Breathing at my side, that heavy animal,   10
That heavy bear who sleeps with me,
Howls in his sleep for a world of sugar,

A sweetness intimate as the water's clasp,
Howls in his sleep because the tight-rope
Trembles and shows the darkness beneath.   15
—The strutting show-off is terrified,
Dressed in his dress-suit, bulging his pants,
Trembles to think that his quivering meat
Must finally wince to nothing at all.

That inescapable animal walks with me,   20
Has followed me since the black womb held,
Moves where I move, distorting my gesture,
A caricature, a swollen shadow,
A stupid clown of the spirit's motive,
Perplexes and affronts with his own darkness,   25
The secret life of belly and bone,
Opaque, too near, my private, yet unknown,
Stretches to embrace the very dear
With whom I would walk without him near,
Touches her grossly, although a word   30
Would bare my heart and make me clear,
Stumbles, flounders, and strives to be fed
Dragging me with him in his mouthing care,
Amid the hundred million of his kind,
The scrimmage of appetite everywhere.   35

QUESTIONS

1) This poem is devoted to an elaborately extended image. It is also a submerged metaphor. The clue to the submerged term is given by the epigraph, which tells us that the bear is a metaphoric equivalent of the body. Since this is the case, what is the special meaning of "me" in line 1?

2) What sort of qualities does Schwartz attribute to the bear?

3) Though it is a somewhat painful proceeding, the exactness of Schwartz's metaphor is illuminated if the metaphoric terms are translated into their literal meanings. What, for example, is meant by the bear's taste for honey, sugar, and candy? by his physical awkwardness? by the fact that he is sleepy?

4) What is the nature of the relationship between the bear and the poet's "self"?

5) Why did Schwartz choose a bear for this metaphor? Would

not some other animal, an elephant, a turtle, a horse, have done as well?

6) What suggestion appears in lines 14–19, where the bear appears dressed on a tightrope? What is significant about the emotion he experiences in this situation?

7) Obviously, the poet feels a conflict between the bear and something else. What is this other entity?

8) What is the poet's attitude toward the bear and what it stands for?

The Sound of Poetry 4

I have never been able to retain the names of feet and metres, or to pay the proper respect to the accepted rules of scansion . . .

—T. S. Eliot, "The Music of Poetry"

METER

Poetry was originally an oral art. The oldest poems, like the *Iliad* and the *Odyssey* by Homer, were composed to be sung or spoken aloud. They were performed to the accompaniment of music by bards or minstrels who carried the words in their memories, and their written versions are merely records of these performances. Although poetry is sometimes rendered aloud in modern times in songs, plays, or poetry readings, it is read silently much more often. In spite of that, it retains enough of the influence of its origin to make its use of sound one of its major resources. If the reader does not read the poem aloud, he is expected to imagine how it would sound if it were actually read. Often enough a reading aloud, with proper stress and intonation, adds a great deal to the understanding of a poem. Most good poetry is too complicated to be grasped through a hearing; but the way a poem sounds is usually so important that it is safe to say that a reader cannot get a good idea of its character unless he thinks of it as something heard as well as something read.

The most prominent audible feature of poetry is *rhythm*. In poetry, as in music, rhythm is the result of an alternating arrangement of contrasting sounds. The English language, like all Germanic languages, has some syllables which are pronounced with more force or emphasis than others; this familiar phenomenon is called *stress* or *accent*. Everyone will recognize that in such words as "father," "savage," "poker," and "hanging" the first syllable is stressed and the second is unstressed, while such words as "before," "resign," "eject," and "respond" present the opposite situation. Stress also appears in natural places in phrases and in spoken language. In such groups of words as "on the top" and "if I dared" the stress falls on the last word. Meaning often determines stress, and the same group of words may be stressed differently, according to their meaning. If we imagine a situation where a boy and a girl are choosing red or black pencils, and want to report that the girl picked the red one, the stress would differ somewhat, depending on whether we answered the question "Who picked the red one?" or "What color did the girl pick?" In the first case the answer would be, "The *girl* picked the red one." In the second it would be, "The girl picked the *red* one." The rhythmic pattern that emerges when words are arranged in such a way that their stressed and unstressed syllables fall into a more or less regular sequence is called *meter*.

This rhythm is clearly felt in strongly accented verse like

> Before the beginning of years
> There came to the making of man
> Time, with a gift of tears;
> Grief, with a glass that ran.

—A. C. SWINBURNE, "Atalanta in Calydon"

The methods of studying versification in English (a study called *prosody*) are drawn from those used for Latin and Greek poetry. But while the rhythm of English verse is based on stress, that is to say, the differing emphasis with which syllables are pronounced, the rhythm of Latin and Greek verse was based on the quality of the vowels, or the length of time given to the pronunciation of each syllable. For this and other reasons, the classical system is not well adapted to the study of English verse. However, it is probably the best that has been devised and is certainly the most widely used. The fact that English prosody is essentially Greek in its principles also explains why nearly all the terms used in it are Greek derivatives.

The basic unit of English meter is a group of two or three syllables called a *foot*. The process of determining the prevailing foot in a line of poetry, and so determining the meter (a process called *scanning* or *scansion*), begins with identifying the syllables as stressed or unstressed. (Stressed syllables are indicated by –, and unstressed ones by ⌣.) Latin and Greek had a large variety of metrical feet, but English has only four that are used regularly. These are:

the iamb ⌣ –   the dactyl – ⌣ ⌣
the trochee – ⌣   the anapest ⌣ ⌣ –

As the following examples show, the different metrical feet create very different rhythms when they are used in verse. The syllables in parentheses in the following examples are omitted from the regular pattern, according to the ways of modifying meter discussed below. (The slant line is used to separate the feet from each other.)

iambs

⌣ – / ⌣ – / ⌣   –
I never saw a moor,
⌣ – / ⌣   – / ⌣   –
I never saw the sea;
⌣   – / ⌣ – / ⌣   – / ⌣   –
Yet know I how the heather looks,
⌣   – / ⌣   – / ⌣   –
And what a wave must be.

—EMILY DICKINSON, "I Never Saw a Moor"

trochees

–   ⌣ / – ⌣ / –   ⌣ / – (⌣)
Souls of poets dead and gone,
–   ⌣ / – ⌣ / –   ⌣ / – (⌣)
What Elysium have ye known,
– ⌣ / –   ⌣ / – ⌣ / –   ⌣
Happy field or mossy cavern,
– ⌣ / –   ⌣ / – ⌣ / –   ⌣
Choicer than the Mermaid Tavern?

—JOHN KEATS, "The Mermaid Tavern"

dactyls

–   ⌣ ⌣ / –   ⌣ ⌣ / – ⌣   ⌣ / – ⌣ (⌣)
Just for a handful of silver he left us,
– ⌣ ⌣ / – ⌣   ⌣ / – ⌣ ⌣ / – (⌣⌣)
Just for a riband to stick in his coat —

Found the one gift of which fortune bereft us,
Lost all the others she let us devote . . .

—ROBERT BROWNING, "The Lost Leader"

anapests

Thou hast conquered, O pale Galilean, the world has grown grey
from thy breath;
We have drunken of things Lethean, and fed on the full-
ness of death.

—A. C. SWINBURNE, "Hymn to Proserpine"

Meters are identified by giving the number of feet to the line
as well as the type of foot. The numbers are expressed in words
derived from Greek, so that a line one foot long is *monometer*,
verse of two feet is *dimeter*, and so on through *trimeter* (three),
tetrameter (four), *pentameter* (five), *hexameter* (six), *heptameter*
(seven), and *octameter* (eight). The identification is given in a
two-word formula combining the name of the meter in adjectival
form with the word giving the number of feet.

Hence, the first, second, and fourth lines of the example
from Emily Dickinson's "I Never Saw a Moor" are in iambic
trimeter, but the third line is one foot longer and is, therefore, in
iambic tetrameter. The lines from Keats's "Mermaid Tavern" are
in trochaic tetrameter (although, as the scansion shows, the unstressed final syllable has been omitted from the first and second
lines). The lines from Swinburne's "Hymn to Proserpine" are
in anapestic hexameter; there is a variation on the basic meter in
the second line, where, as the scansion shows, an unstressed syllable has been omitted.

The most common meter in English verse is iambic pentameter. Lines of iambic pentameter without rhyme are recognized as a distinct form called *blank verse*. This is the most
important verse form used in English, and it is discussed in detail
in Chapter 5. All of Shakespeare's plays, Milton's *Paradise Lost*,
and such long narrative poems as Tennyson's *Idylls of the King*
and Browning's *Ring and the Book* are in blank verse.

As has been noted, some of the examples of meter given above contain variations upon the basic meter. A little actual scansion of poetry will show that no poem ever follows its meter exactly, and a little reflection will show why this is so. The rhythm of a poem that consisted entirely of iambs, trochees, or one of the other metrical feet, without any variation whatever, would quickly become monotonous. Furthermore, it would have no expressiveness, but would be exactly like the regular beating of a drum. Skillful versification consists not of sticking unfailingly to the metrical pattern but of working out interesting and harmonious variations upon it. This may be done by omitting one or more unstressed syllables, or by inverting a foot, that is, replacing an iamb with a trochee, or vice versa. These variations sometimes involve the use of two other metrical feet:

the spondee – –
the pyrrhic ‿ ‿

These feet cannot serve as the prevailing meter of a poem. It is obviously impossible to write a line (or, in fact, more than a word or two) in spondaic feet, using nothing but stresses, or in pyrrhic feet, without any stresses. Nevertheless, these feet are important because they often appear as substitutes for iambs and trochees.

Another element of variation in verse is the syllable that has a degree of stress midway between a full stress and none at all. For example, in the line

‿ –́ / ‿ –́ / ‿ –́ / ‿ –́ / ‿ –
Imparadised in one another's arms ·

—JOHN MILTON, *Paradise Lost*

the last syllable of "imparadised" is not stressed as heavily as the second one. Yet its position as the last syllable of two in an iambic foot and its natural pronunciation give it more emphasis than "in." It is clear, then, that in addition to stressed and unstressed syllables, poetry contains syllables with *half-stress*. They are not exceptional. In

–̆ –́ / ‿ –̆ –́ / ‿̆ –́ / ‿ –̆ –́ / ‿ –
Till Love and Fame to nothingness do sink

—JOHN KEATS, "When I Have Fears"

there is a half-stress on the last syllable of "nothingness." Similarly, in

> The still, sad music of humanity
>
> —WILLIAM WORDSWORTH, "Tintern Abbey"

there is a half-stress on the last syllable of the line. The half-stress does make a difference in the sound of the line, of course, but scansion is considerably simplified if it is counted as a full stress.

In order to see how metrical variation works, let us examine some lines whose basic meter is iambic pentameter. The first represents the pattern without any significant variation:

> When I do count the clock that tells the time
>
> —WILLIAM SHAKESPEARE, "Sonnet 12"

The second varies the pattern slightly:

> Some have at first for wits, then poets past
>
> —ALEXANDER POPE, "An Essay on Criticism"

The variation here is a very common one; the first iamb (⏑ – has been inverted, or replaced by a trochee (– ⏑). In the next example there are two changes:

> Turned critics next, and proved plain fools at last.
>
> —ALEXANDER POPE, "An Essay on Criticism"

Here both the first and fourth iambic feet have had their unstressed syllables changed to stressed ones; or, to say the same thing in a slightly more meaningful way, they have been replaced by spondees.

The following line takes us very far from the iambic pentameter norm:

> In the old age black was not counted fair
>
> —SHAKESPEARE, "Sonnet 127"

Here the first foot is a pyrrhic, the second a spondee, the third a trochee, the fourth a spondee, and only the last foot is an iamb.

Nevertheless, as scansion of the rest of the poem would show, the iamb is the prevailing foot, and the others are variations upon it. English meter is extremely flexible and allows very wide variations. One of the most famous examples of extreme variation is Milton's line

Rocks, caves, lakes, fens, bogs, dens and shades of death

where the first six syllables are all stressed. Occasionally a line of verse will have one more syllable than is to be expected. The two examples here are from Shakespeare's blank verse:

Aumerle, thou weep'st, my tender-hearted cousin

—Richard II

But in a fiction, in a dream of passion

—Hamlet

Also possible, as we have seen from the original examples, are lines in which one or more syllables are omitted.

This flexibility is found, of course, in other meters as well as in iambic pentameter. If we take a typical stanza of iambic tetrameter, we find that it contains similar variations:

The time you won your town the race
We chaired you through the market-place;
Man and boy stood cheering by,
And home we brought you shoulder-high.
—A. E. HOUSMAN, "To an Athlete Dying Young"

The free variations characteristic of English verse make it somewhat difficult for beginning students to identify meters. For one thing, whether a particular syllable should be counted as accented or unaccented is often a matter of opinion. However, this should not cause any confusion, for the meter of the poem depends upon the foot that dominates its rhythm, not upon any particular foot that occurs in it. It may be necessary for the reader to scan three or four or more lines before he is satisfied as to what the prevailing foot is. Generally speaking, the best procedure is to mark the stressed and unstressed syllables and then divide them into feet in the most convenient way. In almost any passage of half a dozen lines the prevailing meter is sure to emerge. Of course, many poems are written in mixed rhythms, with varying meters and line lengths, so that there is no prevailing meter, but a more or less regular pattern of variation. For examples, see "The Dissolution" by John Donne (p. 175) and "Ode: Intimations of Immortality" by William Wordsworth (p. 244).

Because the metrical system that we have described in this chapter is not quite at home in English verse, other ways of analyzing rhythm have occasionally been suggested. The only important innovation of this kind is the one developed by the Victorian poet Gerard Manley Hopkins. Hopkins invented a system called *sprung rhythm*, which made allowance for the fact that stress, rather than quantity, was the controlling element of English verse. Hopkins suggested that each stressed syllable be regarded as constituting a metrical foot and that a varying number of unstressed syllables be allowed between them. He found numerous examples of this kind of rhythm in folk-poetry and in Anglo-Saxon poetry. Further, Hopkins suggested that for convenience the stressed syllable be regarded as the first syllable of each foot. This would make four kinds of feet possible: single stressed syllables, trochees, dactyls, and the foot consisting of one stressed syllable followed by three unstressed ones, called the *First Paeon*. In practice, of course, only the first three would be common. The first four lines of Hopkins's "Felix Randal" exemplify sprung verse and show its most prominent new quality—the varying number of unstressed syllables between the stresses.

Felix Randal the farrier, O he is dead then? my

    duty all ended,

Who have watched his mould of man, big-boned and

    hardy-handsome

Pining, pining, till time when reason rambled in it and some

Fatal four disorders, fleshed there, all contended?

Sprung verse, as Hopkins observed, resembles the rhythm of natural speech; it is therefore appropriate to the conversational and informal style common in modern poetry. Hopkins' innovation in verse has had considerable influence, both as a way of scanning verse and as a guide for creating rhythms.

EXAMPLES. Poems with pronounced rhythm are: Lovelace, "To Lucasta, Going to the Wars," p. 201; Blake, "The Tyger," p. 238; Byron, "The Destruction of Sennacherib," p. 252; Browning, "A Toccata of Galuppi's," p. 280; Shapiro, "Buick," p. 375; Manifold, "Fife Tune," p. 386. Examples of sprung rhythm: Hopkins, "God's Grandeur," p. 304; Lewis, "As One Who Wanders Into Old Workings," p. 352.

OTHER ELEMENTS OF RHYTHM

Another consideration in the rhythm of poetry is the placing of the pauses that occur. Clauses, phrases, and the groupings of words into speech units introduce natural pauses in poetry, just as they do in speech. When such a pause occurs somewhere in the middle of a line, it is called a *caesura*. Unless a line is exceptionally short, it is likely to have a caesura. In Browning's line

> There lay the city thick and plain with spires,

the caesura comes exactly in the middle of the iambic pentameter line, after the word "city." The caesura can occur in the middle of a metric foot or at the end of one. In addition to the caesura, a line of verse may also have (and usually does have) one or more secondary pauses. Byron's

> The beautiful, the brave, the lords of earth and sea

has a caesura after "brave," and secondary pauses after "beautiful" and "earth." These pauses have an appreciable effect on the rhythm of verse, and the placing of the caesura can be varied interestingly, as in these iambic pentameter lines from Milton's *Paradise Lost:*

> Nine times the space // that measures day and night
> To mortal men, // he with his horrid crew
> Lay vanquished, // rolling in the fiery gulf,

Confounded though immortal. // But his doom
Reserved him to more wrath; // for now the thought
Both of lost happiness // and lasting pain
Torments him; // round he throws his baleful eyes
That witnessed huge affliction // and dismay,
Mixed with obdurate pride // and steadfast hate.

The end of a line of verse is the end of a metrical unit, but it
is not necessarily the end of a sentence, clause, or phrase. The poet
has the choice of making the line ending coincide with the natural
dropping of the voice and pause for breath that occurs at the end
of a speech group, or he can carry the speech group over into the
next line, so that it links two lines together. Since the poet's practice in these respects makes a difference in the quality of his verse,
a special terminology has been coined for the way line endings are
treated. A line that has a natural pause at the end (usually indicated by a period, comma or some other mark of punctuation) is
called *end-stopped*. A line that has no such pause is called a *run-on
line* or *enjambment* (see Glossary).

Here is a passage from Oliver Goldsmith's "The Deserted
Village," which consists entirely of end-stopped lines:

Ill fares the land, to hast'ning ills a prey,
Where wealth accumulates, and men decay:
Princes and lords may flourish, or may fade;
A breath can make them, as a breath has made;
But a bold peasantry, their country's pride,
When once destroy'd, can never be supplied.

The following from Browning's "My Last Duchess," by contrast,
consists entirely of run-on lines:

Sir, 'twas not
Her husband's presence only, called that spot
Of joy into the Duchess' cheek: perhaps
Frà Pandolf chanced to say "Her mantle laps
Over my lady's wrist too much," or "Paint
Must never hope to reproduce the faint
Half-flush that dies along her throat:" such stuff
Was courtesy, she thought, and cause enough
For calling up that spot of joy.

This passage is rather unusual, for it is rare to find so long a series of run-on lines.

The end-stopped line is the more conservative and natural way of handling pauses; it makes the pause coincide with the end of the metrical unit and with the rhyme, if there is one. In the periods of English poetry when formal requirements were most severe, it was almost a rule that verse should consist of end-stopped lines. The run-on line subordinates the poem's lines to the rhythms of speech. It therefore has a natural, conversational, and informal effect. It is suitable for drama and dialogue and is common in modern poetry, which often strives for informality. Though there have been times when nearly all poetry consisted of end-stopped lines, it is nearly impossible to write entirely in run-on lines. The usual practice is to mix the two in varying proportions, as in these lines from Theodore Roethke's "A Walk in Late Summer":

> A late rose ravages the casual eye,
> A blaze of being on a central stem.
> It lies upon us to undo the lie
> Of living merely in the realm of time.
> Existence moves toward a certain end—
> A thing all earthly lovers understand.
> That dove's elaborate way of coming near
> Reminds me I am dying with the year.

It is sometimes said that meter is expressive in itself, and that in a good poem one can tell from the sound of the verse what the poem is about. For better or for worse, the metrical resources of poetry are too limited for any such purpose. All that can be claimed for the meter of most poems is that it provides a rhythm which creates a background impression of order. The meter should be appropriate to the thought. A serious poem should not have a jogging, skipping meter, and a humorous one should not have a slow rhythm. Meters can suggest moods, but they cannot express definite feelings. Most of the attempts along this line have been unfortunate, and they seem to prove that the poets were trying to make meter carry more meaning than it could. For example, the anapestic foot is supposed to sound like the hoofbeats of a running horse, and Browning used it for that effect in "How They Brought the Good News from Ghent to Aix":

I sprang to the stirrup, and Joris, and he;
I galloped, Dirck galloped, we galloped all three.

Tennyson's "The Brook" is another famous example of meter used
for expressive effect.

I come from haunts of coot and hern,
I make a sudden sally,
And sparkle out among the fern,
To bicker down a valley.

Probably the final opinion on this subject was given by Pope, who
said that the sound of a poem "must seem an echo to the sense."
The sense, however, is in the words, not in the meter. The meter
can, at best, faintly reflect it. Pope himself performed what is
probably the most successful feat of this kind in such lines as:

When Ajax strives some rock's vast weight to throw,
The line, too, labours and the words move slow.

Here Ajax's efforts are admirably suggested in the clumps of
stressed syllables—"rock's vast weight," "line, too, labours," and
"words move slow."

Not so when swift Camilla scours the plain,
Flies o'er th'unbending corn and skims along the main.

And here the flight is reflected in the regular, smooth, iambic
movement of the verse.

EXAMPLES. Milton, "On the Late Massacre in Piedmont," p. 194;
Blake, "A Poison Tree," p. 238; Browning, "The Bishop Orders
His Tomb," p. 282; Arnold, "Dover Beach," p. 291; Hardy, "The
Convergence of the Twain," p. 49; Lewis, "As One Who Wan-
ders Into Old Workings," p. 352; Hall, "The Morning Porches,"
p. 395.

OTHER SOUND EFFECTS

Though rhythm is easily the most important and most inescapable element of sound in poetry, there are numerous other resources of sound a poet can use. One of the most common of
these is the familiar device of *rhyme*. Rhyme is the similarity in

sound between the syllables at the end of two (or more) lines of poetry that is always found in popular and children's verse,

> As I was going to St. *Ives*
> I met a man with seven *wives.*

The similarity of a single syllable, as in this example, is enough to establish a rhyme, but sometimes the rhyme will include two syllables.

> Perhaps you may ask if the man was a *miser?*
> I answer, no, no, for he always was *wiser.*
>
> —OLIVER GOLDSMITH, "Retaliation"

This situation, where the rhyme consists of a stressed syllable followed by an unstressed one, is known as a *feminine rhyme.* Occasionally a rhyme will include three syllables:

> I'm very good at integral and differential *calculus,*
> I know the scientific names of beings *animalculous* . . .
>
> —W. S. GILBERT, *The Pirates of Penzance*

But this sort of rhyme is probably more appropriate to light verse than serious poetry.

There are at least two variations of rhyme, one common, and one fairly rare, that deserve mention. The common variation is the so-called *off-rhyme* or *slant rhyme,* a rhyme in which the vowel sounds are not really identical, but are similar enough to sound alike.

> Apes and angels playing *tunes*
> On harpsichords or saxo*phones.*
>
> —HERBERT READ, "A World Within a War"

> Only reapers, reaping *early*
> In among the bearded *barley.* . . .
>
> —ALFRED LORD TENNYSON, "The Lady of Shalott"

Some imperfect rhymes are results of historical accidents. Since the times of Shakespeare and Pope the pronunciation of English has changed somewhat. As a result, vowels that were perfect rhymes at one time do not rhyme any longer, though they remain close enough to be accepted as off-rhymes. For example,

Come live with me and be my *love*,
And we will all the pleasures *prove*.

—CHRISTOPHER MARLOWE, "The Passionate Shepherd to his Love"

was originally an exact rhyme, for the vowel in "love" was pronounced in Marlowe's day like the vowel in "prove." Similarly in

Here thou, great ANNA! whom three realms obey,
Dost sometimes counsel take—and sometimes tea.

—ALEXANDER POPE, "The Rape of the Lock"

"tea" was originally pronounced exactly as we pronounce the last
syllable in "obey." The reader will often encounter this situation
in poetry that is more than two hundred years old and should
make allowances for the changes in language that have altered the
effect of some rhymes.

Rhyme, it will be noticed, is based on the similarity of *vowel*
sounds. When consonants are included, they support the resemblance, but similarity of consonants alone does not constitute
rhyme. "Flair" does not rhyme with "floor" and "simple" does
not rhyme with "sample." However, some modern poets have
used the resemblance of consonants rather than vowels as a substitute for rhyme. This is our second and rare variant on the practice of rhyme. The device is drawn from Welsh poetry, where
it is standard, and is called by its Welsh name, *cynganhedd*, which
may be translated (rather self-contradictorily) as "consonant
rhyme." It was used conspicuously by Wilfred Owen in 'Strange
Meeting":

It seemed that out of the battle I *escaped*
Down some profound dull tunnel, long since *scooped*
Through granites which Titanic wars had *groined*.
Yet also there encumbered sleepers *groaned*.

Consonant rhyme is another innovation that is appropriate to the
informality of modern verse.

The function of rhyme is that of tying the poem together,
giving an impression of continuity, shape, and form. Rhyme can
be arranged in a variety of ways to give a number of different
forms. A pair of lines rhyming consecutively is called a *couplet*.

A group of four lines rhyming in some order is a *quatrain*. Some of the standard verse forms are based on elaborate arrangements of rhyme. (See Chapter 5.)

In addition to meter and rhyme, which are parts of the texture of a poem, there are some other devices which a poet may use to ornament or reinforce the meaning of his poem. *Alliteration* is the practice of beginning a number of consecutive or neighboring words with the same consonant, so that a definite effect is achieved.

> *M*any a *m*orning on the *m*oorland did we hear the copses ring.
>
> —ALFRED LORD TENNYSON, "Locksley Hall"

> And the *w*onderful *w*aters knew her, the *w*inds and the viewless *w*ays.
>
> —A. C. SWINBURNE, "Hymn to Proserpine"

> *G*irt in dark *g*rowths, yet *g*limmering with one star.
>
> —DANTE GABRIEL ROSSETTI, "Sleepless Dreams"

Assonance is similarity of vowel sound without the support of consonants which constitutes rhyme. Though sometimes used, especially in modern poetry, as a substitute for rhyme, it is usually found within the line, where it is capable of producing quiet musical effects.

> The army of un*a*lterable l*a*w.
>
> —GEORGE MEREDITH, "Lucifer in Starlight"

> Br*ea*thing like one that hath a w*ea*ry dr*ea*m
>
> —ALFRED LORD TENNYSON, "The Lotos-Eaters"

> Thou foster-ch*i*ld of s*i*lence and slow T*i*me,
>
> —JOHN KEATS, "Ode on a Grecian Urn"

The sound of poetry may be functional as well as ornamental. When a passage imitates or echoes its subject through its sound, we have an effect called *onomatopoeia*. Imitation is a familiar linguistic principle. Many bird names, such as *chickadee* and *whippoorwill*, and many words meaning particular sounds, such as *gurgle*, *splash*, and *hiss*, are clearly onomatopoeic in origin.

Though poetry's capacity for such effects is rather limited, there have been striking examples. Pope's line "The hoarse rough verse should like the torrent roar" uses its open vowels to imitate the stormy sea, and Keats's "The murmurous haunt of flies on summer eves" echoes by its sound the quiet grove he is describing. These lines about a rooster from Wallace Stevens' "Bantams in Pine-Woods" brilliantly suggest the nervous strutting of the bird:

> Chieftain Iffucan of Azcan in caftan
> Of tan with henna hackles, halt!

Most of these phonic effects have diminished in importance since the time when poetry was composed for recitation. Alliteration, for example, was the main structural element of Old English poetry, and in the nineteenth century, when reading aloud was a favorite family pastime, such swinging verses and resounding rhymes as those of Kipling had considerable importance. In modern poetry, however, all of these elements are clearly secondary to the sense of the poem and are characteristically used in inconspicuous ways to knit the poem together and to strengthen its structure.

EXAMPLES. Various types of rhyme, alliteration, assonance, and similar effects may be found in Swinburne's "Garden of Proserpine," p. 297; for an interesting modern use of rhyme, see Moore, "Critics and Connoisseurs," p. 331; for consonant rhyme, Owen, "Arms and the Boy," p. 347, and Thomas, "The Force that Through the Green Fuse," p. 380.

FURTHER READING

Harvey Gross, *Sound and Form in Modern Poetry*, Ann Arbor, Mich., 1964, Chapter II, "The Scansion of English Meters," pp. 24–41.
John Pick, ed., *A Hopkins Reader*, New York and London, 1953, pp. 98–100.

Form and Structure 5

THE SONNET AS A FORM

The importance of organization in poetry will be suggested by a consideration of the following:

> Death stands above me, whispering fear,
>   I know not what is all I know:
> Into his strange language of my ear,
>   There is not a word of low.

With the possible exception of the first, these lines make little sense. Yet all the ingredients of sense are there. The same words rearranged give Walter Savage Landor's little poem:

> Death stands above me, whispering low
>   I know not what into my ear:
> Of his strange language all I know
>   Is, there is not a word of fear.

This is clear, understandable, and expressive language. If we ask why the same words in these two cases are so different in intelligibility, we come to the obvious conclusion that the difference lies in their order, and that their order is important because it establishes relationships among the words. For example, by putting "fear" in the place of "low" in the first line, we have changed the relationship between "whispering" and the word following it. "Fear" becomes the object of "whispering," while "low" is an adverbial modifier. The meaning, of course, is changed, so that the line that reads "whispering fear" means something very different from Landor's original thought, and the rest of the scrambled quatrain can hardly be said to have any meaning at all. Intelligibility, then, is not merely a matter of words, but of the relationships created by the arrangement of words. In short, it depends on *organization.*

Organization controls not only the intelligibility of a poem but also the esthetic impression it produces. Just as an irregular and scattered arrangement of the shapes in a painting evokes one response in the viewer, while a rhythmic and orderly arrangement evokes another, so the various organizational devices of every art have a great deal to do with the feeling a particular work conveys. If, for example, the idea of Landor's quatrain were expressed in this way: "I do not know what to expect of death, but I do not fear it," it is obvious that the prose paraphrase conveys a very different impression from that of the poem, even though the thought is approximately the same.

Organization in poetry involves a kind of partnership between the poet and the reader. The good or proper arrangement of materials is not a natural, absolute thing, but a matter of cultural conditioning. What would seem to be elegant and clear order in one period, or under one set of conditions, might well appear barbarous and unintelligible under different circumstances. Poetic form belongs to the class of things we call *conventions*—tacit agreements or understandings that grow up spontaneously in social groups. A useful analogy appears in language, which is a thoroughly conventional product. Why do speakers of English generally place the subject before the verb and the object after it? This practice is not determined by any rule of nature or the working of the human mind, for there are languages which have different usages. The answer is that the practice has grown up through centuries of custom and has established itself so firmly through usefulness and familiarity that it is universally accepted. In any given situation, a speaker will express himself according to the custom, and his hearer will accept and understand his use of it. In the same way, the effect of poetic organization depends on both the work of the poet and the expectations of the reader. The reader, through his experience, is prepared to make certain interpretations of the features he finds in a poem, and the poet is ready to manipulate these expectations in accordance with his aims.

Though it has a general meaning in other arts, the word

"form" is often used in discussions of poetry to refer specifically to such technical and mechanical matters as rhyme, meter, and stanza arrangement. Couplets, quatrains, sonnets, and so on, are called poetic *forms*. The organization of the thought in a poem may conveniently be called the *structure* of the poem. Poetic forms are comparatively few and fairly well defined. Structures, on the other hand, are too numerous to be classified and exhibit a great deal of variety, for they depend less on tradition and more on the activity of the poet's mind. Generally speaking, it is easy enough to identify the form of a poem. But if the reader is to understand the poem well, he must also obtain some sense of its structure—of the way its thoughts are related to each other. He should know, for example, whether a given idea amplifies, parallels, or contrasts with the ideas around it; he should know whether the poem as a whole constitutes a progression, a series of repetitions, an antithesis, or a combination of these.

The popular poetic form called the *sonnet* offers good illustrations of both form and structure in poetry. In *form* a sonnet is a poem of fourteen iambic pentameter lines, having one of two rhyme schemes. The older form, called the *Italian sonnet,* was developed in Italy and popularized by Petrarch, and it was frequently used by English Renaissance poets. The first eight lines (called the *octave*) of the Italian sonnet has the rhyme pattern *abbaabba*. The last six lines (called the *sestet*) may have any of a number of rhyme schemes; a common one is *cdecde*. These requirements may sound very arbitrary, as if they were deliberately invented by some poet or scholar, but the sonnet is the natural outgrowth of a long tradition, like every other convention. Here is an example of the Italian sonnet:

ON THE GRASSHOPPER AND CRICKET

JOHN KEATS (1795–1821)

The poetry of earth is never dead:
　When all the birds are faint with the hot sun,
　And hide in cooling trees, a voice will run
From hedge to hedge about the new-mown mead;

That is the Grasshopper's—he takes the lead   5
  In summer luxury,—he has never done
  With his delights; for when tired out with fun
He rests at ease beneath some pleasant weed.

The poetry of earth is ceasing never:
  On a lone winter evening when the frost   10
    Has wrought a silence, from the stove there shrills
The Cricket's song, in warmth increasing ever,
  And seems to one in drowsiness half lost,
    The Grasshopper's among some grassy hills.

The second variety of sonnet, called the *English,* or *Shakespearean sonnet,* consists of three quatrains followed by a couplet. The rhyme scheme is *abab cdcd efef gg.* This form arose because the numerous rhymes necessary in the Italian sonnet were hard to find in English; the English poets preserved the fourteen-line length and the iambic pentameter rhythm, but devised a new and easier rhyme scheme. Shakespeare's name is identified with this form, not because he invented it but because his sonnets are the most famous examples of it. The following, Shakespeare's "Sonnet 106," illustrates the form and shows that it is well adapted to the brief and graceful expression of a rather complicated idea. In it the poet says that the descriptions of beautiful people he reads in old poems remind him of his lady, but that even the old poets would have been unable to do justice to her without their special gifts, for those who see her now are unable to praise her sufficiently.

When in the chronicle of wasted time
I see descriptions of the fairest wights,
And beauty making beautiful old rhyme
In praise of ladies dead and lovely knights,
Then, in the blazon of sweet beauty's best,   5
Of hand, of foot, of lip, of eye, of brow,
I see their antique pen would have express'd
Even such a beauty as you master now.
So all their praises are but prophecies
Of this our time, all you prefiguring;   10

2 *wights:* persons 5 *blazon:* originally, the heraldic design on a shield 10 *prefiguring:* anticipating

And, for they look'd but with divining eyes,
They had not skill enough your worth to sing;
For we, which now behold these present days,
Have eyes to wonder, but lack tongues to praise.

As this example shows, the couplet at the end of the Shakespearean sonnet can have a definite air of finality and is an excellent way of finishing off the poem.

The two kinds of sonnets lend themselves to different arrangements of thought, that is, to different structures. The Italian sonnet divides naturally into two parts, the octave and the sestet. The sense of moving from one part of the poem to another is very clear; the octave has its own often-repeated rhymes, and the final rhyme has a concluding sound. The sestet begins with new rhymes, thereby establishing an identity of its own. This division is usually emphasized formally by placing a full pause after the last line of the octave. Such a division lends itself naturally to the expression of a thought that has two parts. Hence, the arrangement of thought—the *structure*—of an Italian sonnet is often a question and answer, a cause and an effect, two elements of a comparison, a generalization followed by a specific application, a problem followed by a solution, and so on. The English sonnet, on the other hand, breaks naturally into four divisions, three quatrains and a couplet. It is therefore a natural medium for ideas which can be expressed in three equal parts followed by a couplet which, because it is too short for the development of a new thought, is generally used to conclude or to sum up. It is obvious here that form and structure are interdependent. If a poet had a three-part idea in mind, he would use the English sonnet form; if he had a two-part idea in mind, he would use the Italian. If, on the other hand, he began his sonnet, as many, if not all poets do, with a strong feeling, but only a vague idea of his thought, his choice of form would go a long way toward determining the structure of his thought.

Many poets who have written sonnets have ignored the special advantages and capacities of the form. Milton, for example, wrote some very great Italian sonnets, but he paid no attention to the convention of separating the octave and the sestet, and many of his sonnets have no pause whatever at the end of the eighth line. Keats's sonnet, "On the Grasshopper and the Cricket," quoted above, shows how form and structure can be made to parallel each other. Both parts of this Italian sonnet support the assertion of the first line, "The poetry of earth is never dead." But they support it in different ways. The octave bases its argument on the summer phenomenon of the grasshopper's song, while the sestet turns to its winter counterpart, the cricket's chirping, as an illustration of "the poetry of earth." The effect of similarity in contrast is skillfully strengthened by the variant of the first line that begins the sestet.

Compare the two-part structure of Keats's sonnet with that of the following, an English sonnet from Edmund Spenser's sonnet sequence *Amoretti:*

SONNET 62

The weary year his race now having run,
The new begins his compass course anew,
With show of morning mild he hath begun,
Betokening peace and plenty to ensue.
So let us, which this change of weather view,   5
Change eke our minds, and former lives amend;
The old year's sins forepast let us eschew,
And fly the faults with which we did offend.
Then shall the new year's joy forth freshly send
Into the glooming world his gladsome ray,   10
And all these storms, which now his beauty blend,
Shall turn to calms and timely clear away.
So, likewise, Love, cheer you your heavy sprite,
And change old year's annoy to new delight.*

* Note that the rhyme of the second and fourth lines of the first quatrain is repeated in the first and third lines of the second quatrain, and that the rhyme of the second and fourth lines in this quatrain appears, in turn, in the first and third lines of the last quatrain. This linkage is a special case, characteristic of the *Amoretti,* but not of sonnets generally.

The fact that each of the three quatrains in this sonnet ends in a period clearly suggests that the thought is complete within the quatrain. The first four lines say that the weather at the beginning of the new year promises good times. The second quatrain urges the poet's lover to follow the example of the new year by forgetting their old grievances and misdeeds. The third one predicts that if they do this the new year will actually be peaceful and beautiful. The couplet then summarizes the message of the sonnet as a whole.

A close relationship between form and structure is found in poetry generally as well as in sonnets. In illustrating and examining the commonest forms used by poets writing English, we shall concentrate on their expressive, organizational, and esthetic qualities. These are often very prominent in particular poems, and the reader should be familiar enough with the conventional forms to be in a position to appreciate them as a part of the effect of the poem as a whole. Further, the poetic forms are interesting cultural products. Each of them reflects, to a greater or lesser degree, the habit of mind of the historical period which invented or made use of it.

EXAMPLES. Shakespeare's sonnets, pp. 172–175; Donne's sonnets, pp. 180–181; Wordsworth, "The World is Too Much With Us," p. 240; Robinson, "The Sheaves," p. 317. Examples of variants on the sonnet form: Sidney, *Astrophel and Stella*, Sonnet 1 ("Loving in truth, and fain in verse my love to show"), p. 169; Meredith, *Modern Love*, p. 292; Hopkins, "The Windhover," p. 303.

RHYMING FORMS

The shortest of the forms using rhyme is the *couplet,* a pair of lines rhyming with each other. Couplets may be written in any meter, of course, but the iambic pentameter couplet has attained so special a position that it must be considered a distinct poetic form. It is called the *heroic couplet,* but this is a misnomer, for the best-known works in this form are not particularly heroic. The iambic pentameter couplet was used by Chaucer in the *Canterbury Tales* and by certain Renaissance dramatists, but it did not achieve its distinctive development until the seventeenth and eighteenth centuries when it was used by Dryden, Pope, and their contemporaries. At this time, it became the fashion to treat each couplet as a self-contained unit of thought, tersely and economically expressing a separate idea. There would naturally be a pause at the end of the second line, and nearly always at the end of the first as well. The result was a tight, closely knit, epigrammatic kind of poetry built up of separate little bricks of thought.

> 'Tis with our judgments as our watches, none
> Go just alike, yet each believes his own.
> In poets as true genius is but rare,
> True taste as seldom is the critic's share,
> Both must alike from Heaven derive their light,
> These born to judge, as well as those to write.
> Let such teach others who themselves excel,
> And censure freely who have written well;
> Authors are partial to their wit, 'tis true,
> But are not critics to their judgment too?

These couplets from Pope's "Essay on Criticism" exemplify the form which dominated English poetry throughout the eighteenth century and remained influential long afterward. Every line is end-stopped; each couplet is syntactically independent; the thought is contained within the couplet, but carefully related to the context. This use of the couplet is noticeably different from that of such poets as Chaucer and Keats, who did not think of the couplets as units of thought. These poets, who wrote before and after the period when the heroic couplet was dominant, usually allowed their thought and syntactic structure to run through long series of couplets and often began a new sentence and a new train of thought with the second line of a couplet, or even in the middle of a line. These lines from Keats's "Endymion" should be compared with those of Pope; the comparison will show clearly that Keats did not, like Pope, regard the couplet as a distinct unit.

> Soon the assembly, in a circle rang'd,
> Stood silent round the shrine: each look was chang'd
> To sudden veneration: women meek
> Beckon'd their sons to silence; while each cheek
> Of virgin bloom paled gently for slight fear.
> Endymion too, without a forest peer,
> Stood, wan, and pale, and with an awed face,
> Among his brothers of the mountain chase.

Pope would have found many things to criticize here. He would have objected to the places where the thought and the sentence continue into the next couplet without a pause (". . . each look was chang'd / To sudden veneration . . ."). He would have objected to the pauses that come in the middle of a line instead of the end. He would have objected, especially, to the appearance of a new thought, and a new person, Endymion, in the second line of a couplet.

The heroic couplet lends itself to a limited number of ways of arranging the thought within the lines. The thought may simply be continued through the two lines, needing the space of both for its expression:

> The man to solitude accustom'd long
> Perceives in ev'ry thing that lives a tongue;
> Not animals alone, but shrubs and trees,
> Have speech for him, and understood with ease.

> —WILLIAM COWPER, "The Needless Alarm"

The second line of the couplet may restate or parallel the thought of the first:

> For gold his sword the hireling ruffian draws,
> For gold the hireling judge distorts the laws.

> —SAMUEL JOHNSON, "The Vanity of Human Wishes"

It is typical of the heroic couplet, however, that its two lines can be made to play off against each other through contrast or antithesis to achieve a balanced and unified effect. For example, the first line may ask a question which the second answers:

> Why has not man a microscopic eye?
> For this plain reason, man is not a fly.

> —ALEXANDER POPE, "Essay on Man"

Or each of the two lines may be devoted to contrasting subjects, thus dividing the couplet into clear halves:

> Self-love, the spring of motion, acts the soul;
> Reason's comparing balance rules the whole.

> —ALEXANDER POPE, "Essay on Man"

Or the contrast may divide the individual lines in half, so that the antithesis is expressed even more economically in each separate line of the couplet. Thus, Dryden, explaining that the reports of a conspiracy against the government were only partly true, wrote:

> Some Truth there was, but dashed and brew'd with Lies;
> To please the Fools, and puzzle all the Wise.
>
> —JOHN DRYDEN, "Absalom and Achitophel"

A stanza of three lines is called a *tercet*. The lines of this stanza may be identical, or they may vary in length and meter. Tercets allow so much freedom in the arrangement of thought that they are best considered a formal rather than a structural device. A tercet may have a single rhyme for all three lines, as in the following example:

> He clasps the crag with crooked hands;
> Close to the sun in lonely lands,
> Ring'd with the azure world, he stands.
>
> —ALFRED LORD TENNYSON, "The Eagle"

Sometimes the first and third lines of the tercet will rhyme with each other, leaving the middle line to rhyme with lines in another stanza. This is the case in Browning's "The Statue and the Bust":

> There's a palace in Florence, the world knows well,
> And a statue watches it from the square,
> And this story of both do our townsmen tell.

A further development of the tercet, the one used by Browning in this poem, is *terza rima*. In *terza rima* the rhyme occurring in the middle of the *aba* tercet becomes the rhyme of the first and last lines in the next tercet, so that the sequence of rhymes runs: *aba bcb cdc ded* and so on. Though *terza rima*, originally an Italian form, was used by Dante in the *Divine Comedy*, its use in English poetry has been limited. Here is an example of it from a version of the story of the city mouse and the country mouse by Sir Thomas Wyatt:

> My mother's maids when they do sew and spin,
> They sing a song made of the fieldish mouse;

That forbecause her livelihood was but thin,
Would needs go see her townish sister's house.
She thought herself endured to grievous pain;
The stormy blasts her cave so sore did souse,
That when the furrows swimmëd with the rain
She must lie cold and wet, in sorry plight.
And worse than that, bare meat there did remain
To comfort her when she her house had dight.

While tercets are fairly rare, *quatrains*, or four-line stanzas, are the most familiar of all English verse forms. Quatrains of one sort or another have been popular in almost every period. As a form the quatrain, which may vary its rhyme scheme and the length and meter of its lines almost indefinitely, presents numerous different possibilities. A few of these have achieved some importance as individual forms. For example, the *ballad stanza*, which has four feet in its first and third lines and three in its second and fourth, and rhymes only in the second and fourth lines, is characteristic of the informal narrative style of the early English ballads.

> Ye Highlands and ye Lawlands,
>   Oh where have you been?
> They have slain the Earl of Murray,
>   And they layd him on the green.
>
> —ANONYMOUS, "The Bonny Earl of Murray"

This quatrain, with its easy formal requirements and songlike quality, is ideally suited to the kind of folk-poetry where story and tune rather than organization are the important things. Most of the ballads in this form are anonymous and have come down through tradition from indefinite origins, but they are surprisingly similar in technique. For one thing, they all use the quatrain as a separate unit, in the same way as the eighteenth-century poets used the couplet, so that the thought and the syntax generally come to a pause at the end of the stanza. A more dignified and formal use of the quatrain is represented by Gray's "Elegy in a Country Churchyard." This poem, written during the period when the heroic couplet was popular, seems to translate the practices connected with the heroic couplet into the use of the quatrain. Its lines are all iambic pentameter, nearly all of them are end-stopped, and the vast majority of the stanzas contain a completed thought, as in this example:

> Full many a gem of purest ray serene,
> The dark unfathom'd caves of ocean bear:
> Full many a flower is born to blush unseen,
> And waste its sweetness on the desert air.

Instead of alternating in the sequence *abab*, the rhymes in a quatrain may be arranged in the pattern *abba*. This is not a common form, but it has been used in one very famous long poem, Tennyson's *In Memoriam* (p. 270). Here is an example from a seventeenth-century poem, the first stanza of Ben Jonson's "Elegy":

> Though beauty be the mark of praise,
> And yours of whom I sing be such
> As not the world can praise too much,
> Yet is't your virtue now I raise.

The quatrain has been a popular rhyme pattern in nearly every period of English poetry, and it appears in contemporary verse more frequently than any other rhyming form.

It is possible to devise an almost indefinite number of stanza forms by combining different meters and rhyme schemes. Poets have invented stanza forms consisting of almost every number of lines up to eighteen or more. For example, adding one line to a quatrain produces a five-line stanza that has its own distinctive quality, as Suckling's "Why So Pale and Wan?" (p. 15) shows, and this pattern of rhyme has had frequent use, in a variety of meters. But the most important standard verse forms after the couplet, tercet, quatrain, and sonnet are *rhyme royal, ottava rima,* and the Spenserian stanza.

Rhyme royal is a stanza of seven lines, usually in iambic pentameter, rhyming *ababbcc*. It was used by Chaucer as a narrative medium and continues to appear from time to time throughout English poetry. This example of it is from a nineteenth-century poem, William Morris' *The Earthly Paradise:*

> Of Heaven or Hell I have no power to sing,
> I cannot ease the burden of your fears,
> Or make quick-coming death a little thing,

> Or bring again the pleasures of past years,
> Nor for my words shall ye forget your tears,
> Or hope again, for aught that I can say,
> The idle singer of an empty day.

Ottava rima, as its name suggests, is an eight-line stanza adapted from the Italian. It has the rhyme scheme *ababababcc*. Introduced into English poetry during the Renaissance, it is found in recent poetry (see Yeats's "Sailing to Byzantium," p. 309). The most famous poem in *ottava rima* is Byron's long comic narrative *Don Juan* (p. 253). This is the first stanza of the first canto (note that Byron uses the rhyme to tell the reader, at the very beginning, how he wants his hero's name to be pronounced):

> I want a hero: an uncommon want,
>   When every year and month sends forth a new one,
> Till, after cloying the gazettes with cant,
>   The age discovers he is not the true one;
> Of such as these I should not care to vaunt,
>   I'll therefore take our ancient friend Don Juan—
> We all have seen him, in the pantomime,
> Sent to the devil somewhat ere his time.

The Spenserian stanza was invented by the author of *The Faery Queen*, who used it as a narrative medium, telling his long story through thousands of these stanzas. Later poets often adopted the Spenserian stanza, though they used it for meditative and descriptive poetry as much as for narration. The Spenserian stanza has fairly complicated specifications. It consists of nine lines, all iambic pentameter except the last, which is hexameter. Its rhyme scheme is *ababbcbcc*. Here is an example of it, a stanza from Shelley's "Adonais" that describes the coming of spring:

> Through wood and stream and field and hill and Ocean
> A quickening life from the Earth's heart has burst
> As it has ever done, with change and motion,
> From the great morning of the world when first
> God dawned on Chaos; in its stream immersed,
> The lamps of Heaven flash with a softer light;
> All baser things pant with life's sacred thirst;
> Diffuse themselves; and spend in love's delight,
> The beauty and the joy of their renewèd might.

Like the Italian sonnet, the Spenserian stanza allows for a "turn" or change of thought, either a reversal or a renewal. It does this by means of the fifth line, which repeats the rhyme of the fourth. The long last line, called an *alexandrine* (see Glossary), can be used for a concluding thought, like the final couplet of the sonnet, or for a particularly resounding or elegant effect.

EXAMPLES. Couplets exhibiting various styles and meters: Southwell, "The Burning Babe," p. 170; Marvell, "To His Coy Mistress," p. 204; Housman, "To an Athlete Dying Young," p. 306; Frost, "Once By the Pacific," p. 6; Lowell, "The Crucifix" (irregular), p. 388. Tercets and *terza rima:* Shelley, "Ode to the West Wind," p. 80; Browning, "A Toccata of Galuppi's," p. 280; Roethke, "The Waking," p. 368; Hall, "The Morning Porches," p. 395.

Quatrains in various styles and meters: "Sir Patrick Spens," p. 161; Donne, "The Ecstasy," p. 177; Blake, "Preface to *Milton*," p. 237; Scott, "Proud Maisie," p. 250; Landor, "Dirce," p. 251; Keats, "La Belle Dame Sans Merci," p. 262; Longfellow, "The Jewish Cemetery at Newport," p. 265; Tennyson, from *In Memoriam,* p. 270; Hardy, "Channel Firing," p. 301; Watkins, "The Mummy," p. 359.

Five-line stanzas: Shelley, "The World's Great Age Begins Anew," p. 259; Shakespeare, "Fear No More the Heat o' the Sun," p. 171; Betjeman, "In Westminster Abbey," p. 387.

Unconventional stanza forms: Herrick, "To Daffodils," p. 184; Herbert, "Discipline," p. 189; Gray, "Ode on the Death of a Favourite Cat," p. 232; Wordsworth, "The Solitary Reaper," p. 241; Keats, "Ode on a Grecian Urn," p. 263; Browning, "Soliloquy of the Spanish Cloister," p. 277; Moore, "Critics and Connoisseurs," p. 331; MacNeice, "Schizophrene," p. 364; Auden, "Voltaire at Ferney," p. 362; Thomas, "A Refusal to Mourn the Death, By Fire, of a Child in London," p. 382.

Irregular rhyme patterns: Tennyson, "The Kraken," p. 142; Arnold, "Dover Beach," p. 291; Eliot, "The Love Song of J. Alfred Prufrock," p. 339; MacLeish, "The Silent Slain," p. 124; Auden, "Musée des Beaux Arts," p. 361.

BLANK VERSE AND FREE VERSE

There are two standard verse-forms that do not make use of rhyme. The oldest and most important of these is *blank verse*. It consists of iambic pentameter lines and is the form of many of the greatest long poems in English, including Shakespeare's plays, Milton's *Paradise Lost*, and Wordsworth's *Prelude*. Blank verse is an extremely flexible and subtle form. Since it has no rhyme, the form does not intrude upon the reader's attention, distracting him from the content of the poem, as sometimes happens in stanzaic forms, yet its regular meter, when properly handled, conveys a quiet sense of rhythm and organization. Variation can be introduced by pauses within the line, end-stopped or run-on lines, and the usual metrical variants. At times it is fashionable to have the blank verse line more or less self-contained, or end-stopped; at other times the run-on line is favored.

Three examples will suggest the variety that blank verse can achieve. The first is from *Dr. Faustus* by Christopher Marlowe, who is generally accepted as the first English poet to make effective use of blank verse. The quoted passage is from a highly emotional moment in the play. Faustus, after having sold his soul to the Devil and led a life of crime, is sinking into hell and tries desperately to avoid his fate at the last minute. He asks the stars to save him by transforming him into a cloud. At a time like this the poetry might well be violent and irregular, but Marlowe's conception of blank verse was such that his lines have a steady rhythm, and every line is end-stopped.

> You stars that reigned at my nativity,
> Whose influence hath allotted death and hell,
> Now draw up Faustus, like a foggy mist,
> Into the entrails of yon lab'ring clouds,
> That, when you vomit forth into the air,
> My limbs may issue from your smoky mouths,
> So that my soul may but ascend to heaven!

For a contrasting example, we turn to *King Lear*, a play written about fifteen years after *Dr. Faustus*, and so belonging to the same historical period. The dramatic situation in this example is comparable to the one from Marlowe's play. The old king, driven out into the storm by the ingratitude of his daughters, is going mad, and turns the anger he feels upon unjust men in general, warning them that the storm will expose them.

> Tremble, thou wretch,
> That hast within thee undivulged crimes,
> Unwhipp'd of justice: hide thee, thou bloody hand;
> Thou perjured, and thou simular man of virtue
> That art incestuous: caitiff, in pieces shake,
> That under covert and convenient seeming
> Hast practised on man's life close pent-up guilts
> Rive your concealing continents, and cry
> These dreadful summoners grace.

The energy of the feeling often carries the thought over into the next line, and on the other hand, the caesura occurs in abrupt and unexpected places. The iambic pentameter unit has nearly disappeared, for it is seldom heard beneath the other rhythms that have been superimposed over the form, rhythms that begin and end in the middle of the line at varying points. Obviously, Shakespeare's use of blank verse here is much freer than Marlowe's.

Blank verse remains as popular among modern poets as it has been in the past. It is often used for narrative and lyric poety, and, as in earlier periods of literature, is the natural medium for poetic drama. Here is an example of modern blank verse from "Birches" by Robert Frost:

> When I see birches bend to left and right
> Across the line of straighter darker trees,
> I like to think some boy's been swinging them.
> But swinging doesn't bend them down to stay
> As ice-storms do. Often you must have seen them
> Loaded with ice a sunny winter morning
> After a rain.

The rhythm of Frost's lines is hardly perceptible, for the metrical variants mask the meter. "Often you must have seen them" is very unrhythmical, and "As ice-storms do" has three consecutive stresses. The pauses fall where they may and land at the ends of the lines only by coincidence. The sentences and syntactical groupings are short and simple, as in speech. In general, the casual, conversational quality of these lines makes them characteristic of modern blank verse.

Free verse has neither rhyme nor a regular meter, and its sound is distinguished from that of prose only by a general rhythmical quality. Critics used to regard the free verse form as an absence of any form at all; actually, if it is well handled, it is quite demanding, for it requires the poet to improvise his rhythms at every point in the poem instead of following some traditional pattern. In free verse the lines may be of very different lengths, and the thought may begin and end anywhere. Free verse gives the poet very little guidance; it requires him to use his own judgment in manipulating the rhythms, pauses, and proportions of his poem. In the same way it demands close attention from the reader, who cannot rely upon convention as a basis for guidance and comparison. Two contrasting examples of free verse will show the different effects the form is capable of. The first, from Walt Whitman, one of its most famous practitioners, is loose, energetic, variable in its rhythms:

> I am enamour'd of growing out-doors,
> Of men that live among cattle or taste of the ocean or woods,
> Of the builders and steerers of ships and the wielders of axes and
>   mauls, and the drivers of horses,
> I can eat and sleep with them week in and week out.

Very different is the free verse of the American poet who signed herself "H. D." (Hilda Doolittle). In this passage from "Orchard" every word and syllable is carefully chosen to achieve a tight, restrained effect:

> O rough-hewn
> god of the orchard,
> I bring you an offering—
> do you, alone unbeautiful,
> son of the god,
> spare us from loveliness.

EXAMPLES. Blank verse: Tennyson, "Tithonus," p. 274; Browning, "The Bishop Orders His Tomb," p. 282. Free verse: Whitman,

"To a Locomotive in Winter," p. 287; Pound, "Lament of the Frontier Guard," p. 324; Williams, "The Poor," p. 323; Jeffers, "Hurt Hawks," p. 328; Bishop, "The Fish," p. 372.

VARIETIES OF STRUCTURE

In discussing poetic forms, we have been able to choose a few that are most common and to give illustrations of them. It would be impossible to do this with poetic structures, for the ways of arranging thought in poetry and the kinds of relationships that can exist among them are very numerous. In logic, mathematics, and other scientific ways of thinking, ideas are related according to fixed procedures. This is not true, however, of poetry; the poet uses his imagination in an opposite way, to find new ways of relating the details of his experience. There are, to be sure, some poetic structures that are more familiar than others, but these are, for that reason, likely to be least significant and meaningful as elements in a poem.

While it may be impossible to give any satisfactory catalogue or listing of poetic structures, it is well worth while to examine a few more or less representative ones as illustrations of the way in which the thoughts, ideas, feelings—all that is included in the *content* of a poem—work with and against each other. The ways in which they parallel, conflict with, or augment each other are felt as a design, a drama, or a framework. One of the important things in reading poetry is to be aware of the interrelationships among the various parts of its content. At the very least, one should know where one idea stops and another begins; as a second step, one should grasp the relationship between the ideas; finally, some impression of the poem as a whole, unified formation of thoughts should emerge. For the most part, these relationships are improvisations on the poet's part; tradition plays only a small part in them. In only two of the standard poetic forms, the sonnet and the ode, is the structure more or less dictated by customary practice.

The simplest poetic structure is parallelism, the repeated assertion of an idea in the form of statements having essentially the same meaning. A poem would not be expected to dwell on the same idea for very long, but sometimes variety of expression rather than progress in thought is emphasized. The following, for example, expresses the same idea in a number of ways before it moves to a conclusion:

TO THE VIRGINS, TO MAKE MUCH OF TIME

ROBERT HERRICK (1591–1674)

> Gather ye rosebuds while ye may,
>   Old time is still a-flying;
> And this same flower that smiles today
>   Tomorrow will be dying.
>
> The glorious lamp of heaven, the sun,   5
>   The higher he's a-getting,
> The sooner will his race be run,
>   And nearer he's to setting.
>
> That age is best which is the first,
>   When youth and blood are warmer;   10
> But being spent, the worse, and worst
>   Times still succeed the former.
>
> Then be not coy, but use your time,
>   And, while ye may, go marry;
> For, having lost but once your prime,   15
>   You may forever tarry.

After making his point in the first line, the poet offers several examples to support his contention that pleasant things do not last indefinitely. Having dwelt on this idea for most of three stanzas, he then turns, in the last stanza, and not before, to the conclusion that logically follows from it.

Actual repetition, as distinguished from parallelism, is common in poetry, of course. It can take the form of simple reiteration, or, less obviously, of grammatical constructions so similar that an effect of repetition is achieved. A repeated word, line, or passage is called a *refrain*. This feature is often found in oral poetry, where, as in the case of the ballad "Edward" (p. 163), it is used as a rhythmic element. However, refrains are not confined to primitive poetry. They are often found in the poetry of all periods, where they may be used for the purpose of gaining emphasis. In the following example the repetitions follow an established pattern, for the poem is written in the form of a *villanelle*. In the villanelle, the number of lines and the rhyme scheme are prescribed; its distinguishing feature is the repetition of the first and third lines alternately at the ends of the succeeding stanzas, and then together, as a couplet, at the end of the poem.

THE HOUSE ON THE HILL

EDWIN ARLINGTON ROBINSON (1869–1935)

They are all gone away,
   The House is shut and still,
There is nothing more to say.

Through broken walls and gray
   The winds blow bleak and shrill: 5
They are all gone away.

Nor is there one to-day
   To speak them good or ill:
There is nothing more to say.

Why is it then we stray   10
   Around the sunken sill?
They are all gone away,

And our poor fancy-play
   For them is wasted skill:
There is nothing more to say.   15

There is ruin and decay
   In the House on the Hill:
They are all gone away,
There is nothing more to say.

The repetitions in Robinson's villanelle are explained by their context. The essential effect is a gathering emphasis upon the loneliness and desertion of the scene, until the last two lines create their effect of devastating finality.

Paradoxically, repetition can be used to express changing, rather than identical, thoughts. In the following example, the refrain gains this effect by interacting wtih the rest of the poem in a subtle manner:

THE TIDE RISES, THE TIDE FALLS

HENRY WADSWORTH LONGFELLOW (1807–1882)

The tide rises, the tide falls,
The twilight darkens, the curlew calls;
Along the sea-sands damp and brown
The traveller hastens toward the town,
    And the tide rises, the tide falls.   5

Darkness settles on roofs and walls,
But the sea, the sea in the darkness calls;
The little waves, with their soft, white hands,
Efface the footprints in the sands,
    And the tide rises, the tide falls.   10

The morning breaks; the steeds in their stalls
Stamp and neigh, as the hostler calls;
The day returns, but nevermore
Returns the traveller to the shore,
    And the tide rises, the tide falls.   15

The theme of this poem is change. Its point is that while the movements of other things change, those of the sea do not. In the first stanza the tide is seen as a part of a whole changing land-scape, and its action harmonizes with the other actions as a nor-mal process. In the second stanza other movements cease; but, as the refrain emphasizes, the tides continue, now operating in oppo-sition to everything else. In the final stanza the movements of human activities are more vigorous than any preceding ones, and a clear change has taken place, for the traveler has moved on. But the sea is unchanged and now seems quiet and subdued by contrast with the other movements. The unvarying refrain is, of course, a perfect expression of the persistence of the tides; but its implications shift as its relations with its context change.

One of the commonest poetic structures is the alternation of contrasting elements. This may take place within the line, or from line to line, as in the neoclassic couplet, or it may take the form of a switching back and forth in one stanza after another, or an entire poem may be divided into two parts. This balancing of opposites is called *antithesis;* the following stanza from Shelley's "Adonais" illustrates it.

> The One remains, the many change and pass;
> Heaven's light forever shines, Earth's shadows fly;
> Life, like a dome of many-coloured glass,
> Stains the white radiance of Eternity,
> Until Death tramples it to fragments.—Die,   5
> If thou wouldst be with that which thou dost seek!
> Follow where all is fled!—Rome's azure sky,
> Flowers, ruins, statues, music, words are weak
> The glory they transfuse with fitting truth to speak.

Although the poem as a whole laments the death of his fellow-poet, Keats, Shelley is now approaching the idea that death is not an evil, as it is usually thought to be. He is ready to bring forward the neo-Platonic doctrine that life offers only inferior forms of an ideal existence we can enter upon only after death. Hence, the first five lines of the stanza develop the idea that the life Keats has left is varied and transitory, while the ideal is single, unified, and eternal. Each of the first two lines expresses this antithesis in a brief contrast. After the injunction of the fifth and sixth lines, the last three lines return to the antithesis of the actual and the ideal, stating that the beautiful things encountered in life are only weak reflections of some greater glory.

Another common structural design is the *climax.* In poetry, as in fiction or drama, a climax is a moment of highest intensity following a gradual building up of tension. Generally the reader's curiosity is awakened and made more urgent by an awareness of something missing that is to be supplied at the end. A good example of poetic climax occurs in Archibald MacLeish's "The Silent Slain." This short poem is about the legendary medieval hero Roland, whose army was massacred by the Saracens. It is supposed to be spoken by a member of the army that went to rescue him, but arrived too late. The thirteen-line poem consists of a single sentence describing in emotional and jumbled fashion how the soldiers heard Roland's horn giving the signal of distress in the distance, turned back, heard the battle in the distance, and arrived at the battlefield.

THE SILENT SLAIN

We too, we too, descending once again
The hills of our own land, we too have heard
Far off—Ah, que ce cor a longue haleine—
The horn of Roland in the passages of Spain,
The first, the second blast, the failing third,   5
And with the third turned back and climbed once more
The steep road southward, and heard faint the sound
Of swords, of horses, the disastrous war,
And crossed the dark defile at last, and found
At Roncevaux upon the darkening plain   10
The dead against the dead and on the silent ground
The silent slain—

3 *Ah, que ce cor a longue haleine:* "Ah, what a long blast this horn has." From the original poem describing this incident, *Le Chanson de Roland.*

The poem ends in this way, cut off abruptly by the shock the speaker experiences when he sees the soldiers who have just been killed.

EXAMPLES. Parallelism: King, "Sic Vita," p. 185; Herrick, "To Anthea," p. 183; Thomas, "The Force that Through the Green Fuse," p. 380. Repetition: "The Complaint of Chaucer to His Purse," p. 165; Donne, "A Hymn to God the Father," p. 179; Watkins, "The Mummy," p. 359. Antithesis: Blake, "The Clod and the Pebble," p. 69; Stevens, "The Glass of Water," p. 134. Climax: Shakespeare, Sonnet 146 ("Poor soul, the centre of my sinful earth"), p. 174; Tennyson, *In Memoriam*, LIV ("O, yet we trust that somehow good"), p, 271; Dickinson, "After great pain a formal feeling comes," p. 294; Yeats, "To a Friend Whose Work Has Come to Nothing," p. 309; Empson, "Homage to the British Museum," p. 153.

LOGICAL STRUCTURE

Poetry can, of course, make use of the structures of meaning that are found in prose. It can develop its ideas logically, through ordinary reasoning, causal analysis, analogies, and the use of evidence. However, these do not usually prove anything when they occur in verse, but provide skeletons of order and coherence. The poet seems to go through the motions of logical argument, and even though his logic may be unsound, the rational framework may enhance the effectiveness of his ideas. One of the commonest types of these quasilogical structures in verse is the joining of a general idea with a specific instance. Poetry is typically concrete and specific, and it is usual to find that a poem with this sort of structure devotes more space and emphasis to the physical than to the abstract. Nevertheless, general or abstract comment, expressed or implied, is often necessary to complete the physical actuality that is described, to relate it to general experience, or to draw a conclusion from it.

This necessity can be explained in another way. A poem does, it is true, invariably register an individual reaction; but it also seeks to convey this reaction in a coherent way. This procedure involves making a bridge between perception and the thought one has about it, between the particular event and a general awareness, between the singleness of a feeling or sensation and its meaningful application. The different ways of moving between these psychological poles amount to differing structural effects. The movement may be inductive, a perception that some specific condition is general or universal:

> I peel and portion
> A tangerine and spit the pips and feel
> The drunkenness of things being various.
>
> —LOUIS MACNEICE, "Snow"

The different actions involved in eating the tangerine have impressed the poet with the fact that all reality displays the same variety. An example of the reverse kind of reasoning, the deductive moment from a general statement to a particular instance of it, occurs in Dryden's description of his character, Achitophel:

> Great wits are sure to madness near allied,
> And thin partitions do their bounds divide;
> Else why should he, with wealth and honour blest,
> Refuse his age the needful hours of rest?
> Punish a body which he could not please,
> Bankrupt of life, yet prodigal of ease?
>
> —JOHN DRYDEN, "Absalom and Achitophel"

Though this passage has the form of an argument, the general rule expressed in the first two lines is less important as a logical tool than as a part of the description. The notion that genius and madness are related helps to explain Achitophel's behavior and to clarify his nature, even if it is not true.

Another method of reasoning that has its place in poetry is *analogy*, or argument based on a similarity between the subject of the argument and something else. It resembles comparative figures of speech such as metaphor and simile, but it can usually be distinguished from them because it has an intellectual, as well as an emotive, quality. It depends on similarities of structure or relationships rather than resemblances of quality or appearance. Analogy and other comparisons may be difficult to tell apart, but we usually feel that an analogy is present if the comparison is used to make an argumentative point and if the resemblance is a matter of logical thought or perception.

THE COMING OF WISDOM WITH TIME

WILLIAM BUTLER YEATS (1865–1939)

> Though leaves are many, the root is one;
> Through all the lying days of my youth
> I swayed my leaves and flowers in the sun;
> Now I may wither into the truth.

The poet sees an analogy between himself and the tree. He has produced pretty things in his youth, like the leaves and flowers of the tree; but these achievements were ephemeral, like the leaves and flowers, and he expects to find that just as the life of the tree depends on a single root, so his own depends on some single, unstated truth which he hopes to learn as he grows old.

These logical structures present facts and their significance side by side. But poets nearly always prefer to merge fact and significance into a single unity without logical structure. Instead of using a two-part construction consisting of fact plus interpretation, the poet in these cases presents the fact in such a way that the meaning rises naturally from it, without further comment. He makes the object, event, or experience speak for itself; the work of generalization and application is done, more or less unconsciously, by the reader. The following short poem exemplifies this common structure:

THE CHERRY TREES

EDWARD THOMAS (1878–1917)

The cherry trees bend over and are shedding
On the old road where all that passed are dead
Their petals, strewing the grass as for a wedding
This early May morn when there is none to wed.

No shift from description or the specific scene to general comment takes place here. The comment is in the description. The scene of the flowering trees beautifying the unused road clearly dramatizes the contrast between the transitory lives of the men who once traveled on the road and the enduring processes of nature.

Sometimes a poet will make use of an ostensibly logical structure to reach conclusions that are obviously irrational. He sets his ideas in an order that enables him to demonstrate that black is white, that love is hate, or that death is life. Such a structure may be called ironic or paradoxical. It seems to turn itself over as it develops, like a pancake, ending with the assertion of an idea that seems logically inconsistent with its beginning. Unlike the antithesis, which deals with opposites and their relation, the paradox moves from the fact of opposition to some basis for a resolution of it. This basis, however, is usually a matter of emotion or intuition rather than logic, in spite of the logical framework within which it is found. The following poem illustrates paradoxical structure:

TO ALTHEA, FROM PRISON

RICHARD LOVELACE (1618–1657)

When Love with unconfinéd wings
Hovers within my gates,
And my divine Althea brings
To whisper at the grates;
When I lie tangled in her hair   5
And fettered to her eye,
The birds that wanton in the air
Know no such liberty.

When flowing cups run swiftly round,
With no allaying Thames,   10
Our careless heads with roses bound,
Our hearts with loyal flames;
When thirsty grief in wine we steep,
When healths and draughts go free,
Fishes, that tipple in the deep,   15
Know no such liberty.

When, like committed linnets, I
With shriller throat shall sing
The sweetness, mercy, majesty,
And glories of my King;   20
When I shall voice aloud how good
He is, how great should be,

10 *no allaying Thames:* that is, without diluting water 17 *committed linnets:* imprisoned finches

Enlargéd winds, that curl the flood,
Know no such liberty.

Stone walls do not a prison make,   25
Nor iron bars a cage;
Minds innocent and quiet take
That for an hermitage.
If I have freedom in my love,
And in my soul am free,   30
Angels alone, that soar above,
Enjoy such liberty.

The poet argues that, in spite of the fact that he is in prison, freedom is obtainable through love, drink, song, and independence of mind. To say that Lovelace is denying that he is imprisoned is too simple. The physical fact of imprisonment is necessary to the success of the argument that true liberty can be achieved through the resources Lovelace praises. The victory of the imagination over actuality is stated in the famous paradox of lines 25 and 26. Rationally, these assertions make no sense; but if we have been accepting Lovelace's views up to this point, his conclusions are irresistible.

EXAMPLES. Marvell, "On a Drop of Dew," p. 202; Donne, "A Valediction: Forbidding Mourning," p. 176; Gray, "Ode on the Death of a Favourite Cat," p. 232; Frost, "Desert Places," p. 311; Day Lewis, "As One Who Wanders Into Old Workings," p. 352; Bishop, "The Fish," p. 372.

FURTHER READING

Cleanth Brooks, *The Well-Wrought Urn*, New York, 1947, pp. 176-181.
J. V. Cunningham, "Logic and Lyric," *Modern Philology*, LI (August 1953), 33-41.
Paul Goodman, *Theory of Literature*, Chicago, 1954, pp. 202-215.
John Crowe Ransom, *The World's Body*, pp. 270-303 ("Shakespeare at Sonnets").

EXAMPLES

BALLADE
OF A TOYOKUNI COLOUR-PRINT
To W. A.

WILLIAM ERNEST HENLEY

(1849–1903)

Was I a Samurai renowned,
Two-sworded, fierce, immense of bow?
A histrion angular and profound?
A priest? a porter?—Child, although
I have forgotten clean, I know   5
That in the shade of Fujisan,
What time the cherry-orchards blow,
I loved you once in old Japan.

As here you loiter, flowing-gowned
And hugely sashed, with pins a-row   10
Your quaint head as with flamelets crowned,
Demure, inviting—even so,
When merry maids in Miyako
To feel the sweet o' the year began,
And green gardens to overflow,   15
I loved you once in old Japan.

Clear shine the hills; the rice-fields round
Two cranes are circling; sleepy and slow,
A blue canal the lake's blue bound
Breaks at the bamboo bridge; and lo!   20
Touched with the sundown's spirit and glow,
I see you turn, with flirted fan,
Against the plum-tree's bloomy snow. . . .
I loved you once in old Japan!

Toyokuni: Utagawa Toyokuni, Japanese print-
maker of the eighteenth and nineteenth centuries 1 *Samurai:* a knight or warrior 3 *histrion:*
actor 6 *Fujisan:* Mount Fujiyama

Envoy

Dear, 'twas a dozen lives ago;   25
But that I was a lucky man
The Toyokuni here will show:
I loved you—once—in old Japan.

QUESTIONS

1) The ballade is a special form that calls for the repetition of the
refrain at the end of each stanza. (See also "The Complaint of Chaucer
to His Purse," p. 165.) What is the relation of the refrain to each of
the first three stanzas?

2) Is the force of the refrain in the first three stanzas exactly the
same? How does the subject matter of each of these stanzas point to
a different part of the refrain in each case?

3) The change in punctuation in the last occurrence of the refrain
introduces a significant change of emphasis. What is stressed there?

4) Did the speaker really know the girl in the picture? What
experience is he undergoing?

5) What quality is found in Henley's description of "old Japan,"
the setting of the supposed love affair? Does he seem to know Japan
through firsthand experience?

6) What is peculiar about the construction of the sentences at
the beginning of the third stanza? Is there some explanation that can
be offered for this?

7) What paradox appears in line 5? How can it be resolved?

DEAF AND DUMB

A Group by Woolner

ROBERT BROWNING (1812–1890)

Only the prism's obstruction shows aright
The secret of a sunbeam, breaks its light
Into the jewelled bow from blankest white;
    So may a glory from defect arise:

Deaf and Dumb: The subject of this poem was a statue
of two children who were deaf mutes. 3 *bow:* rainbow

Only by Deafness may the vexed Love wreak   5
Its insuppressive sense on brow and cheek,
Only by Dumbness adequately speak
        As favored mouth could never, through the eyes.

QUESTIONS

1) What parallel is developed between the children and the prism?

2) What relation between the concrete and the abstract does Browning exploit?

3) How many pieces of evidence does Browning offer for the generalization he states in line 4?

4) How useful or valid is this generalization?

5) Could Browning's statement about the prism be written as a syllogism or a chain of syllogisms?

6) What function does the generalization perform within the poem? Is this function in any way similar to the major premise of a syllogism?

7) How convincing is the analogy between the prism and the deaf and dumb children? What effect does this have on the value of the poem?

MY HEART LEAPS UP

WILLIAM WORDSWORTH (1770–1850)

My heart leaps up when I behold
    A rainbow in the sky:
So was it when my life began;
So is it now I am a man;
So be it when I shall grow old,   5
    Or let me die!
The Child is father of the Man;
And I could wish my days to be
Bound each to each by natural piety.

QUESTIONS

1) The logic of this deceptively simple poem is based upon the unspoken assumption, familiar to readers of Wordsworth's poetry, that the capacity to respond to nature is connected with virtue and

constitutes a "natural piety." How does this belief explain the exceptionally strong emphasis in lines 5 and 6?

2) What connection is there between the generalization of line 7 and the specific statements in the rest of the poem?

3) What is the effect of the parallel grammatical construction of lines 3–5?

4) The poem moves rather quickly from its beginning to its conclusion, omitting a number of implied thoughts. State some of these missing ideas.

OPPOSITION

SIDNEY LANIER (1842–1881)

Of fret, of dark, of thorn, of chill,
 Complain no more; for these, O heart,
Direct the random of the will
 As rhymes direct the rage of art.

The lute's fixed fret, that runs athwart   5
 The strain and purpose of the string,
For governance and nice consort
 Doth bar his wilful wavering.

The dark hath many dear avails;
 The dark distills divinest dews   10
The dark is rich with nightingales,
 With dreams, and with the heavenly Muse.

Bleeding with thorns of petty strife,
 I'll ease (as lovers do) my smart
With sonnets to my lady Life   15
 Writ red in issues from the heart.

What grace may lie within the chill
 Of favor frozen fast in scorn!
When Good's a-freeze, we call it Ill!
 This rosy Time is glacier-born.   20

5 *lute:* a stringed instrument with some resemblance to a guitar; *fret:* a ridge on the fingering board 8 *his:* that is, the lute's 9 *avails:* benefits, advantages.

Of fret, of dark, of thorn, of chill,
　　Complain thou not, O heart; for these
Bank-in the current of the will
　　To uses, arts, and charities.

QUESTIONS

1) Explain the paradox expressed by this poem. Is this a new or striking idea?

2) What is the effect achieved by the repetition of the first lines in lines 21 and 22? What is the effect of the slight change in word order?

3) Which of the stanzas have antithetical structures? Which individual lines have such structures?

4) What is the submerged metaphor of the final three lines?

THE GLASS OF WATER

WALLACE STEVENS (1879–1956)

That the glass would melt in heat,
That the water would freeze in cold,
Shows that this object is merely a state,
One of many, between two poles. So,
In the metaphysical, there are these poles.　　　　　5

Here in the centre stands the glass. Light
Is the lion that comes down to drink. There
And in that state, the glass is a pool.
Ruddy are his eyes and ruddy are his claws
When light comes down to wet his frothy jaws　　　10

And in the water winding weeds move round.
And there and in another state—the refractions,
The *metaphysica*, the plastic parts of poems
Crash in the mind—But, fat Jocundus, worrying
About what stands here in the centre, not the glass,　　15

13 *metaphysica:* the Latin term for things that lie beyond physical reality 14 *Jocundus:* a character improvised for this poem; his name is the Latin word for "cheerful."

But in the centre of our lives, this time, this day,
It is a state, this spring among the politicians
Playing cards. In a village of the indigenes,
One would have still to discover. Among the dogs and dung,
One would continue to contend with one's ideas.   20

QUESTIONS

1) This poem makes use of an analogy between the glass of water and "the centre of our lives," (line 16). What similarity is pointed out in the first stanza?

2) What are the two "states" mentioned in lines 8 and 17? What are the "poles" that are comparable to heat and cold which affect the glass of water?

3) What is the significance of the aggressively realistic details in the final stanza—"the politicians/Playing cards" and "the dogs and dung"?

4) What is it that "One would have still to discover" in line 19?

5) Why does Stevens choose as his analogue for so important a thing as the subject of this poem—"the centre of our lives"—so trivial an object as a glass of water?

DEATH, BE NOT PROUD
From Holy Sonnets

JOHN DONNE (1573–1631)

Death, be not proud, though some have callèd thee
Mighty and dreadful, for thou are not so;
For those whom thou think'st thou dost overthrow
Die not, poor Death; nor yet canst thou kill me.
From rest and sleep, which but thy pictures be,   5
Much pleasure; then from thee much more must flow;
And soonest our best men with thee do go—
Rest of their bones and souls' delivery!
Thou'rt slave to fate, chance, kings, and desperate men,
And dost with poison, war, and sickness dwell;   10
And poppy or charms can make us sleep as well
And better than thy stroke. Why swell'st thou then?
One short sleep past, we wake eternally,
And Death shall be no more: Death, thou shalt die.

12 *why swell'st thou?* why are you so proud?

QUESTIONS

1) What is the unstated (but entirely familiar) assumption behind the statement that death's victims do not die?

2) What is the rather startling argument of lines 5–6? To what type of argument does it belong? Is it convincing? Is it effective as poetry?

3) How many of the usual ideas about death does Donne take issue with? How many of these contradictory notions seem acceptable?

4) What arguments does Donne use to support his opening command, "Death, be not proud"?

5) Characterize Donne's attitude toward death. Is he bitter? resigned? defiant?

6) On what intuitional basis does the idea of the last line rest? In what way does it exaggerate or modify conventional belief?

The Creative Power of Poetry 6

Because it is capable of varying effects, and because poets as well as readers have different conceptions of its nature, poetry lends itself to a number of widely differing functions. In the form of songs or ballads it is one of the oldest and simplest of organized entertainments. Accounts of moving or amusing episodes in language that has rhyme, rhythm, and perhaps a refrain have always been a source of delight and are still a common form of entertainment for children.

According to the Latin poet Horace, poetry has the function of teaching as well as delighting. Once we move away from the very simplest poems, we are likely to find that most serious poetry has a moral quality. It seeks not merely to express a view of something but also to suggest the sort of behavior appropriate to that view. There is a large body of distinguished religious verse in English whose dominant purpose is moral teaching. Everything else these poems contain is merely a way of implementing some moral lesson. There are also many poems which, while they are not actually religious, have the purpose of formulating moral values. Pope's "Essay on Man" is one of the best-known examples of such poetry. It contains many direct moral injunctions like

> Know then thyself, presume not God to scan;
> The proper study of mankind is man.

However, in poetry generally the moral element is less obtrusive, taking its place with the esthetic and the intellectual as one of the components usually demanded by significant art.

Poetry may also serve as a historical record, and this has always been regarded as one of its most important and most interesting functions. It preserves the customs, ideas, and feelings of other times and sometimes even reports historical events. We have poetry from times and places which have left little or no written history, so that historians naturally turn to the poetry for information. Even if an official record of a particular period is available, the poetry written at the time may be far more valuable to historians because of its vividness, candor, and intimacy. Chroniclers rarely consider it necessary to report information about the habits, beliefs, and environment of daily life, for they cannot imagine that such commonplace facts will ever be forgotten, or that they will ever be of value. The *Iliad* and the *Odyssey*, in addition to being the earliest and greatest poems of Western civilization, are the fullest record we have of a remote period, and they contain much historical information that might otherwise have been lost. In the *Odyssey*, for example, we learn that a princess, Nausicaa, helps her women do the laundry, and that a king, Odysseus, is skillful at ploughing and carpentry. It is clear, therefore, that in Homer's time royal families were not exempted from hard physical labor.

It is usually difficult to get a clear idea of the real beliefs and convictions of a past age. Attitudes in any age that everyone accepts unquestioningly are, of course, the most influential ones, but because they are too obvious to be openly stated, and too familiar to be analyzed, they are rarely recorded accurately by contemporary observers. However, it is very possible, in fact, it is nearly inevitable, that a poet of the time, in writing about love or battles or narrating an enjoyable story, will provide excellent examples of the prevailing attitudes and opinions. In Chaucer's amusing "Nun's Priest Tale," the wife of the cock Chauntecleer explains the cause of his bad dreams by a long lecture containing many of the principles of medieval medicine. Among other bits of learned lore, she tells him that dreams containing red things are caused by an excess of the fluid called "choler" in the body, and that dreams containing black things are caused by an excess of "melancholy." Similarly, in the medieval ballad "Sir Patrick Spens" (p. 161), the captain gives the order to prepare his ship for a voyage, whereupon one of the sailors objects:

> Late, late yestreen I saw the new moone
>   Wi the auld moone in hir arme,
> And I feir, I feir, my deir master,
>   That we will cum to harme.

The stanza reminds us that everyday activities in the Middle Ages were likely to be controlled by astrological portents and similar superstitions.

With rare exceptions, poets do not regard themselves as historians. The historical value of good poetry is merely incidental to its other values. Nevertheless, the trained literary historian, through careful study and analysis, is often able to use literature as a way of gaining valuable insights into the mind and spirit of a remote period. The more or less casual reader is bound to learn a great deal about other views of life in reading poetry of the past; even better, he often gains a more vivid impression of people, ideas, and events than is available in any other medium.

But poetry's strongest claim to attention is based on the fact that it can function as a source of new and original knowledge. In describing the nature of poetry, Chapter 1 pointed out that there are things for which individual words or expressions do not exist. This fact is indicative of another, even more significant one: there are whole areas of experience which have been given so little attention that we have not even developed a vocabulary for discussing them. Such deficiencies are characteristic of knowledge in general. Everyone realizes that he is not equally aware of everything in his experience, but knows some things well and is ignorant of others. What is true of individuals is true of the culture as a whole.

Perhaps the best way of showing that every society is insensitive in certain areas is to compare the differing knowledge of familiar things that is available in different cultures. There are certain primitive tribes that do not recognize the existence of more than three colors; they have terms for white and black, and only one term for every other color, so that red, blue, green, brown, and so on are all considered to be the same color. To us who speak English this seems to be an extremely primitive development of color awareness, but it is important to realize that our own awareness of some parts of our experience may be fully as primitive. To take a trivial but suggestive example, most people who speak English know only one word for banana. As far as we are concerned, there *is* only one kind of banana, though it may exhibit certain variations in shape, color, and ripeness. But in the

Philippine Islands, where many kinds of bananas are grown, people distinguish between eating and cooking bananas and recognize different varieties having different names, much as we distinguish among varieties of apples.

Thus, the experience of an individual or of a whole culture is like a checkerboard of neighboring areas, some of which get intense attention, while others are hardly noticed. In the development of a culture heavy stress is laid on those aspects of experience that are made important by circumstances, while others are ignored, just as roads put through wild territory will lead from one city to another and bypass the countryside. Travelers who use the roads will say that they have seen the country; actually, they have seen only the small part of it that lies beside the roads. A minute's reflection will show that everything we know is known in that way. In trying to understand the chaotic sea of experiences that surrounds us at every moment, the mind seems to throw a net into it and to draw out a handful of impressions with which it can work. But the great bulk of what is there remains behind, and even if it is picked up by the senses, it does not enter the thoughts.

Since there is always a vast field of such unnoticed and unobserved reality even in experiences that are very familiar, there is always an opportunity for the sort of poetry that brings it to our attention. Such poetry adds to our perception and knowledge. It fills in a blank space on the map of our awareness. It enables us to see in familiar things aspects that we did not know were there, just as a microscope enables us to see surprising details of structure in material that can be seen well enough for ordinary purposes by the naked eye.

It is natural to allow most of the details of everyday life to go by without much attention. They usually seem too trivial, too complicated, or too depressing to deserve thought and expression. But this economy of attention, which is certainly necessary in practical life, interferes with our full knowledge of experience. One of the most important qualifications a poet can have is curiosity about matters of little practical value. His poem may well begin with a feeling that some familiar experience has a significance that has been overlooked, and a willingness to explore it until he has grasped this elusive quality and can express it in a way that will enable the reader to grasp it as well. In this short poem William Carlos Williams has sharply isolated the sense that the commonplace is significant:

THE RED WHEELBARROW

so much depends
upon

a red wheel
barrow

glazed with rain
water

beside the white
chickens

It may be objected that insights of this kind are not knowledge. To say that is to assume that knowledge is limited to practical information that can be used for some other purpose, like a chronology of historical events or a train schedule. Because we live in a time which tends to judge everything by its applicability to something else, we have to make a deliberate effort to remind ourselves of the obvious fact that some of the experiences we seek must be ends in themselves. Even after we have admitted that such innately satisfying experiences exist, it is hard to include the acquisition of knowledge among them. "Useless knowledge" is a contemptuous phrase. But some highly respectable fields of study, such as philosophy, history, theology, literature, and much pure science, consist entirely of information that is, from a practical point of view, "useless." In short, there is a kind of knowledge that is generally recognized to be an end in itself, to have no "use" but that of being known. Its value lies in the satisfaction of knowing it. This is the kind of knowledge that poetry contains. Reading poetry does not help us to do anything; it simply helps us to gain a greater awareness of our experiences than we can achieve ourselves.

It would be easy to infer from what has just been said that

poetry is valuable because it furnishes illuminating comment upon actual experience. While poetry often does contain such comment, it is well to remember that the effect of the poem lies within itself, not in its relation to actuality. This is easily demonstrated. If one were to read a poem about the sea that described its destructive power (Robert Frost's "Once by the Pacific," [p. 6], is a good example), one would not have to check the accuracy of the poet's insight by visiting the sea itself to see if it really did seem destructive. If the sea's appearance when the reader saw it contradicted the impression described by the poem, that would not interfere with the poem's effect. Even if the reader had never seen the ocean, he would not be under much of a handicap in appreciating the poem. Further, the effect of a poem does not become attached to the actuality that the poem takes as its subject. At best, an actual experience of the sea may remind the reader of the words of the poem, which in turn may repeat their effect. It is clear, then, that a poem does not offer a copy of, or a comment upon, actuality, but a sensation of insight peculiar to itself. Its value does not depend upon its "truth" to reality, but on its ability to provide, within itself, a clear and coherent experience. The following poem illustrates this point. It is not about a recognizable subject and cannot be "true" to anyone's previous experience; nevertheless, it is intelligible, suggestive, and meaningful.

THE KRAKEN

ALFRED LORD TENNYSON (1809–1892)

Below the thunders of the upper deep,
Far, far beneath in the abysmal sea,
His ancient, dreamless, uninvaded sleep
The Kraken sleepeth: faintest sunlights flee
About his shadowy sides; above him swell   5
Huge sponges of millennial growth and height;
And far away into the sickly light,
From many a wondrous grot and secret cell
Unnumbered and enormous polypi

Winnow with giant arms the slumbering green.   10
There hath he lain for ages, and will lie
Battening upon huge sea worms in his sleep,
Until the latter fire shall heat the deep;
Then once by man and angels to be seen,
In roaring he shall rise and on the surface die.   15

The information that the kraken is a sea monster in Scandinavian mythology does not add much to the effect of the poem. The description itself, vigorously imagined and sharply sketched, offers the reader a new and authentic reality. The unanswered questions that arise within the poem are a part of its mystifying effect. It presents itself for contemplation, without commenting on anything. Whatever relation it may have to the reader's other experiences—whatever *meaning*, in the narrow sense of the term, it may have—is not within the poem itself, but is only made possible by it.

A little poem by Emily Dickinson about the situation in a household the day after a member of the family has died is an excellent example of poetry working in this way. It is easy to see why this subject has not had much attention and is ripe for exploration; it is overshadowed by the more dramatic episode of death itself. Yet the reader will recognize that Emily Dickinson has isolated an aspect of the event that is meaningful.

The bustle in a house
The morning after death
Is solemnest of industries
Enacted upon earth,—

The sweeping up the heart,
And putting love away,
We shall not want to use again
Until eternity.

In the middle of its unbearable emotional trial, the family returns to its everyday tasks and finds that these are a way of recovering from grief. As they set the house in order, they set their feelings in order; hope of a future reunion replaces their immediate sorrow. Readers who have been through this experience will probably acknowledge that the poem brings into focus a feeling of their own that was crowded out by more intense feelings. But it is more important to note that even readers who have no firsthand knowledge of their own about the subject can participate fully in the insight offered by the poem. The poem is not merely an addition to, or amplification of, other experience; it is a more or less autonomous experience in itself.

The poetic device used by Emily Dickinson can be recognized as the process of imaginative comparison that was described in Chapter 3 as typical of poetry. The poet has brought together two things not generally associated, recovery from grief, and housekeeping, and has established a meaningful relationship between the two. By demonstrating how one is like the other, she identifies the quality common to both that is the subject of her poem. Thus, she makes one unit of her comparison light up the dark side of the other. Similarly, G. M. Hopkins, also writing about the experience of grief in "No worst, there is none" (p. 305), describes the sudden and absolute quality it has at its onset by comparing it to a fall from a cliff:

> O the mind, mind has mountains; cliffs of fall
> Frightful, sheer, no-man-fathomed. . . .

In the following short poem, A. E. Housman swiftly formulates two impressive images to drive home the doctrine that original sin cannot be expunged by any human effort:

> Stars, I have seen them fall,
> But when they drop and die
> No star is lost at all
> From all the star-sown sky.
> The toil of all that be   5
> Helps not the primal fault:
> It rains into the sea,
> And still the sea is salt.

Thus, an idea that has lost much of its force because it is so familiar has its meaning renewed by a comparison with something else that is familiar, but has never been regarded from the particular point of view taken by Housman.

These examples show how imaginative comparisons can produce isolated flashes of awareness. But poetry is also capable of generating extended and systematic bodies of knowledge. In fact, most images of the kind we have been discussing are not merely the results of chance moments of inspiration, but parts of coherent views of life that are different enough from ordinary attitudes to lead the poets to insights that are missed by the rest of us. By using its own characteristic methods poetry can and often does develop more or less complete philosophies. Because it uses the power of the imagination to probe experience, it has from time to time been able to see meanings in things that seemed meaningless, to find fresh solutions for the great problems of existence, and generally to introduce order into spiritual chaos. Insights contributed by poets at different moments in history have opened new areas of thought and feeling, enabled men to formulate firm bases of belief for their actions and principles, and acted as creative forces in the world of ideas.

Cases in which a poet's philosophy has become a general historical influence are often used to prove the importance of poetry. However, as we have already seen, the thought of a poem cannot be extracted from it without being, to some degree, falsified. If the insight expressed in the poem is applied to some actual social or philosophic problem, it ceases to be just the same insight. As a result of such inevitable distortions, it has happened that poets have "inspired" their readers to actions and opinions which the poets themselves would have disapproved. Poetry does not require the evidence of overt historical achievements to justify it; its real justification lies in its direct effect on the individual reader.

It often happens, however, that a poet's vision of life powerfully influences so great a number of readers that it becomes a public and historic phenomenon as well as a private and esthetic one. Two instances of this, brief and necessarily greatly simplified, will be enough to show how poetry can play a vital role as a cultural force.

People have always seen beauty in nature, but the main source of the particular attitude toward it that is common today is the poetry and philosophy of the English romantic poet, William Wordsworth. Primitive man and the pagan Greeks and Romans expressed their feeling for nature by imagining that it was filled with gods. In the Christian era, however, such beliefs were out of place. Nature could be no more to Europeans who lived before Wordsworth's time than a source of comfort and quiet, and an example of the harmonious orderliness of the universe. But Wordsworth revived the pagan feeling that nature as a whole was alive and sacred. He tells us that as a boy he was deeply moved by the physical beauty of such natural sights as waterfalls and sunsets. When he grew older and meditated upon the power nature had to stir his emotions, he drew certain philosphical conclusions about it. He sensed a subtle, continuous drama in the movements and activities of the woods, so that a hill looming over the water seemed to follow him reprovingly when he stole a boat, and the trees in a secluded spot seemed to reproach him when he violated their calm by tearing a branch from a hazel tree (see the excerpt from "The Prelude," p. 242). He said:

> Even the loose stones that cover the highway
> I gave a moral life: I saw them feel,
> Or linked them to some feeling . . . .

In short, nature was alive, conscious, and full of meaning to Wordsworth. It was the physical manifestation of a divine being who spoke to man through it and used it to teach morality and sensitivity to beauty and to ennoble human character. Living things like trees and flowers seemed happy because they lived in harmony with the whole of nature, and Wordsworth felt that man, who was a part of nature, would be happier if he lived close to it and followed its ways.

Although other poets and thinkers had had such ideas before, Wordsworth found his own way to this view of nature. In this sense it was original with him. His contribution can be fairly evaluated only if we recognize that other attitudes toward nature are possible. It can, with considerable justice, be considered violent, cruel, barbarous, ugly, or indifferent to the well-being of man. But Wordsworth's feeling that nature was holy and benign, and the poetry that expressed it, became part of the ordinary culture of English-speaking countries. People learned it as they learned their language and national customs, accepting unquestioningly without much thought of alternate beliefs the idea that nature contains a mysterious "presence" whose influence is spiritually uplifting. Even people who have never heard of Wordsworth and who are indifferent to poetry in general may enjoy the countryside, may take a particular pleasure in watching birds and animals, and may feel that cutting down trees is a violation of something sacred. They would be far less likely to have these feelings if Wordsworth had not had so great an influence.

In philosophy, as in plane geometry, a handful of axioms can lead to a whole system of thought. Wordsworth's feelings about nature formed the basis for an elaborate system of social, political, spiritual, educational, and philosophical beliefs that followed naturally from them. For example, he expressed the idea in many of his early poems that true wisdom came not from deliberate analysis but from effortless communion with nature. He attributed the social evils of his time to the destructive moral effects of removing people from country environments to the artificial and pernicious life of the city. Many of these opinions were less individual than his nature philosophy, and none of them were as influential (Wordsworth himself changed his mind about many of them), but they entered the cultural life of Europe through his poetry and played more or less important parts in it.

Probably the best example of a twentieth-century poet who, like Wordsworth in the nineteenth century, has strongly influenced the thought of his time is T. S. Eliot. His obscure and complicated poem *The Waste Land*, which was first published in 1922, expressed a criticism of modern life that many contemporaries felt to be perceptive and valid. Eliot took the view that the cause for the ugliness and insensitivity of modern life, and for its lack of dignity or nobility, was the loss of religious faith. One of the devices that occur in his poem is the elaborately extended metaphor that is called *allegory*. Eliot compared the spiritual condition of modern life to a kingdom described in the legends about the Holy Grail. In the legends the kingdom is barren because its king is sick; when his health is restored, the land becomes fertile again. Through a complex of symbols and allusions, Eliot suggests that spiritual life, like the kingdom in the legend, can be made fruitful again if religious beliefs and the virtues that go with them are restored.

Long before *The Waste Land* was written, observers had

pointed out that the sort of progress that puts mechanization ahead of human needs and feelings is destructive, and many reformers had worked to relieve the poverty and crime that it produced. Eliot's contribution was that of convincing his readers through powerful ironic contrasts that the disorder present in modern society was fundamentally spiritual. Eliot's attitude, like Wordsworth's, carried with it a number of social, political, and religious implications, but none of them has been as widely accepted as his diagnosis of the modern condition. It is commonplace nowadays to feel that modern life, however comfortable, pleasant, and exciting it may be, lacks the sense of direction that could be supplied by some powerful religious belief.

The organization and propagation of beliefs appears to be one of the normal functions of poetry. Many of the world's greatest poets, such as Lucretius, Milton, Dante, and Pope, have used their art in this way, although many equally great poets, such as Homer, Shakespeare, and Chaucer, have not done so explicitly. When he seeks to create order out of the chaos of confusing experiences man encounters in life, the poet returns to the role played by his forerunners in antiquity. The work of a philosophical poet resembles ancient religious myths which explained the system of the universe and sought to guide people's conduct and foretell the future in the light of that system. It was a common practice among the Greeks to make long trips to some shrine which was reputed to be able to answer any question that might be put to it. The answers of these oracles, often ambiguous and obscure, were regarded as keys to the riddles set by the gods for man to solve. The preaching of such Old Testament prophets as Jeremiah and Isaiah was also an interpretation of the universe and man's position in it and a force intended to mold behavior and morality. Philosophical poetry does not command the same degree of belief as religious prophecy, but it does resemble it in using the senses and emotions to formulate an intelligible view of life.

Further Reading

M. H. Abrams, *The Mirror and the Lamp*, New York, 1958 (Norton), pp. 272–285 ("The Poem as Heterocosm").

Hazard Adams, *The Contexts of Poetry*, Boston, 1963, pp. 181–193 ("A Theory: The Literary Cosmos").

I. A. Richards, *Principles of Literary Criticism*, New York, 1950, Chapters XXII and XXXII ("The Availability of the Poet's Experience" and "The Imagination").

Susanne K. Langer, *Feeling and Form*, New York, 1953, pp. 208–235 ("Poesis").

EXAMPLES

THE NEW HOUSE

EDWARD THOMAS (1878–1917)

Now first, as I shut the door,
   I was alone
In the new house; and the wind
   Began to moan.

Old at once was the house,   5
   And I was old;
My ears were teased with the dread
   Of what was foretold.

Nights of storm, days of mist, without end;
   Sad days when the sun   10
Shone in vain; old griefs and griefs
   Not yet begun.

All was foretold me; naught
   Could I foresee;
But I learned how the wind would sound   15
   After these things should be.

QUESTIONS

1) The house is clearly not the real subject of the poem. What is the real subject?

2) Explain the paradox of line 5, "Old at once was the house."

3) What does the poet mean by saying that he learned how the wind would sound far in the future?

4) What bearing does the poem have on the general problem of knowledge? Does the poet learn anything? Does the reader?

ON FIRST LOOKING INTO CHAPMAN'S HOMER

JOHN KEATS (1795–1821)

Much have I travell'd in the realms of gold,
And many goodly states and kingdoms seen;
Round many western islands have I been
Which bards in fealty to Apollo hold.
Oft of one wide expanse had I been told   5
That deep-browed Homer ruled as his demesne;
Yet did I never breathe its pure serene
Till I heard Chapman speak out loud and bold:
Then felt I like some watcher of the skies
When a new planet swims into his ken;   10
Or like stout Cortez when with eagle eyes
He star'd at the Pacific—and all his men
Look'd at each other with a wild surmise—
Silent, upon a peak in Darien.

6 *demesne:* domain 14 *Darien:* in Panama

QUESTIONS

In this poem, Keats seeks to express feelings of the kind that usually defy expression. He had been shown the translation of Homer written by the seventeenth-century poet George Chapman and found the discovery so exciting that he spent most of the night reading it with his friend Charles Cowden Clarke. Early the next morning, Clarke reports, Keats sent him this sonnet describing his reaction to the Chapman translation.

1) What does Keats mean by "the realms of gold"?

2) What is the "one wide expanse" in line 5?

3) What do the two events mentioned in lines 9–12 have in common with Keats's reading of Chapman?

4) Is it possible to identify the "wild surmise" of line 13? Would the poem have been improved if this had been made explicit?

5) Do "Cortez"—who should, of course, have been Balboa—and his men react to the discovery in the same way?

6) Why is the discoverer "silent"? What would have been the

effect if Keats had added a few lines to this poem, explaining his thoughts? Would they have helped to clarify Keats's feelings about reading Chapman?

KUBLA KHAN

SAMUEL TAYLOR COLERIDGE (1772–1834)

In Xanadu did Kubla Khan
A stately pleasure dome decree:
Where Alph, the sacred river, ran
Through caverns measureless to man
   Down to a sunless sea.   5
So twice five miles of fertile ground
With walls and towers were girdled round:
And there were gardens bright with sinuous rills,
Where blossomed many an incense-bearing tree;
And here were forests ancient as the hills,   10
Enfolding sunny spots of greenery.

But oh! that deep romantic chasm which slanted
Down the green hill athwart a cedarn cover!
A savage place! as holy and enchanted
As e'er beneath a waning moon was haunted   15
By woman wailing for her demon lover!
And from this chasm, with ceaseless turmoil seething
As if this earth in fast thick pants were breathing;
A mighty fountain momently was forced:
Amid whose swift half-intermitted burst   20
Huge fragments vaulted like rebounding hail,
Or chaffy grain beneath the thresher's flail:
And 'mid these dancing rocks at once and ever
It flung up momently the sacred river.
Five miles meandering with a mazy motion   25
Through wood and dale the sacred river ran,
Then reached the caverns measureless to man,
And sank in tumult to a lifeless ocean:
And 'mid this tumult Kubla heard from far
Ancestral voices prophesying war!   30
   The shadow of the dome of pleasure
    Floated midway on the waves;

> Where was heard the mingled measure
> From the fountain and the caves.
> It was a miracle of rare device,   35
> A sunny pleasure dome with caves of ice!
>
> A damsel with a dulcimer
> In a vision once I saw:
> It was an Abyssinian maid,
> And on her dulcimer she played,   40
> Singing of Mount Abora.
> Could I revive within me
> Her symphony and song,
> To such a deep delight 'twould win me,
> That with music loud and long,   45
> I would build that dome in air,
> That sunny dome! those caves of ice!
> And all who heard should see them there,
> And all should cry, Beware! Beware!
> His flashing eyes, his floating hair!   50
> Weave a circle round him thrice,
> And close your eyes with holy dread,
> For he on honey-dew hath fed,
> And drunk the milk of Paradise.

QUESTIONS

According to Coleridge, this poem was written with very little intellectual control. He said that it came to him in a dream and that he wrote it down from memory, but was interrupted after starting what was to have been a much longer poem. It is, therefore, only a fragment. Even if Coleridge's account is not entirely accurate, the poem is obviously incomplete and doesn't make much "sense" in the usual meaning of the word. Yet it is one of the best-known English poems.

1) How much relation do the things described in the poem—the palace, the chasm with its fountain, the "sacred river" flowing to a sea inside caverns, and the maiden, whose song has magical properties—have to reality? How believable are they?

2) How much relation do the elements of the poem have to each other? Does it seem likely that this aspect of the poem would be improved if the poem were completed?

3) What suggestion does the last section of the poem, beginning with line 37, make about the status of the pleasure dome and its landscape?

4) Does the poem have any moral or lesson?

5) Most of the details of this poem were suggested by a travel book Coleridge had read. Does that improve the realism or authenticity of the poem?

6) What qualities does this poem have in common with Tennyson's "The Kraken" (p. 142)?

HOMAGE TO THE BRITISH MUSEUM

WILLIAM EMPSON (1906–   )

There is a supreme God in the ethnological section;
A hollow toad shape, faced with a blank shield.
He needs his belly to include the Pantheon,
Which is inserted through a hole behind.
At the navel, at the points formally stressed, at the
       organs of sense,   5
Lice glue themselves, dolls, local deities,
His smooth wood creeps with all the creeds of the world.

Attending there let us absorb the cultures of nations
And dissolve into our judgement all their codes.
Then, being clogged with a natural hesitation   10
(People are continually asking one the way out),
Let us stand here and admit that we have no road.
Being everything, let us admit that is to be something.
Or give ourselves the benefit of the doubt;
Let us offer our pinch of dust all to this God,   15
And grant his reign over the entire building.

3 *Pantheon:* the entire group of gods

QUESTIONS

1) What is the ambiguity of the term "supreme God" in the first line? Does the rest of the poem have any bearing upon this double meaning?

2) What is the purpose of Empson's detailed description of this unattractive object?

3) What attitude toward the "creeds of the world" and the various beliefs of mankind does the exhibit arouse, according to line 8–9?

4) In lines 10–12, Empson develops a wide general attitude from a specific, and rather trivial situation. Explain this.

5) What reason does Empson give for recommending the worship of this deity? To what extent does his reason resemble traditional theological attitudes?

6) To what extent is the poem satirical? Against what is the satire directed?

7) Describe the qualities of originality in this poem. Consider its tone, its subject, its thought processes, and its conclusion.

8) What is the force of "the entire building" in the last line? (The British Museum is the largest museum in England and includes many departments devoted to various fields of study, such as history, anthropology, literature, and ancient cultures.)

9) What is the paradox of line 13? What relation does this comment have to man? What role does skepticism play in this line?

LAMARCK ELABORATED

"The environment creates the organ"

RICHARD WILBUR (1921—   )

The Greeks were wrong who said our eyes have rays;
Not from these sockets or these sparkling poles
Comes the illumination of our days.
It was the sun that bored these two blue holes.

It was the song of doves begot the ear   5
And not the ear that first conceived of sound:
That organ bloomed in vibrant atmosphere,
As music conjured Ilium from the ground.

The yielding water, the repugnant stone,
The poisoned berry and the flaring rose   10
Attired in sense the tactless finger-bone
And set the taste-buds and inspired the nose.

9 *Ilium:* ancient Troy

Out of our vivid ambiance came unsought
All sense but that most formidably dim.
The shell of balance rolls in seas of thought.   15
It was the mind that taught the head to swim.

Newtonian numbers set to cosmic lyres
Whelmed us in whirling worlds we could not know,
And by the imagined floods of our desires
The voice of Sirens gave us vertigo.   20

The epigraph expresses the theory of the pre-Darwinian naturalist
Lamarck, who thought that living forms could be directly modified
by environment. As the title indicates, the poem applies this principle
to particular instances, explaining them deductively.

QUESTIONS

1) What is the relation between the epigraph and the first three
stanzas?

2) What is exceptional about the use of the words "tactless" in
line 11 and "inspired" in line 12? (Consult a dictionary, if necessary,
to determine the root meanings of these words.)

3) In stanza four, what is the sense "most formidably dim"?

4) What is the meaning of line 16? Distinguish, in particular,
between what Wilbur seems to mean by "mind" and by "head."
What fact of consciousness is explained by this stanza?

5) What is the relation of the final stanza to the fourth? What
two kinds of unknowns are described in it?

6) Does Wilbur believe the assertions of the first three stanzas—
that the light of the sun created eyes, and so on? If not, why does he
make them?

7) Does he believe the assertion in the fourth stanza? If not, why
does he make it?

8) In what way does the poem as a whole suggest the possible
usefulness of ideas that can be imagined, but not really believed?

9) In what way does the poem suggest a view of the universe
and of man's place in it?

THE SECOND COMING

WILLIAM BUTLER YEATS (1865–1939)

Turning and turning in the widening gyre
The falcon cannot hear the falconer;
Things fall apart; the centre cannot hold;
Mere anarchy is loosed upon the world,
The blood-dimmed tide is loosed, and everywhere   5
The ceremony of innocence is drowned;
The best lack all conviction, while the worst
Are full of passionate intensity.

Surely some revelation is at hand;
Surely the Second Coming is at hand.   10
The Second Coming! Hardly are those words out
When a vast image out of *Spiritus Mundi*
Troubles my sight: somewhere in sands of the desert
A shape with lion body and the head of a man,
A gaze blank and pitiless as the sun,   15
Is moving its slow thighs, while all about it
Reel shadows of the indignant desert birds.
The darkness drops again; but now I know
That twenty centuries of stony sleep
Were vexed to nightmare by a rocking cradle,   20
And what rough beast, its hour come round at last,
Slouches towards Bethlehem to be born?

1 *gyre:* a circular path 2 *the falcon cannot hear:* in falconry,
the bird flies in a circle around his trainer and is recalled by
a whistle 12 *Spiritus Mundi:* the Spirit of the World 14 *A
shape with lion body:* Yeats has borrowed the male sphinx
of Egyptian mythology

QUESTIONS

1) What is being described in the first section? Is it a particular
situation or a general condition?

2) What are the "twenty centuries"? Why do you suppose they
were, in Yeats's opinion, centuries of "stony sleep"?

3) What event does Yeats foresee in the final line? Why is it put
in the form of a question?

4) What irony is present in the terms "revelation," "Second Coming," and *Spiritus Mundi?*

5) Should the "rough beast" be more definite? why?

6) Does the poem contain a prediction? What is it?

7) How does Yeats's "Second Coming" differ from the event normally meant by this phrase? Does Yeats's original application of the phrase become convincing as the poem proceeds? At what point does the reader become aware that Yeats means something new by "Second Coming"?

8) How does Yeats make his "original myth" vivid and believable? Are there any elements in it that are not original?

AN ANTHOLOGY
OF ENGLISH
AND
AMERICAN POEMS

Section 2

Anonymous Medieval Ballads

SIR PATRICK SPENS

The king sits in Dumferling toune,
  Drinking the blude-reid wine;
"O whar will I get guid sailor,
  To sail this schip of mine."

Up and spak an eldern knicht,   5
  Sat at the kings richt kne:
"Sir Patrick Spens is the best sailor
  That sails upon the se."

The king has written a braid letter,
  And signd it wi his hand,   10
And sent it to Sir Patrick Spens,
  Was walking on the sand.

The first line that Sir Patrick red,
  A loud lauch lauched he;
The next line that Sir Patrick red,   15
  The teir blinded his ee.

"O wha is this has don this deid,
  This ill deid don to me,
To send me out this time o' the yeir,
  To sail upon the se!   20

"Mak haste, mak haste, my mirry men all,
  Our guid schip sails the morne":
"O say na sae, my master deir,
  For I feir a deadlie storme.

"Late late yestreen I saw the new moone,   25
  Wi the auld moone in hir arme,
And I feir, I feir, my deir master,
  That we will cum to harme."

O our Scots nobles wer richt laith
  To weet their cork-heild schoone: 30
Bot lang owre a' the play wer playd,
  Thair hats they swam aboone.

O lang, lang may their ladies sit,
  Wi thair fans into their hand,
Or eir they se Sir Patrick Spens   35
  Cum sailing to the land.

O lang, lang may the ladies stand,
  Wi thair gold kems in thair hair,
Waiting for thair ain deir lords,
  For they'll see thame na mair.   40

Haf owre, haf owre to Aberdour,
  It's fiftie fadom deip,
And thair lies guid Sir Patrick Spens,
  Wi the Scots lords at his feit.

29 *laith:* loathe, that is, unwilling 32 *aboon:*
above 38 *kems:* combs

THE TWA CORBIES

As I was walking all alane
I heard twa corbies making a mane;
The tane unto the t'other say,
"Where sall we gang and dine to-day?"

"—In behint yon auld fail dyke,   5
I wot there lies a new-slain Knight;
And naebody kens that he lies there,
But his hawk, his hound, and lady fair.

"His hound is to the hunting gane,
His hawk to fetch the wild-fowl hame,   10
His lady's ta'en another mate,
So we may make our dinner sweet.

The Twa Corbies: The Two Ravens; 2 *mane:*
moan 3 *tane:* one 5 *fail dyke:* wall of earth 7
kens: knows

"Ye'll sit on his white hause-bane,
And I'll pick out his bonny blue een
Wi' ae lock o' his gowden hair   15
We'll theek our nest when it grows bare.

"Mony a one for him makes mane,
But nane sall ken where he is gane;
O'er his white banes, when they are bare,
The wind sall blaw for evermair."   20

13 *hause-bane:* neck bone 14 *een:* eyes 15
gowden: golden 16 *theek:* thatch

EDWARD

Why does your brand sae drap wi' bluid,
      Edward, Edward?
Why does your brand sae drap wi' bluid,
   And why sae sad gang ye, O?"
"O I ha'e killed my hawk sae guid,   5
      Mither, mither,
O I ha'e killed my hawk sae guid,
   And I had nae mair but he, O."

"Your hawk's bluid was never sae reid,
      Edward, Edward.   10
Your hawk's bluid was never sae reid,
   My dear son I tell thee, O."
"O I ha'e killed my reid-roan steed,
      Mither, mither,
O I ha'e killed my reid-roan steed,   15
   That erst was sae fair and free, O."

"Your steed was auld and ye ha'e gat mair,
      Edward, Edward.
Your steed was auld and ye ha'e gat mair:
   Som other dule ye dree, O."   20

1 *brand:* sword; *drap:* drip 4 *gang:* go 8 *nae mair:* no more
13 *reid-roan:* red roan 16 *erst:* formerly 20 *dule:* woe; *dree:*
suffer

"O I ha'e killed my fader dear,
  Mither, mither,
O I ha'e killed my fader dear,
  Alas and wae is me, O!"

"And whatten penance wul ye dree for that,   25
    Edward, Edward?
And whatten penance wul ye dree for that,
  My dear son, now tell me, O?"
"I'll set my feet in yonder boat,
    Mither, mither,   30
I'll set my feet in yonder boat,
  And I'll fare over the sea, O."

"And what wul ye do wi' your towers and your ha',
    Edward, Edward?
And what wul ye do wi' your towers and your ha',   35
  That were sae fair to see, O?"
"I'll let thame stand til they down fa',
    Mither, mither,
I'll let thame stand til they down fa',
  For here never mair maun I be, O."   40

"And what wul ye leave to your bairns and your wife,
    Edward, Edward,
And what wul ye leave to your bairns and your wife,
  Whan ye gang over the sea, O?"
"The warldes room, late them beg thrae life,   45
    Mither, mither,
The warldes room, late them beg thrae life,
  For thame never mair wul I see, O."

"And what wul ye leave to your ain mither dear,
    Edward, Edward?   50
And what wul ye leave to your ain mither dear,
  My dear son, now tell me, O?"
"The curse of hell frae me sal ye bear,
    Mither, mither,
The curse of hell frae me sal ye bear,   55
  Sic counseils ye gave to me, O."

24 *wae:* woe 25 *whatten:* what 33 *ha':* hall 40 *maun:* must 41
bairns: children 45 *late:* let 53 *sal:* shall 56 *sic:* such

Geoffrey Chaucer

(CA. 1340–1400)

THE COMPLAINT OF CHAUCER
TO HIS PURSE

To yow, my purse, and to noon other wight
Complayne I, for ye be my lady dere!
I am so sory, now that ye been lyght;
For certes, but ye make me hevy chere,
Me were as leef be layd upon my bere;   5
For which unto your mercy thus I crye:
Beth hevy ageyn, or elles mot I dye!

Now voucheth sauf this day, or yt be nyght,
That I of yow the blisful soun may here,
Or see your colour lyk the sonne bryght,   10
That of yelownesse hadde never pere.
Ye be my lyf, ye be myn hertes stere,
Quene of comfort and of good companye:
Beth hevy ageyn, or elles moote I dye!

Now purse, that ben to me my lyves lyght   15
And saveour, as doun in this world here,
Out of this toune helpe me thurgh your myght,
Syn that ye wole nat ben my tresorere;
For I am shave as nye as any frere.
But yet I pray unto your curtesye: 20
Beth hevy ageyn, or elles moote I dye!

1 *wight:* person 4 *hevy chere:* gloomy appearance or behavior 7 *mot:* must 8 *voucheth sauf:* permit; *or:* ere,
before 12 *stere:* rudder, guide 16 *as doun in this world
here:* as in this world down here 19 *frere:* friar

Lenvoy de Chaucer

O conquerour of Brutes Albyon,
Which that by lyne and free eleccion
Been verray kyng, this song to yow I sende;
And ye, that mowen alle oure harmes amende,   25
Have mynde upon my supplicacion!

22 *Brutes Albyon:* Albion is England, supposed to have
been founded by a Roman named Brutus. The "conqueror"
addressed is the king. 24 *verray:* rightful 25 women . . .
amende: can remedy all our ills

Sir Thomas Wyatt

(1503–1542)

FORGET NOT YET

Forget not yet the tried intent
Of such a truth as I have meant,
My great travail so gladly spent,
    Forget not yet.

Forget not yet when first began   5
The weary life ye know, since whan
The suit, the service none tell can,
    Forget not yet.

Forget not yet the great assays,
The cruel wrong, the scornful ways,   10
The painful patience in denays,
    Forget not yet.

6 *whan:* when 7 *suit:* courtship 9 *assays:* tests of
devotion 11 *denays:* denials

Forget not yet, forget not this,
How long ago hath been and is
The mind that never meant amiss,   15
   Forget not yet.

Forget not then thine own approved,
The which so long hath thee so loved,
Whose steadfast faith yet never moved,
   Forget not this.   20

Sir Edward Dyer

(1543–1607)

MY MIND TO ME A KINGDOM IS

My mind to me a kingdom is;
   Such present joys therein I find
That it excels all other bliss
   That earth affords or grows by kind.
Though much I want which most would have,   5
Yet still my mind forbids to crave.

No princely pomp, no wealthy store,
   No force to win the victory,
No wily wit to salve a sore,
   No shape to feed a loving eye;   10
To none of these I yield as thrall,—
For why? My mind doth serve for all.

I see how plenty surfeits oft,
   And hasty climbers soon do fall;
I see that those which are aloft   15
   Mishap doth threaten most of all;
They get with toil, they keep with fear.
Such cares my mind could never bear.

4 *by kind:* naturally 5 *want:* lack

Content I live, this is my stay;
  I seek no more than may suffice;
I press to bear no haughty sway;   20
  Look, what I lack my mind supplies;
Lo, thus I triumph like a king,
Content with that my mind doth bring.

Some have too much, yet still do crave;   25
  I little have, and seek no more.
They are but poor, though much they have,
  And I am rich with little store.
They poor, I rich; they beg, I give;
They lack, I leave; they pine, I live.   30

I laugh not at another's loss;
  I grudge not at another's gain;
No worldly waves my mind can toss;
  My state at one doth still remain.
I fear no foe, I fawn no friend;   35
I loathe not life, nor dread my end.

Some weigh their pleasure by their lust,
  Their wisdom by their rage of will;
Their treasure is their only trust;
  A cloakéd craft their store of skill.   40
But all the pleasure that I find
Is to maintain a quiet mind.

My wealth is health and perfect ease;
  My conscience clear my chief defense;
I neither seek by bribes to please,   45
  Nor by deceit to breed offense.
Thus do I live; thus will I die.
Would all did so as well as I!

35 *fawn:* fawn upon

Sir Philip Sidney

(1554–1586)

FROM ASTROPHEL AND STELLA

1

Loving in truth, and fain in verse my love to show,
That she, dear she, might take some pleasure of my pain,
Pleasure might cause her read, reading might make her know,
Knowledge might pity win, and pity grace obtain,
I sought fit words to paint the blackest face of woe,   5
Studying inventions fine, her wits to entertain:
Oft turning others' leaves, to see if thence would flow
Some fresh and fruitful showers upon my sunburnt brain.
But words came halting forth, wanting Invention's stay,
Invention, Nature's child, fled stepdame Study's blows,   10
And others' feet still seemed but strangers in my way.
Thus, great with child to speak, and helpless in my throes,
Biting my truant pen, beating myself for spite:
"Fool," said my Muse to me, "look in thy heart, and write!"

1 *fain:* eager 9 *stay:* help

31

With how sad steps, Oh Moon, thou climb'st the skies!
How silently, and with how wan a face!
What, may it be that even in heavenly place
That busy archer his sharp arrows tries?
Sure, if that long-with-love-acquainted eyes   5
Can judge of love, thou feel'st a lover's case,
I read it in thy looks; thy languished grace,
To me, that feel the like, thy state descries.
Then, even of fellowship, Oh Moon, tell me,

4 *that busy archer:* Cupid 8 *descries:* discloses

Is constant love deemed there but want of wit?   10
Are beauties there as proud as here they be?
Do they above love to be loved, and yet
Those lovers scorn whom that love doth possess?
Do they call virtue there ungratefulness?

39

Come sleep! Oh sleep, the certain knot of peace,
The baiting place of wit, the balm of woe,
The poor man's wealth, the prisoner's release,
Th' indifferent judge between the high and low;
With shield of proof shield me from out the prease   5
Of those fierce darts Despair at me doth throw;
Oh make in me those civil wars to cease;
I will good tribute pay, if thou do so.
Take thou of me smooth pillows, sweetest bed,
A chamber deaf to noise and blind to light,   10
A rosy garland and a weary head;
And if these things, as being thine by right,
Move not thy heavy grace, thou shalt in me,
Livelier than elsewhere, Stella's image see.

2 *baiting place:* a place for feeding horses while traveling; hence, a
place of renewal 5 *shield of proof:* a sure defense; *prease:* press,
multitude

*R*obert *S*outhwell

(1561–1595)

THE BURNING BABE

As I in hoary winter's night stood shivering in the snow,
Surprise I was with sudden heat which made my heart to glow;
And lifting up a fearful eye to view what fire was near,
A pretty babe all burning bright did in the air appear;

Who, scorchéd with excessive heat, such floods of tears did shed   5
As though his floods should quench his flames which with his tears
        were fed.
"Alas," quoth he, "but newly born in fiery heats I fry,
Yet none approach to warm their hearts or feel my fire but I!
My faultless breast the furnace is, the fuel wounding thorns,
Love is the fire, and sighs the smoke, the ashes shame and scorns;   10
The fuel justice layeth on, and mercy blows the coals,
The metal in this furnace wrought are men's defiléd souls,
For which, as now on fire I am to work them tò their good,
So will I melt into a bath to wash them in my blood."
With this he vanished out of sight and swiftly shrunk away,   15
And straight I calléd unto mind that it was Christmas day.

William Shakespeare

(1564–1616)

FEAR NO MORE THE HEAT
O' THE SUN

Fear no more the heat o' the sun,
    Nor the furious winter's rages;
Thou thy worldly task hast done,
    Home art gone, and ta'en thy wages:
Golden lads and girls all must,   5
As chimney-sweepers, come to dust.

Fear no more the frown o' the great;
    Thou art past the tyrant's stroke;
Care no more to clothe and eat;
    To thee the reed is as the oak: 10
The scepter, learning, physic, must
All follow this, and come to dust.

Fear no more the lightning flash,
    Nor the all-dreaded thunder stone;

Fear not slander, censure rash;   15
    Thou hast finished joy and moan:
All lovers young, all lovers must
Consign to thee, and come to dust.

No exorciser harm thee!
Nor no witchcraft charm thee!   20
Ghost unlaid forbear thee!
Nothing ill come near thee!
Quiet consummation have;
And renowned be thy grave!

FULL FATHOM FIVE

Full fathom five thy father lies;
    Of his bones are coral made;
Those are pearls that were his eyes:
    Nothing of him that doth fade,
But doth suffer a sea change   5
Into something rich and strange.
Sea nymphs hourly ring his knell:
    Ding-dong.
Hark! now I hear them—Ding-dong, bell.

SONNETS

29

When, in disgrace with fortune and men's eyes,
I all alone beweep my outcast state,
And trouble deaf heaven with my bootless cries,
And look upon myself, and curse my fate,
Wishing me like to one more rich in hope,   5
Featured like him, like him with friends possessed,
Desiring this man's art and that man's scope,
With what I most enjoy contented least;
Yet in these thoughts myself almost despising,

5 *bootless:* useless 6 *Featured like him:* resembling him

Haply I think on thee—and then my state,   10
Like to the lark at break of day arising
From sullen earth, sings hymns at heaven's gate;
For thy sweet love remembered such wealth brings
That then I scorn to change my state with kings.

30

When to the sessions of sweet silent thought
I summon up remembrance of things past,
I sigh the lack of many a thing I sought,
And with old woes new wail my dear time's waste:
Then can I drown an eye, unused to flow,   5
For precious friends hid in death's dateless night,
And weep afresh love's long since canceled woe,
And moan the expense of many a vanished sight:
Then can I grieve at grievances foregone,
And heavily from woe to woe tell o'er   10
The sad account of fore-bemoanéd moan,
Which I new pay as if not paid before.
But if the while I think on thee, dear friend,
All losses are restored and sorrows end.

8 *expense:* passing 9 *foregone:* surrendered

71

No longer mourn for me when I am dead
Than you shall hear the surly sullen bell
Give warning to the world that I am fled
From this vile world, with vilest worms to dwell:
Nay, if you read this line, remember not   5
The hand that writ it; for I love you so,
That I in your sweet thoughts would be forgot,
If thinking on me then should make you woe.
Oh, if, I say, you look upon this verse
When I perhaps compounded am with clay,   10
Do not so much as my poor name rehearse,
But let your love even with my life decay;
Lest the wise world should look into your moan,
And mock you with me after I am gone.

73

That time of year thou mayst in me behold
When yellow leaves, or none, or few, do hang
Upon those boughs which shake against the cold,
Bare ruined choirs, where late the sweet birds sang.
In me thou see'st the twilight of such day   5
As after sunset fadeth in the west;
Which by and by black night doth take away,
Death's second self, that seals up all in rest.
In me thou see'st the glowing of such fire,
That on the ashes of his youth doth lie,   10
As the deathbed whereon it must expire,
Consumed with that which it was nourished by.
This thou perceiv'st, which makes thy love more strong,
To love that well which thou must leave ere long.

130

My mistress' eyes are nothing like the sun;
Coral is far more red than her lips' red;
If snow be white, why then her breasts are dun;
If hairs be wires, black wires grow on her head.
I have seen roses damasked, red and white,   5
But no such roses see I in her cheeks;
And in some perfumes is there more delight
Than in the breath that from my mistress reeks.
I love to hear her speak, yet well I know
That music hath a far more pleasing sound;   10
I grant I never saw a goddess go;
My mistress, when she walks, treads on the ground.
And yet, by heaven, I think my love as rare
As any she belied with false compare.

5 *damasked:* used as ornaments 14 *she:* used here as a noun

146

Poor soul, the center of my sinful earth,
Thrall to these rebel powers that thee array,
Why dost thou pine within and suffer dearth,
Painting thy outward walls so costly gay?

2 *Thrall:* slave 3 *dearth:* deprivation

Why so large cost, having so short a lease,   5
Dost thou upon thy fading mansion spend?
Shall worms, inheritors of this excess,
Eat up thy charge? Is this thy body's end?
Then, soul, live thou upon thy servant's loss,
And let that pine to aggravate thy store;   10
Buy terms divine in selling hours of dross;
Within be fed, without be rich no more.
So shalt thou feed on death, that feeds on men,
And death once dead, there's no more dying then.

10 *aggravate:* increase; *store:* wealth 11 *dross:* waste

John Donne

(1573–1631)

THE DISSOLUTION

She is dead; and all which die
    To their first elements resolve;
And we were mutual elements to us,
    And made of one another.
    My body then doth hers involve,   5
And those things whereof I consist, hereby
In me abundant grow, and burdenous,
    And nourish not, but smother.
    My fire of passion, sighs of air,
Water of tears, and earthly sad despair,   10
    Which my materials be,
But near worn out by love's security,
She, to my loss, both by her death repair,
    And I might live long wretched so
But that my fire doth with my fuel grow.   15
    Now as those active kings
    Whose foreign conquest treasure brings,

Receive more, and spend more, and soonest break:
This (which I am amazed that I can speak)
    This death hath with my store   20
      My use increased.
And so my soul more earnestly released
Will outstrip hers; as bullets flown before
A latter bullet may o'ertake, the powder being more.

A VALEDICTION:
FORBIDDING MOURNING

As virtuous men pass mildly away,
   And whisper to their souls to go,
Whilst some of their sad friends do say,
   The breath goes now, and some say, no;

So let us melt, and make no noise,   5
   No tear-floods, nor sigh-tempests move,
'Twere profanation of our joys
   To tell the laity our love.

Moving of th' earth brings harms and fears,
   Men reckon what it did and meant;   10
But trepidation of the spheres,
   Though greater far, is innocent.

Dull sublunary lovers' love
   (Whose soul is sense) cannot admit
Absence, because it doth remove   15
   Those things which elemented it.

But we by a love so much refined
   That our selves know not what it is,
Inter-assuréd of the mind,
   Care less, eyes, lips, and hands to miss.   20

8 *the laity:* outsiders 11 *trepidation of the spheres:* in Ptolemaic astronomy, the apparent irregularity of planetary movements was explained by the theory that the spheres in which the planets revolved experienced tremblings or "trepidations." 13 *sublunary:* beneath the moon, therefore, ordinary 16 *elemented:* made it up

Our two souls therefore, which are one,
   Though I must go, endure not yet
A breach, but an expansion,
   Like gold to airy thinness beat.

If they be two, they are two so   25
   As stiff twin compasses are two;
Thy soul, the fixed foot, makes no show
   To move, but doth, if th' other do.

And though it in the center sit,
   Yet when the other far doth roam,   30
It leans and harkens after it,
   And grows erect, as that comes home.

Such wilt thou be to me, who must
   Like th' other foot, obliquely run;
Thy firmness makes my circle just,   35
   And makes me end where I begun.

35 *just:* correct

THE ECSTASY

Where, like a pillow on a bed,
   A pregnant bank swelled up to rest
The violet's reclining head,
   Sat we two, one another's best.
Our hands were firmly cemented   5
   With a fast balm, which thence did spring.
Our eye-beams twisted, and did thread
   Our eyes upon one double string;
So to intergraft our hands, as yet
   Was all the means to make us one;   10
And pictures in our eyes to get
   Was all our propagation.
As 'twixt two equal armies, Fate
   Suspends uncertain victory,
Our souls (which to advance their state,   15
   Were gone out) hung 'twixt her and me.
And whilst our souls negotiate there,
   We like sepulchral statues lay;

All day the same our postures were,
    And we said nothing all the day.   20
If any, so by love refined
    That he soul's language understood,
And by good love were grown all mind,
    Within convenient distance stood,
He (though he know not which soul spake,   25
    Because both meant, both spake the same)
Might thence a new concoction take,
    And part far purer than he came.
This ecstasy doth unperplex
    (We said) and tell us what we love;   30
We see by this it was not sex,
    We see we saw not what did move;
But as all several souls contain
    Mixture of things, they know not what,
Love these mixed souls doth mix again,   35
    And makes both one, each this and that.
A single violet transplant,
    The strength, the color, and the size
(All which before was poor, and scant)
    Redoubles still, and multiplies.   40
When love, with one another so
    Interinanimates two souls,
That abler soul, which thence doth flow,
    Defects of loneliness controls.
We then, who are this new soul, know,   45
    Of what we are composed, and made,
For, th' atomies of which we grow,
    Are souls, whom no change can invade.
But O alas, so long, so far
    Our bodies why do we forbear?   50
They are ours, though they are not we; we are
    The intelligences, they the sphere.
We owe them thanks because they thus,
    Did us, to us, at first convey,

27 *concoction:* mixture 32 *move:* motivate 47 *atomies:* atoms 50 *forbear:* withhold 52 *intelligences,
sphere:* in the old astronomy, each of the "spheres"
in the universe was supposed to be controlled by an
"intelligence."

Yielded their forces, sense, to us,   55
  Nor are dross to us, but allay.
On man heaven's influence works not so
  But that it first imprints the air,
So soul into the soul may flow,
  Though it to body first repair.   60
As our blood labors to beget
  Spirits as like souls as it can,
Because such fingers need to knit
  That subtle knot which makes us man:
So must pure lovers' souls descend   65
  T' affections, and to faculties
Which sense may reach and apprehend;
  Else a great Prince in prison lies.
To our bodies turn we then, that so
  Weak men on love revealed may look;   70
Love's mysteries in souls do grow,
  But yet the body is his book.
And if some lover, such as we,
  Have heard this dialogue of one,
Let him still mark us; he shall see   75
  Small change when we are to bodies gone.

56 *allay:* alloy 60 *repair:* go to

A HYMN TO GOD THE FATHER

Wilt Thou forgive that sin where I begun,
  Which is my sin, though it were done before?
Wilt Thou forgive that sin through which I run,
  And do run still, though still I do deplore?
    When Thou hast done, Thou hast not done,   5
      For I have more.

Wilt Thou forgive that sin which I have won
  Others to sin? and made my sin their door?
Wilt Thou forgive that sin which I did shun
  A year or two, but wallowed in a score?   10
    When Thou hast done, Thou hast not done,
      For I have more.

I have a sin of fear, that when I have spun
  My last thread, I shall perish on the shore;
Swear by Thy self, that at my death Thy Son   15
  Shall shine as he shines now and heretofore;
    And, having done that, Thou hast done,
      I fear no more.

HOLY SONNETS

7

At the round earth's imagined corners blow
Your trumpets, angels, and arise, arise
From death, you numberlesss infinities
Of souls, and to your scattered bodies go,
All whom the flood did, and fire shall o'erthrow;   5
All whom war, dearth, age, agues, tyrannies,
Despair, law, chance, hath slain, and you whose eyes
Shall behold God, and never taste death's woe.
But let them sleep, Lord, and me mourn a space,
For, if all above these, my sins abound,   10
'Tis late to ask abundance of Thy grace,
When we are there; here on this lowly ground,
Teach me how to repent; for that's as good
As if Thou hadst sealed my pardon, with Thy blood.

9

If poisonous minerals, and if that tree
Whose fruit threw death on else immortal us,
If lecherous goats, if serpents envious
Cannot be damned, Alas! why should I be?
Why should intent or reason, born in me,   5
Make sins, else equal, in me more heinous?
And mercy being easy, and glorious
To God, in his stern wrath why threatens he?
But who am I, that dare dispute with thee,
O God? O! of thine only worthy blood,   10

1 *that tree:* an allusion to the legend of the Garden of Eden

And my tears, make a heavenly Lethean flood,
And drown in it my sin's black memory;
That thou remember them, some claim as debt,
I think it mercy, if thou wilt forget.

11 *Lethean:* Lethe, one of the four rivers of the Greek underworld, brought forgetfulness to those who drank its water.

14

Batter my heart, three personed God; for you
As yet but knock, breathe, shine, and seek to mend;
That I may rise and stand, o'erthrow me and bend
Your force to break, blow, burn and make me new.
I, like an usurped town to another due,   5
Labour to admit you, but Oh, to no end;
Reason, your viceroy in me, me should defend,
But is captived and proves weak or untrue.
Yet dearly I love you and would be loved fain,
But am betrothed unto your enemy: 10
Divorce me, untie or break that knot again,
Take me to you, imprison me, for I
Except you enthrall me, never shall be free,
Nor ever chaste, except you ravish me.

*B*en *J*onson

(1573–1637)

A FIT OF RIME AGAINST RIME

Rime, the rack of finest wits,
That expresseth but by fits
     True conceit,
Spoiling senses of their treasure,
Cozening judgment with a measure,   5

3 *conceit:* imagination 5 *cozening:* cheating

But false weight;
Wresting words from their true calling,
Propping verse for fear of falling
        To the ground;
Jointing syllables, drowning letters,   10
Fast'ning vowels as with fetters
        They were bound!
Soon as lazy thou wert known,
All good poetry hence was flown,
        And art banished.   15
For a thousand years together
All Parnassus' green did wither,
        And wit vanished.
Pegasus did fly away,
At the well no Muse did stay,   20
        But bewailed
So to see the fountain dry,
And Apollo's music die,
        All light failed!
Starveling rhymes did fill the stage;   25
Not a poet in an age
        Worth a crowning;
Not a work deserving bays,
Nor a line deserving praise,
        Pallas frowning;   30
Greek was free from rime's infection,
Happy Greek by this protection
        Was not spoiled.
Whilst the Latin, queen of tongues,
Is not yet free from rime's wrongs,   35
        But rests foiled.
Scarce the hill again doth flourish,
Scarce the world a wit doth nourish
        To restore

17 *Parnassus:* the mountain sacred to
Apollo, hence, associated with song and
art 19 *Pegasus:* the mythical winged horse
who is said to have started the flow of
Hippocrene, the fountain of inspiration,
with a blow of his hoof 23 *Apollo:* the god
of song and poetry 30 *Pallas:* another
name for Athene, the goddess of wisdom
36 *hill:* that is, Parnassus

Phoebus to his crown again, 40
And the Muses to their brain,
 As before.
Vulgar languages that want
Words and sweetness, and be scant
 Of true measure, 45
Tyrant rhyme hath so abused,
That they long since have refused
 Other caesure.
He that first invented thee,
May his joints tormented be, 50
 Cramped forever.
Still may syllables jar with time,
Still may reason war with rime,
 Resting never.
May his sense when it would meet 55
The cold tumor in his feet,
 Grow unsounder;
And his title be long fool,
That in rearing such a school
 Was the founder. 60

40 *Phoebus:* another name for Apollo 43
vulgar languages: those spoken by the common people unlike Latin and Greek 48
caesure: caesura, or method of division

*R*obert *H*errick
(1591–1674)

O ANTHEA, WHO MAY COMMAND
HIM ANYTHING

Bid me to live, and I will live
 Thy protestant to be:
Or bid me love, and I will give
 A loving heart to thee.

2 *protestant:* a protestor of love

A heart as soft, a heart as kind,   5
  A heart as sound and free
As in the whole world thou canst find,
  That heart I'll give to thee.

Bid that heart stay, and it will stay,
  To honor thy decree;   10
Or bid it languish quite away,
  And't shall do so for thee.

Bid me to weep, and I will weep,
  While I have eyes to see;
And having none, yet I will keep   15
  A heart to weep for thee.

Bid me despair, and I'll despair,
  Under that cypress tree;
Or bid me die, and I will dare
  E'en death, to die for thee.   20

Thou art my life, my love, my heart,
  The very eyes of me;
And hast command of every part,
  To live and die for thee.

TO DAFFODILS

Fair daffodils, we weep to see
  You haste away so soon;
As yet the early-rising sun
  Has not attained his noon.
    Stay, stay,   5
   Until the hasting day
     Has run
   But to the even-song;
And, having prayed together, we
   Will go with you along.   10

We have short time to stay, as you;
  We have as short a spring;
As quick a growth to meet decay,
  As you, or any thing.
    We die,   15
  As your hours do, and dry
    Away

Like to the summer's rain;
    Or as the pearls of morning's dew,
        Ne'er to be found again.

THE RESURRECTION POSSIBLE
AND PROBABLE

For each one body that i'th' earth is sown,
There's an uprising but of one for one:
But for each grain, that in the ground is thrown,
Threescore or fourscore spring up thence for one:
So that the wonder is not half so great,   5
Of ours, as is the rising of the wheat.

DISCONTENTS IN DEVON

More discontents I never had
    Since I was born, than here;
Where I have been, and still am sad
    In this dull Devonshire:
Yet justly too I must confess;   5
    I ne'er invented such
Ennobled numbers for the press
    Than where I loathed so much.

Henry King

(1592–1669)

SIC VITA

Like to the falling of a star,
Or as the flights of eagles are,
Or like the fresh spring's gaudy hue,
Or silver drops of morning dew,
Or like a wind that chafes the flood,   5
Or bubbles which on water stood:

Sic Vita: Such is life (Latin)

Even such is man, whose borrowed light
Is straight called in, and paid to night.
  The wind blows out, the bubble dies;
  The spring entombed in autumn lies;   10
  The dew dries up, the star is shot;
  The flight is past, and man forgot.

George Herbert

(1593–1633)

REDEMPTION

Having been tenant long to a rich Lord,
  Not thriving, I resolved to be bold,
  And make a suit unto him, to afford
A new small-rented lease, and cancel th' old.

In Heaven at his manor I him sought: 5
  They told me there, that he was lately gone
  About some land, which he had dearly bought
Long since on earth, to take possession.

I straight return'd, and knowing his great birth,
  Sought him accordingly in great resorts;   10
  In cities, theatres, gardens, parks, and courts:
At length I heard a ragged noise and mirth
  Of thieves and murderers: there I him espied,
  Who straight, *Your suit is granted*, said, and died.

VIRTUE

Sweet day, so cool, so calm, so bright,
  The bridal of the earth and sky:
The dew shall weep thy fall tonight;
  For thou must die.

2 *bridal:* wedding

Sweet rose, whose hue, angry and brave,   5
  Bids the rash gazer wipe his eye:
Thy root is ever in its grave,
    And thou must die.

Sweet spring, full of sweet days and roses,
  A box where sweets compacted lie;   10
My music shows ye have your closes,
    And all must die.

Only a sweet and virtuous soul,
  Like seasoned timber, never gives;
But though the whole world turn to coal,   15
    Then chiefly lives.

10 *sweets:* perfumes 11 *closes:* a musical term,
meaning the ends of passages 15 *coal:* to ashes,
in the fire at the Day of Judgment

JORDAN (I)

Who says that fictions only and false hair
Become a verse? Is there in truth no beauty?
Is all good structure in a winding stair?
May no lines pass, except they do their duty
  Not to a true, but painted chair?   5

Is it no verse, except enchanted groves
And sudden arbors shadow coarse-spun lines?
Must purling streams refresh a lover's loves?
Must all be veiled while he that reads, divines,
  Catching the sense at two removes?   10

Shepherds are honest people; let them sing:
Riddle who list, for me, and pull for prime:
I envy no man's nightingale or spring;
Nor let them punish me with loss of rhyme,
  Who plainly say, *My God, My King.*   15

11 *Riddle who list etc.:* Let those who want to write
complex poems, hoping to produce something good
by luck; *pull for prime:* an expression from a card
game, meaning to draw for a valuable card

JORDAN (II)

When first my lines of heavenly joys made mention,
   Such was their luster, they did so excel,
That I sought out quaint words, and trim invention;
   My thoughts began to burnish, sprout, and swell,
Curling with metaphors a plain intention,   5
   Decking the sense, as if it were to sell.

Thousands of notions in my brain did run,
   Offering their service, if I were not sped:
I often blotted what I had begun;
   This was not quick enough, and that was dead.   10
Nothing could seem too rich to clothe the sun,
   Much less those joys which trample on his head.

As flames do work and wind when they ascend,
   So did I weave myself into the sense;
But while I bustled, I might hear a friend   15
   Whisper, "How wide is all this long pretense!
There is in love a sweetness ready penned:
   Copy out only that, and save expense."

8 *sped:* suited 16 *wide:* useless

THE PULLEY

   When God at first made man,
Having a glass of blessings standing by,
   "Let us," said he, "pour on him all we can.
Let the world's riches, which dispersèd lie,
   Contract into a span."   5

   So strength first made a way;
Then beauty flowed, then wisdom, honor, pleasure.
   When almost all was out, God made a stay,
Perceiving that, alone of all his treasure,
   Rest in the bottom lay.   10

   "For if I should," said he,
"Bestow this jewel also on my creature,

He would adore my gifts instead of me,
And rest in Nature, not the God of Nature;
  So both should losers be.   15

"Yet let him keep the rest,
But keep them with repining restlessness.
  Let him be rich and weary, that at least,
If goodness lead him not, yet weariness
  May toss him to my breast."   20

DISCIPLINE

Throw away Thy rod,
Throw away Thy wrath:
    O my God,
Take the gentle path.

For my heart's desire   5
Unto Thine is bent:
    I aspire
To a full consent.

Not a word or look
I affect to own,   10
    But by book,
And Thy Book alone.

Though I fail, I weep:
Though I halt in pace,
    Yet I creep   15
To the throne of grace.

Then let wrath remove;
Love will do the deed:
    For with love
Stony hearts will bleed.   20

Love is swift of foot;
Love's a man of war,
    And can shoot,
And can hit from far.

Who can 'scape his bow?   25
That which wrought on Thee,
        Brought Thee low,
Needs must work on me.

Throw away Thy rod;
Though man frailties hath,   30
        Thou art God:
Throw away Thy wrath.

THE PEARL

Matt. XIII

I know the ways of learning: both the head
And pipes that feed the press, and make it run;
What reason hath from nature borrowèd,
Or of itself, like a good housewife, spun
In laws and policy; what the stars conspire;   5
What willing nature speaks, what forced by fire;
Both the old discoveries, and the new-found seas,
The stock and surplus, cause and history;
All these stand open, or I have the keys;
        Yet I love Thee.   10

I know the ways of honor: what maintains
The quick returns of courtesy and wit;
In vies of favors whether party gains
When glory swells the heart, and moldeth it
To all expressions both of hand and eye,   15
Which on the world a true-love-knot may tie,
And bear the bundle wheresoe'er it goes;
How many drams of spirit there must be
To sell my life unto my friends or foes;
        Yet I love Thee.   20

The Pearl: the "pearl of great price" to which the kingdom of heaven is compared in Matthew 13:45 2 *press:*
probably a printing press 13 *vies:* rivalries; *whether:*
which

I know the ways of pleasure: the sweet strains,
The lullings and the relishes of it;
The propositions of hot blood and brains;
What mirth and music mean; what love and wit
Have done these twenty hundred years and more;   25
I know the projects of unbridled store;
My stuff is flesh, not brass; my senses live,
And grumble oft that they have more in me
Than he that curbs them, being but one to five;
    Yet I love Thee.   30

I know all these, and have them in my hand;
Therefore not sealed, but with open eyes
I fly to Thee, and fully understand
Both the main sale and the commodities;
And at what rate and price I have Thy love,   35
With all the circumstances that may move.
Yet through these labryinths, not my groveling wit,
But Thy silk twist let down from heaven to me
Did both conduct and teach me how by it
    To climb to Thee.   40

26 *store:* treasure 32 *sealed:* blinded, as falcons were in
training

Thomas Carew

(1595–1639)

A SONG

Ask me no more where Jove bestows,
When June is past, the fading rose;
For in your beauty's orient deep,
These flowers, as in their causes, sleep.

3 *orient:* lustrous or pearly 4 *causes:* origins

Ask me no more whither do stray   5
The golden atoms of the day;
For in pure love heaven did prepare
Those powders to enrich your hair.

Ask me no more whither doth haste
The nightingale when May is past;   10
For in your sweet dividing throat
She winters, and keeps warm her note.

Ask me no more where those stars light,
That downwards fall in dead of night;
For in your eyes they sit, and there   15
Fixéd become, as in their sphere.

Ask me no more if east or west
The phoenix builds her spicy nest;
For unto you at last she flies,
And in your fragrant bosom dies.   20

11 *dividing:* melodious 18 *phoenix:* the legendary bird who died in flames every thousand
years, then rose from her ashes. She built her
nest with the branches of spice-bearing plants.

Edmund Waller

(1606–1687)

OF ENGLISH VERSE

Poets may boast, as safely vain,
Their works shall with the world remain;
Both, bound together, live or die,
The verses and the prophecy.

But who can hope his lines should long   5
Last in a daily changing tongue?

While they are new, envy prevails;
And as that dies, our language fails.

When architects have done their part,
The matter may betray their art;   10
Time, if we use ill-chosen stone,
Soon brings a well-built palace down.

Poets that lasting marble seek
Must carve in Latin or in Greek;
We write in sand, our language grows,   15
And, like the tide, our work o'erflows.

Chaucer his sense can only boast,
The glory of his numbers lost!
Years have defaced his matchless strain,
And yet he did not sing in vain.   20

The beauties which adorned that age,
The shining subjects of his rage,
Hoping they should immortal prove,
Rewarded with success his love.

This was the generous poet's scope,   25
And all an English pen can hope,
To make the fair approve his flame,
That can so far extend their fame.

Verse, thus designed, has no ill fate
If it arrive but at the date   30
Of fading beauty; if it prove
But as long-lived as present love.

John Milton

(1608–1674)

ON THE LATE MASSACRE IN PIEDMONT

Avenge, O Lord, thy slaughtered saints, whose bones   3
  Lie scattered on the Alpine mountains cold,
  Even them who kept thy truth so pure of old
  When all our fathers worshiped stocks and stones,
Forget not: in thy book record their groans   5
  Who were thy sheep and in their ancient fold
  Slain by the bloody Piemontese that rolled
  Mother with infant down the rocks. Their moans
  The vales redoubled to the hills, and they
  To Heaven. Their martyred blood and ashes sow   10
  O'er all th' Italian fields where still doth sway
The triple tyrant: that from these may grow
  A hundredfold, who having learnt thy way
  Early may fly the Babylonian woe.

On the Late Massacre: the subject was a massacre of a sect
called the Waldenses living in northern Italy 12 *the triple
tyrant:* the Catholic church, with its doctrine of the Trinity
14 *the Babylonian woe:* Catholicism

METHOUGHT I SAW MY LATE ESPOUSÉD SAINT

Methought I saw my late espouséd saint
  Brought to me like Alcestis from the grave,
  Whom Jove's great son to her glad husband gave,
  Rescued from death by force though pale and faint.

2 *Alcestis:* she agreed to accept death in her husband's
place, but was brought back from the underworld
through the efforts of Hercules

Mine, as whom washed from spot of childbed taint,   5
   Purification in the old law did save,
   And such, as yet once more I trust to have
Full sight of her in Heaven without restraint,
Came vested all in white, pure as her mind.
   Her face was veiled, yet to my fancied sight,   10
   Love, sweetness, goodness, in her person shined
So clear, as in no face with more delight.
   But O, as to embrace me she inclined,
   I waked, she fled, and day brought back my night.

5 *as whom washed . . . :* his dead wife is compared to
women purified after childbirth by ritual washing, in accordance with Old Testament law 13 *inclined:* leaned

LYCIDAS

*In this monody the author bewails a learned
friend, unfortunately drowned in his passage from
Chester on the Irish Seas, 1637. And by occasion
foretells the ruin of our corrupted clergy then in
their height.*

Yet once more, O ye laurels, and once more,
Ye myrtles brown, with ivy never sere,
I come to pluck your berries harsh and crude,
And with forced fingers rude
Shatter your leaves before the mellowing year.   5
Bitter constraint, and sad occasion dear,
Compels me to disturb your season due;
For Lycidas is dead, dead ere his prime,
Young Lycidas, and hath not left his peer.
Who would not sing for Lycidas? He knew   10
Himself to sing, and build the lofty rhyme.
He must not float upon his watery bier
Unwept, and welter to the parching wind,
Without the meed of some melodious tear.

Lycidas: Milton's conventional name for Edward King, the
"learned friend" whose death he is lamenting. 3 *crude:* unripe 13
welter: tumbled about on the waves 14 *meed:* reward

Begin then, Sisters of the sacred well,   15
That from beneath the seat of Jove doth spring,
Begin, and somewhat loudly sweep the string.
Hence with denial vain, and coy excuse;
So may some gentle Muse
With lucky words favor my destined urn,   20
And as he passes turn,
And bid fair peace be to my sable shroud.
For we were nursed upon the self-same hill,
Fed the same flock, by fountain, shade, and rill.

Together both, ere the high lawns appeared   25
Under the opening eyelids of the morn,
We drove afield, and both together heard
What time the gray-fly winds her sultry horn,
Battening our flocks with the fresh dews of night,
Oft till the star that rose, at evening, bright,   30
Toward Heaven's descent had sloped his westering wheel.
Meanwhile the rural ditties were not mute,
Tempered to the oaten flute,
Rough Satyrs danced, and Fauns with cloven heel
From the glad sound would not be absent long,   35
And old Damoetas loved to hear our song.
    But O the heavy change, now thou art gone,
Now thou art gone, and never must return!
Thee, Shepherd, thee the woods, and desert caves,
With wild thyme and the gadding vine o'ergrown,   40
And all their echoes mourn.
The willows and the hazel copses green
Shall now no more be seen,
Fanning their joyous leaves to thy soft lays.
As killing as the canker to the rose,   45
Or taint-worm to the weanling herds that graze,
Or frost to flowers, that their gay wardrobe wear,
When first the white-thorn blows;

15 *Sisters:* the Muses, or goddesses of the arts, who were associated
with the Pierian spring near Mt. Olympus ("the seat of Jove") 19
Muse: poet. The antecedent of "he" in line 21 20 *urn:* a burial con-
tainer 29 *Battening:* feeding 30 *the star:* the planet Venus 35 *Satyrs,
Fauns:* pleasure-loving minor deities, usually depicted with
goats' feet 36 *Damoetas:* Milton's conventional name for a Cambridge teacher 40 *gadding:* wandering

Such, Lycidas, thy loss to shepherd's ear.
　　Where were ye, Nymphs, when the remorseless deep 　　　50
Closed o'er the head of your loved Lycidas?
For neither were ye playing on the steep,
Where your old bards, the famous Druids, lie,
Nor on the shaggy top of Mona high,
Nor yet where Deva spreads her wizard stream. 　　　　　55
Ay me, I fondly dream!
Had ye been there!—for what could that have done?
What could the Muse herself that Orpheus bore,
The muse herself, for her enchanting son,
Whom universal Nature did lament, 　　　　　　　　　60
When by the rout that made the hideous roar,
His gory visage down the stream was sent,
Down the swift Hebrus to the Lesbian shore?
　　Alas! What boots it with uncessant care
To tend the homely slighted shepherd's trade, 　　　　　65
And strictly meditate the thankless Muse?
Were it not better done as others use,
To sport with Amaryllis in the shade,
Or with the tangles of Neaera's hair?
Fame is the spur that the clear spirit doth raise 　　　70
(That last infirmity of noble mind)
To scorn delights, and live laborious days;
But the fair guerdon when we hope to find,
And think to burst out into sudden blaze,
Comes the blind Fury with the abhorrèd shears, 　　　75
And slits the thin-spun life. "But not the praise,"
Phoebus replied, and touched my trembling ears:
"Fame is no plant that grows on mortal soil,
Nor in the glistering foil
Set off to the world, nor in broad rumor lies, 　　　　80
But lives and spreads aloft by those pure eyes,

---

54 *Mona:* refers to the Isle of Man and to Anglesey, both islands in the Irish Sea, where King was drowned 55 *Deva:* the river Dee, which was supposed to have prophetic power 57 *the Muse herself:* Calliope, the mother of Orpheus. Orpheus was torn apart by wild women, and his head was flung into the river Hebrus 65 *shepherd's trade:* poetry 68-69 *Amaryllis, Neaera:* conventional names for nymphs 73 *guerdon:* reward 75 *the blind Fury:* Atropos, the third Fate, who cuts the thread of man's life 77 *Phoebus:* Apollo, the god of poetry 79 *foil:* setting or background

And perfect witness of all-judging Jove;
As he pronounces lastly on each deed,
Of so much fame in Heaven expect thy meed."
   O fountain Arethuse, and thou honored flood,   85
Smooth-sliding Mincius, crowned with vocal reeds,
That strain I heard was of a higher mood;
But now my oat proceeds,
And listens to the Herald of the Sea,
That came in Neptune's plea.   90
He asked the waves, and asked the felon winds,
What hard mishap hath doomed this gentle swain?
And questioned every gust of rugged wings
That blows from off each beakèd promontory;
They knew not of his story,   95
And sage Hippotades their answer brings,
That not a blast was from his dungeon strayed;
The air was calm, and on the level brine,
Sleek Panope with all her sisters played.
It was that fatal and perfidious bark,   100
Built in the eclipse, and rigged with curses dark,
That sunk so low that sacred head of thine.
   Next Camus, reverend sire, went footing slow,
His mantle hairy, and his bonnet sedge,
Inwrought with figures dim, and on the edge   105
Like to that sanguine flower inscribed with woe.
"Ah, who hath reft" (quoth he) "my dearest pledge?"
Last came, and last did go,
The Pilot of the Galilean Lake;
Two massy keys he bore of metals twain   110
(The golden opes, the iron shuts amain).

---

85 *Arethuse:* Arethusa was a nymph who was purchased by the god of the river Alpheus from Greece across the sea to Sicily, where she was transformed into a stream by Diana. 86 *Mincius:* a river in Italy mentioned by Virgil 88 *oat:* shepherd's pipe made of straw 89 *Herald of the Sea:* Triton, the messenger of Neptune 96 *Hippotades:* Aeolus, god of the winds 99 *Panope:* a sea nymph 101 *Built in the eclipse:* that is, at an unlucky time 103 *Camus:* the deity of the river Cam, in Cambridge 106 *that sanguine flower:* the markings on the hyacinth are supposed to resemble the Greek word for "Alas!" 107 *reft:* broken, destroyed 109 *Pilot:* St. Peter was originally a fisherman on the Sea of Galilee, he keeps the keys of heaven

He shook his mitered locks, and stern bespake:
"How well could I have spared for thee, young swain,
Enow of such as for their bellies' sake
Creep and intrude, and climb into the fold! 115
Of other care they little reckoning make,
Than how to scramble at the shearers' feast,
And shove away the worthy bidden guest.
Blind mouths! that scarce themselves know how to hold
A sheep-hook, or have learned aught else the least 120
That to the faithful herdman's art belongs!
What recks it them? What need they? They are sped;
And when they list, their lean and flashy songs
Grate on their scrannel pipes of wretched straw;
The hungry sheep look up, and are not fed, 125
But swollen with wind, and the rank mist they draw,
Rot inwardly, and foul contagion spread;
Besides what the grim wolf with privy paw
Daily devours apace, and nothing said.
But that two-handed engine at the door 130
Stands ready to smite once, and smite no more."
    Return Alpheus, the dread voice is past,
That shrunk thy streams; return, Sicilian Muse,
And call the vales, and bid them hither cast
Their bells, and flowerets of a thousand hues. 135
Ye valleys low where the mild whispers use,
Of shades and wanton winds, and gushing brooks,
On whose fresh lap the swart star sparely looks,
Throw hither all your quaint enameled eyes,
That on the green turf suck the honeyed showers, 140
And purple all the ground with vernal flowers.
Bring the rathe primrose that forsaken dies,
The tufted crow-toe, and pale jessamine,
The white pink, and the pansy freaked with jet,

---

112 *mitered locks:* he wears the miter, or bishop's hat 120 *sheep-hook:* the bishop's staff is shaped like a shepherd's crook 122 *they are sped:* they are satisfied 123 *list:* wish 124 *scrannel:* weak 128 *the grim wolf:* probably, Satan 130 *two-handed engine:* a problematic metaphor, meaning some weapon of revenge 132 *Alpheus:* the god who pursued Arethusa to Sicily (line 85) 138 *the swart star:* Sirius, called "swart" because the ancients thought it was red; it is associated with midsummer 142 *rathe:* early 144 *freaked:* spotted

The glowing violet,   145
The musk-rose, and the well-attired woodbine,
With cowslips wan that hang the pensive head,
And every flower that sad embroidery wears.
Bid amaranthus all his beauty shed,
And daffodillies fill their cups with tears,   150
To strew the laureate hearse where Lycid lies.
For so to interpose a little ease,
Let our frail thoughts dally with false surmise.
Ay me! Whilst thee the shores, and sounding seas
Wash far away, where'er thy bones are hurled,   155
Whether beyond the story Hebrides,
Where thou perhaps under the whelming tide
Visitest the bottom of the monstrous world;
Or whether thou to our moist vows denied,
Sleep'st by the fable of Bellerus old,   160
Where the great Vision of the guarded mount
Looks toward Namancos and Bayona's hold;
Look homeward Angel now, and melt with ruth;
And, O ye dolphins, waft the hapless youth.
    Weep no more, woeful shepherds weep no more,   165
For Lycidas, your sorrow, is not dead,
Sunk though he be beneath the watery floor;
So sinks the day-star in the ocean bed,
And yet anon repairs his drooping head,
And tricks his beams, and with new-spangled ore,   170
Flames in the forehead of the morning sky:
So Lycidas sunk low, but mounted high,
Through the dear might of him that walked the waves,
Where other groves, and other streams along,
With nectar pure his oozy locks he laves,   175
And hears the unexpressive nuptial song,
In the blest kingdoms meek of joy and love.
There entertain him all the saints above,

156 *Hebrides:* islands northwest of Scotland 158 *monstrous:* filled
with monsters 160 *Bellerus:* a giant who is supposed to be buried on
the shore of Cornwall 161 *the guarded mount:* St. Michael's Mount
in Cornwall 162 *Namancos:* a place on the north coast of Spain
Bayona: Bayonne, an old fortress town on the coast of France 163
Angel: addressed to St. Michael; *ruth:* pity 168 *the day-star:* the
sun 170 *tricks:* arranges

In solemn troops, and sweet societies
That sing, and singing in their glory move,   180
And wipe the tears forever from his eyes.
Now Lycidas the shepherds weep no more;
Henceforth thou art the Genius of the shore,
In thy large recompense, and shalt be good
To all that wander in that perilous flood.   185
   Thus sang the uncouth swain to the oaks and rills,
While the still morn went out with sandals gray;
He touched the tender stops of various quills,
With eager thought warbling his Doric lay.
And now the sun had stretched out all the hills,   190
And now was dropped into the western bay;
At last he rose, and twitched his mantle blue:
Tomorrow to fresh woods, and pastures new.

183 *Genius:* guardian spirit 186 *uncouth:* rough, uncivilized 188
quills: the stalks of which the shepherd's flute was made 180 *Doric:*
rustic

*R*ichard *L*ovelace

(1618–1658)

TO LUCASTA, GOING
TO THE WARS

Tell me not, Sweet, I am unkind
That from the nunnery
Of thy chaste breast and quiet mind,
To war and arms I fly.

True, a new mistress now I chase,   5
The first foe in the field;
And with a stronger faith embrace
A sword, a horse, a shield.

Yet this inconstancy is such
As you too shall adore;   10
I could not love thee, Dear, so much,
Loved I not honor more.

Andrew Marvell

(1621–1678)

ON A DROP OF DEW

See how the orient dew,
Shed from the bosom of the morn
  Into the blowing roses,
Yet careless of its mansion new,
For the clear region where 'twas born   5
  Round in itself incloses,
  And in its little globe's extent
Frames as it can its native element;
How it the purple flower does slight,
  Scarce touching where it lies,   10
But gazing back upon the skies,
  Shines with a mournful light
    Like its own tear,
Because so long divided from the sphere.
  Restless it rolls and unsecure,   15
    Trembling lest it grow impure,
  Till the warm sun pity its pain,
And to the skies exhale it back again.
    So the soul, that drop, that ray
Of the clear fountain of eternal day,   20
Could it within the human flower be seen,
  Rememb'ring still its former height,
  Shuns the sweet leaves and blossoms green;

1 *orient:* lustrous, shining 4 *careless of:* indifferent to
14 *the sphere:* the sky

And recollecting its own light,
Does, in its pure and circling thoughts, express   25
The greater heaven in an heaven less.
   In how coy a figure wound,
   Every way it turns away;
   So the world excluding round,
   Yet receiving in the day;   30
   Dark beneath but bright above,
   Here disdaining, there in love;
   How loose and easy hence to go,
   How girt and ready to ascend;
   Moving but on a point below,   35
   It all about does upwards bend.
Such did the manna's sacred dew distil,
White and entire, though congealed and chill;
Congealed on earth, but does, dissolving, run
Into the glories of th' almighty sun.   40

27 *coy:* elusive

THE DEFINITION OF LOVE

My love is of a birth as rare
As 'tis for object strange and high;
It was begotten by despair
Upon impossibility.

Magnanimous despair alone   5
Could show me so divine a thing,
Where feeble hope could ne'er have flown,
But vainly flapped its tinsel wing.

And yet I quickly might arrive
Where my extended soul is fixed,   10
But fate does iron wedges drive,
And always crowds itself betwixt.

For fate with jealous eye does see
Two perfect loves, nor lets them close;

8 *tinsel:* a thin, metallic material that is showy, but
fragile

Their union would her ruin be,   15
And her tyrannic power depose.

And therefore her decrees of steel
Us as the distant poles have placed,
Though love's whole world on us doth wheel,
Not by themselves to be embraced;   20

Unless the giddy heaven fall,
And earth some new convulsion tear,
And, us to join, the world should all
Be cramped into a planisphere.

As lines, so loves, oblique may well   25
Themselves in every angle greet;
But ours so truly parallel,
Though infinite, can never meet.

Therefore the love which us doth bind,
But fate so enviously debars,   30
Is the conjunction of the mind,
And opposition of the stars.

24 *planisphere:* a notion of the earth flattened, with
the poles together, used in astrology 31, 32 *conjunction, opposition:* astrological terms

TO HIS COY MISTRESS

Had we but world enough, and time,
This coyness, lady, were no crime.
We would sit down and think which way
To walk, and pass our long love's day;
Thou by the Indian Ganges' side   5
Shouldst rubies find; I by the tide
Of Humber would complain. I would
Love you ten years before the Flood;

5 *Ganges:* a river in India 7 *Humber:* a river in
England 8 *ten years before the Flood:* the
Biblical deluge, associated with Noah. It
would be a long time from this period to
"the conversion of the Jews."

And you should, if you please, refuse
Till the conversion of the Jews.   10
My vegetable love should grow
Vaster than empires, and more slow.
An hundred years should go to praise
Thine eyes, and on thy forehead gaze;
Two hundred to adore each breast,   15
But thirty thousand to the rest;
An age at least to every part,
And the last age should show your heart.
For, lady, you deserve this state,
Nor would I love at lower rate.   20
　　But at my back I always hear
Time's wingèd chariot hurrying near;
And yonder all before us lie
Deserts of vast eternity.
Thy beauty shall no more be found,   25
Nor in thy marble vaults shall sound
My echoing song; then worms shall try
That long preserved virginity,
And your quaint honor turn to dust,
And into ashes all my lust.   30
The grave's a fine and private place,
But none, I think, do there embrace.
　　Now therefore, while the youthful hue
Sits on thy skin like morning dew,
And while thy willing soul transpires   35
At every port with instant fires,
Now let us sport us while we may;
And now, like am'rous birds of prey,
Rather at once our time devour,
Than languish in his slow-chapped power.   40
Let us roll all our strength, and all
Our sweetness, up into one ball;
And tear our pleasures with rough strife
Thorough the iron gates of life.
Thus, though we cannot make our sun   45
Stand still, yet we will make him run.

27 *try*: test 35 *transpires*: breathes out 36 *instant*: immediate 40 *slow-chapped*: having jaws
that move slowly

Henry Vaughan

(1622–1695)

THE RETREAT

Happy those early days, when I
Shined in my angel infancy;
Before I understood this place
Appointed for my second race,
Or taught my soul to fancy aught   5
But a white, celestial thought;
When yet I had not walked above
A mile or two from my first love,
And looking back, at that short space,
Could see a glimpse of His bright face;   10
When on some gilded cloud or flower
My gazing soul would dwell an hour,
And in those weaker glories spy
Some shadows of eternity;
Before I taught my tongue to wound   15
My conscience with a sinful sound,
Or had the black art to dispense
A several sin to every sense,
But felt through all this fleshly dress
Bright shoots of everlastingness.   20
    Oh, how I long to travel back,
And tread again that ancient track!
That I might once more reach that plain
Where first I left my glorious train;
From whence the enlightened spirit sees   25
That shady city of palm trees.
But, ah! my soul with too much stay

4 *second race:* introducing the theme of the
poem, the idea that there is an earlier life 26
shady city: the Heavenly City 27 *stay:* delay

Is drunk, and staggers in the way.
Some men a forward motion love;
But I by backward steps would move,   30
And when this dust falls to the urn,
In that state I came, return.

30 *urn:* for holding the ashes of the dead

THEY ARE ALL GONE INTO THE WORLD OF LIGHT

They are all gone into the world of light!
  And I alone sit lingering here;
Their very memory is fair and bright,
  And my sad thoughts doth clear.

It glows and glitters in my cloudy breast   5
  Like stars upon some gloomy grove,
Or those faint beams in which this hill is dressed
  After the sun's remove.

I see them walking in an air of glory,
  Whose light doth trample on my days;   10
My days, which are at best but dull and hoary,
  Mere glimmering and decays.

O holy hope, and high humility,
  High as the heavens above!
These are your walks, and you have showed them me   15
  To kindle my cold love.

Dear, beauteous death! the jewel of the just,
  Shining nowhere but in the dark;
What mysteries do lie beyond thy dust,
  Could man outlook that mark!   20

He that hath found some fledged bird's nest may know
  At first sight if the bird be flown;
But what fair well or grove he sings in now,
  That is to him unknown.

4 *clear:* clarify 20 *that mark:* the boundary of death

And yet, as angels in some brighter dreams   25
  Call to the soul when man doth sleep,
So some strange thoughts transcend our wonted themes,
  And into glory peep.

If a star were confined into a tomb,
  Her captive flames must needs burn there;   30
But when the hand that locked her up gives room,
  She'll shine through all the sphere.

O Father of eternal life, and all
  Created glories under Thee!
Resume Thy spirit from this world of thrall   35
  Into true liberty!

Either disperse these mists, which blot and fill
  My perspective still as they pass;
Or else remove me hence unto that hill
  Where I shall need no glass.   40

35 *Resume:* take up again; *thrall:* slavery 39 *that hill:* the hill
of Zion in Jerusalem, symbolic of deliverance

$\mathcal{A}$lexander $\mathcal{P}$ope

(1688–1744)

THE RAPE OF THE LOCK

An Heroi-Comical Poem

This poem is based upon an actual incident. A young nobleman named Lord Petre had jokingly cut a lock of hair from the head of the beautiful Miss Arabella Fermor. The trick angered Miss Fermor and, according to Pope, "created an estrangement between the two families, though they had lived so long in great friendship before." John Caryll, a relative of Miss Fermor's, and a

*friend of Pope's, who is mentioned in the third
line, suggested that he write a poem turning the
episode into a joke, as a means of bringing the
friends together again. A first, and much shorter,
version of the poem was published in 1712. The
final form, published in 1717, is the result of much
revision and expansion.*

Canto I

What dire offence from amorous causes springs,
What mighty contests rise from trivial things,
I sing—This verse to CARYLL, Muse! is due:
This, even Belinda may vouchsafe to view;
Slight is the subject, but not so the praise,   5
If she inspire, and he approve my lays.
   Say what strange motive, goddess! could compel
A well-bred lord to assault a gentle belle?
O say what stranger cause, yet unexplored,
Could make a gentle belle reject a lord?   10
In tasks so bold, can little men engage,
And in soft bosoms dwells such mighty rage?
   Sol through white curtains shot a tim'rous ray,
And oped those eyes that must eclipse the day:
Now lap-dogs give themselves the rousing shake,   15
And sleepless lovers, just at twelve awake:
Thrice rung the bell, the slipper knock'd the ground,
And the press'd watch return'd a silver sound.
Belinda still her downy pillow press'd,
Her guardian sylph prolong'd the balmy rest: 20
'Twas he had summon'd to her silent bed
The morning-dream that hover'd o'er her head;
A youth more glittering than a birth-night beau,
(That ev'n in slumber caused her cheek to glow)
Seem'd to her ear his winning lips to lay,   25
And thus in whispers said, or seem'd to say:
   "Fairest of mortals, thou distinguish'd care
Of thousand bright inhabitants of air!

17 *the slipper knock'd:* to call the maid, who has not answered
the bell 18 *the press'd watch:* a repeater watch. It had a bell
which rang hours and quarters when a pin was pressed
23 *birth-night:* the festive occasion of a royal birthday

If e'er one vision touch'd thy infant thought,
Of all the nurse and all the priest have taught;   30
Of airy elves by moonlight shadows seen,
The silver token, and the circled green,
Or virgins visited by angel powers,
With golden crowns and wreaths of heavenly flowers;
Hear and believe! thy own importance know,   35
Nor bound thy narrow views to things below.
Some secret truths, from learned pride conceal'd,
To maids alone and children are reveal'd:
What, though no credit doubting wits may give?
The fair and innocent shall still believe.   40
Know, then, unnumbered spirits round thee fly,
The light militia of the lower sky:
These, though unseen, are ever on the wing,
Hang o'er the box, and hover round the ring.
Think what an equipage thou hast in air,   45
And view with scorn two pages and a chair.
As now your own, our beings were of old,
And once inclosed in woman's beauteous mould;
Thence, by a soft transition, we repair
From earthly vehicles to these of air.   50
Think not, when woman's transient breath is fled,
That all her vanities at once are dead;
Succeeding vanities she still regards,
And though she plays no more, o'erlooks the cards.
Her joy in gilded chariots, when alive,   55
And love of ombre, after death survive.
For when the fair in all their pride expire,
To their first elements their souls retire:
The sprites of fiery termagants in flame
Mount up, and take a Salamander's name.   60
Soft yielding minds to water glide away,
And sip, with nymphs, their elemental tea.

32 *silver token:* a gift left by fairies; *circled green:* so-called "fairy rings" in the grass, thought to be circles where the fairies danced 44 *the box:* a theater box; *the ring:* a circular drive in Hyde Park frequented by fashionable people 46 *a chair:* a sedan chair; an enclosed chair carried on poles by two servants 54 *o'erlooks the cards:* watches the game 56 *ombre:* the card game played in Canto III 60 *Salamander:* a spirit who was supposed to live in fire

The graver prude sinks downward to a gnome,
In search of mischief still on earth to roam.
The light coquettes in sylphs aloft repair,   65
And sport and flutter in the fields of air.
  "Know further yet; whoever fair and chaste
Rejects mankind, is by some sylph embraced:
For spirits, freed from mortal laws, with ease
Assume what sexes and what shapes they please.   70
What guards the purity of melting maids,
In courtly balls, and midnight masquerades,
Safe from the treach'rous friend, the daring spark,
The glance by day, the whisper in the dark,
When kind occasion prompts their warm desires,   75
When music softens, and when dancing fires?
'Tis but their sylph, the wise celestials know,
Though honour is the word with men below.
  "Some nymphs there are, too conscious of their face,
For life predestined to the gnomes' embrace.   80
These swell their prospects and exalt their pride,
When offers are disdain'd and love denied:
Then gay ideas crowd the vacant brain,
While peers, and dukes, and all their sweeping train,
And garters, stars, and coronets appear,   85
And in soft sounds, 'Your Grace' salutes their ear.
'Tis these that early taint the female soul,
Instruct the eyes of young coquettes to roll,
Teach infant cheeks a bidden blush to know,
And little hearts to flutter at a beau.   90
  "Oft when the world imagine women stray,
The sylphs through mystic mazes guide their way,
Through all the giddy circle they pursue,
And old impertinence expel by new.
What tender maid but must a victim fall   95
To one man's treat, but for another's ball?
When Florio speaks, what virgin could withstand,
If gentle Damon did not squeeze her hand?

73 *spark:* a dandy 85 *garters, stars, and coronet:* marks of
rank or distinction 86 "*Your Grace*": the form of address appropriate to a duchess 89 *a bidden blush:* one produced by
rouge 97, 98 *Florio, Damon:* names invented for the hypo-
thetical lovers.

With varying vanities, from ev'ry part,
They shift the moving toy-shop of their heart;   100
Where wigs with wigs, with sword-knots sword-knots strive,
Beaux banish beaux, and coaches coaches drive.
This erring mortals levity may call,
Oh, blind to truth! the sylphs contrive it all.
    "Of these am I, who thy protection claim,   105
A watchful sprite, and Ariel is my name.
Late, as I ranged the crystal wilds of air,
In the clear mirror of thy ruling star
I saw, alas! some dread event impend,
Ere to the main this morning sun descend;   110
But heaven reveals not what, or how, or where:
Warn'd by the sylph, oh, pious maid, beware!
This to disclose is all thy guardian can:
Beware of all, but most beware of man!"
    He said; when Shock, who thought she slept too long,   115
Leap'd up, and waked his mistress with his tongue.
'Twas then, Belinda, if report say true,
Thy eyes first open'd on a billet-doux;
Wounds, charms, and ardors, were no sooner read,
But all the vision vanish'd from thy head.   120
    And now, unveil'd, the toilet stands display'd,
Each silver vase in mystic order laid.
First, robed in white, the nymph intent adores,
With head uncover'd, the cosmetic powers.
A heav'nly image in the glass appears,   125
To that she bends, to that her eye she rears;
Th' inferior priestess, at her altar's side,
Trembling, begins the sacred rites of pride.
Unnumber'd treasures ope at once, and here
The various offerings of the world appear;   130
From each she nicely culls with curious toil,
And decks the goddess with the glitt'ring spoil.
This casket India's glowing gems unlocks,
And all Arabia breathes from yonder box.
The tortoise here and elephant unite,   135
Transform'd to combs, the speckled and the white.

---

101 *sword-knots:* the fashionable adornment of a ribbon tied
to the hilt of a sword 121 *toilet:* dressing table

Here files of pins extend their shining rows,
Puffs, powders, patches, Bibles, billet-doux.
Now awful beauty puts on all its arms;
The fair each moment rises in her charms,   140
Repairs her smiles, awakens every grace,
And calls forth all the wonders of her face:
Sees by degrees a purer blush arise,
And keener lightnings quicken in her eyes.
The busy sylphs surround their darling care,   145
These set the head, and those divide the hair,
Some fold the sleeve, while others plait the gown;
And Betty's praised for labours not her own.

138 *patches:* bits of black fabric or court plaster which women
stuck to their faces as adornments

Canto II

Not with more glories, in th' ethereal plain,
The sun first rises o'er the purpled main,
Than, issuing forth, the rival of his beams
Launch'd on the bosom of the silver Thames.
Fair nymphs and well-dress'd youths around her shone,   5
But every eye was fix'd on her alone.
On her white breast a sparkling cross she wore,
Which Jews might kiss, and infidels adore.
Her lively looks a sprightly mind disclose,
Quick as her eyes, and as unfix'd as those: 10
Favours to none, to all she smiles extends;
Oft she rejects, but never once offends.
Bright as the sun, her eyes the gazers strike,
And, like the sun, they shine on all alike.
Yet graceful ease, and sweetness void of pride,   15
Might hide her faults, if belles had faults to hide:
If to her share some female errors fall,
Look on her face, and you'll forget them all.
    This nymph, to the destruction of mankind,
Nourish'd two locks, which graceful hung behind   20
In equal curls, and well conspired to deck
With shining ringlets the smooth ivory neck.
Love in these labyrinths his slaves detains,

And mighty hearts are held in slender chains.
With hairy springes we the birds betray,   25
Slight lines of hair surprise the finny prey,
Fair tresses man's imperial race insnare,
And beauty draws us with a single hair.

Th' adventurous baron the bright locks admired;
He saw, he wish'd, and to the prize aspired.   30
Resolved to win, he meditates the way,
By force to ravish, or by fraud betray;
For when success a lover's toils attends,
Few ask, if fraud or force attain'd his ends.

For this, ere Phœbus rose, he had implored   35
Propitious Heaven, and every power adored:
But chiefly Love—to Love an altar built,
Of twelve vast French romances, neatly gilt.
There lay three garters, half a pair of gloves;
And all the trophies of his former loves: 40
With tender billet-doux he lights the pyre,
And breathes three amorous sighs to raise the fire.
Then prostrate falls, and begs with ardent eyes
Soon to obtain, and long possess the prize:
The powers gave ear, and granted half his prayer,   45
The rest, the winds dispersed in empty air.

But now secure the painted vessel glides,
The sun-beams trembling on the floating tides;
While melting music steals upon the sky,
And soften'd sounds along the waters die;   50
Smooth flow the waves, the zephyrs gently play,
Belinda smiled, and all the world was gay.
All but the sylph—with careful thoughts oppress'd,
Th' impending woe sat heavy on his breast.
He summons straight his denizens of air;   55
The lucid squadrons round the sails repair:
Soft o'er the shrouds aërial whispers breathe,
That seem'd but zephyrs to the train beneath.
Some to the sun their insect-wings unfold,
Waft on the breeze, or sink in clouds of gold;   60
Transparent forms, too fine for mortal sight,
Their fluid bodies half dissolved in light.
Loose to the wind their airy garments flew,

25 *springes:* traps 35 *Phœbus:* the sun

Thin glittering textures of the filmy dew,
Dipp'd in the richest tincture of the skies,   65
Where light disports in ever-mingling dyes;
While ev'ry beam new transient colours flings,
Colours that change whene'er they wave their wings.
Amid the circle on the gilded mast,
Superior by the head, was Ariel placed;   70
His purple pinions op'ning to the sun,
He raised his azure wand, and thus begun:
    "Ye sylphs and sylphids, to your chief give ear;
Fays, fairies, genii, elves, and dæmons, hear:
Ye know the spheres, and various tasks assign'd   75
By laws eternal to the aërial kind.
Some in the fields of purest ether play,
And bask and whiten in the blaze of day.
Some guide the course of wand'ring orbs on high,
Or roll the planets through the boundless sky.   80
Some less refined beneath the moon's pale light
Pursue the stars that shoot athwart the night,
Or suck the mists in grosser air below,
Or dip their pinions in the painted bow,
Or brew fierce tempests on the wintry main,   85
Or o'er the glebe distil the kindly rain.
Others on earth o'er human race preside,
Watch all their ways, and all their actions guide:
Of these the chief the care of nations own,
And guard with arms divine the British throne.   90
    "Our humbler province is to tend the fair,
Not a less pleasing, though less glorious care;
To save the powder from too rude a gale,
Nor let the imprison'd essences exhale;
To draw fresh colours from the vernal flowers;   95
To steal from rainbows, ere they drop in showers,
A brighter wash; to curl their waving hairs,
Assist their blushes and inspire their airs;
Nay, oft, in dreams, invention we bestow,
To change a flounce, or add a furbelow.   100
    "This day, black omens threat the brightest fair
That e'er deserved a watchful spirit's care;

86 *glebe:* a cultivated field 100 *furbelow:* fabric formed into
pleats or flounces as an ornament on a dress

Some dire disaster, or by force, or slight;
But what, or where, the Fates have wrapp'd in night.
Whether the nymph shall break Diana's law,   105
Or some frail China jar receive a flaw;
Or stain her honour or her new brocade;
Forget her prayers, or miss a masquerade;
Or lose her heart, or necklace, at a ball;
Or whether Heaven has doom'd that Shock must fall.   110
Haste, then, ye spirits! to your charge repair:
The flutt'ring fan be Zephyretta's care;
The drops to thee, Brillante, we consign;
And, Momentilla, let the watch be thine;
Do thou, Crispissa, tend her fav'rite lock;   115
Ariel himself shall be the guard of Shock.
    "To fifty chosen sylphs, of special note,
We trust th' important charge, the petticoat:
Oft have we known that seven-fold fence to fail,
Though stiff with hoops, and arm'd with ribs of whale;   120
Form a strong line about the silver bound,
And guard the wide circumference around.
    "Whatever spirit, careless of his charge,
His post neglects, or leaves the fair at large,
Shall feel sharp vengeance soon o'ertake his sins,   125
Be stopp'd in vials, or transfix'd with pins;
Or plunged in lakes of bitter washes lie,
Or wedged whole ages in a bodkin's eye:
Gums and pomatums shall his flight restrain,
While clogg'd he beats his silken wings in vain: 130
Or alum styptics with contracting power
Shrink his thin essence like a rivell'd flower:
Or, as Ixion fix'd, the wretch shall feel
The giddy motion of the whirling mill,
In fumes of burning chocolate shall glow,   135
And tremble at the sea that froths below!"
    He spoke; the spirits from the sails descend;
Some, orb in orb, around the nymph extend;
Some thrid the mazy ringlets of her hair;

105 *Diana:* goddess of chastity 112 *Zephyretta:* this, and the
names in the following lines are fanciful names for the spirits
128 *bodkin:* needle 132 *rivell'd:* shrunken 134 *mill:* used for
grinding chocolate

Some hang upon the pendants of her ear: 140
With beating hearts the dire event they wait,
Anxious and trembling for the birth of Fate.

Canto III

Close by those meads, for ever crown'd with flowers,
Where Thames with pride surveys his rising towers,
There stands a structure of majestic frame,
Which from the neighb'ring Hampton takes its name.
Here Britain's statesmen oft the fall foredoom   5
Of foreign tyrants, and of nymphs at home;
Here thou, great ANNA! whom three realms obey,
Dost sometimes counsel take—and sometimes tea.
    Hither the heroes and the nymphs resort,
To taste a while the pleasures of a court;   10
In various talk th' instructive hours they pass'd,
Who gave the ball, or paid the visit last;
One speaks the glory of the British Queen,
And one describes a charming Indian screen;
A third interprets motions, looks, and eyes;   15
At every word a reputation dies.
Snuff, or the fan, supply each pause of chat,
With singing, laughing, ogling, *and all that.*
    Meanwhile, declining from the noon of day,
The sun obliquely shoots his burning ray;   20
The hungry judges soon the sentence sign,
And wretches hang that jurymen may dine;
The merchant from th' exchange returns in peace,
And the long labours of the toilet cease.
Belinda now, whom thirst of fame invites,   25
Burns to encounter two adventurous knights,
At ombre singly to decide their doom;
And swells her breast with conquests yet to come.
Straight the three bands prepare in arms to join,
Each band the number of the sacred nine.   30
Soon as she spreads her hand, th' aërial guard

---

3 *structure of majestic frame:* Hampton Court Palace 7 *great
ANNA:* Queen Anne, who reigned 1702–1714; the three
realms were England, France, and Ireland 27 *ombre:* a card
game for three players

Descend, and sit on each important card:
First Ariel perch'd upon a Matadore,
Then each according to the rank he bore;
For sylphs, yet mindful of their ancient race,   35
Are, as when women, wondrous fond of place.
  Behold, four Kings in majesty revered,
With hoary whiskers and a forky beard;
And four fair Queens, whose hands sustain a flower,
Th' expressive emblem of their softer power;   40
Four knaves in garbs succinct, a trusty band;
Caps on their heads, and halberts in their hand;
And party-colour'd troops, a shining train,
Drawn forth to combat on the velvet plain.
  The skilful nymph reviews her force with care: 45
"Let Spades be trumps!" she said, and trumps they were.
  Now move to war her sable Matadores,
In show like leaders of the swarthy Moors.
Spadillio first, unconquerable lord!
Led off two captive trumps, and swept the board.   50
As many more Manillio forced to yield,
And march'd a victor from the verdant field.
Him Basto follow'd; but his fate more hard
Gain'd but one trump, and one plebeian card.
With his broad sabre next, a chief in years,   55
The hoary Majesty of Spades appears,
Puts forth one manly leg, to sight reveal'd,
The rest, his many-colour'd robe conceal'd.
The rebel Knave, who dares his prince engage,
Proves the just victim of his royal rage.   60
Ev'n mighty Pam, that kings and queens o'erthrew,
And mow'd down armies in the fights of Lu,
Sad chance of war! now destitute of aid,
Falls undistinguish'd by the victor Spade!
  Thus far both armies to Belinda yield;   65
Now to the baron fate inclines the field.
His warlike Amazon her host invades,
Th' imperial consort of the crown of Spades.
The Club's black tyrant first her victim dyed,
Spite of his haughty mien, and barb'rous pride: 70

33 *Matadore:* this, like the terms in the following lines, refers
to the cards and their values 41 *succinct:* tight-fitting

What boots the regal circle on his head,
His giant limbs, in state unwieldy spread;
That long behind he trails his pompous robe,
And, of all monarchs, only grasps the globe?
The baron now his Diamonds pours apace;   75
Th' embroider'd King who shows but half his face,
And his refulgent Queen, with powers combined
Of broken troops an easy conquest find.
Clubs, Diamonds, Hearts, in wild disorder seen,
With throngs promiscuous strow the level green.   80
Thus when dispersed a routed army runs,
Of Asia's troops, and Afric's sable sons,
With like confusion different nations fly,
Of various habit, and of various dye,
The pierced battalions disunited fall,   85
In heaps on heaps; one fate o'erwhelms them all.
    The Knave of Diamonds tries his wily arts,
And wins (oh shameful chance!) the Queen of Hearts.
At this, the blood the virgin's cheek forsook,
A livid paleness spreads o'er all her look;   90
She sees, and trembles at th' approaching ill,
Just in the jaws of ruin, and Codille.
And now (as oft in some distemper'd state)
On one nice trick depends the gen'ral fate,
An Ace of Hearts steps forth: the King unseen   95
Lurk'd in her hand, and mourn'd his captive Queen:
He springs to vengeance with an eager pace,
And falls like thunder on the prostrate Ace.
The nymph exulting fills with shouts the sky;
The walls, the woods, and long canals reply.   100
    O thoughtless mortals! ever blind to fate,
Too soon dejected, and too soon elate.
Sudden, these honours shall be snatch'd away,
And cursed for ever this victorious day.
    For lo! the board with cups and spoons is crown'd,   105
The berries crackle, and the mill turns round:
On shining altars of Japan they raise
The silver lamp; the fiery spirits blaze:
From silver spouts the grateful liquors glide,
While China's earth receives the smoking tide: 110
At once they gratify their scent and taste,
And frequent cups prolong the rich repast.

Straight hover round the fair her airy band;
Some, as she sipp'd, the fuming liquor fann'd,
Some o'er her lap their careful plumes display'd,   115
Trembling, and conscious of the rich brocade.
Coffee (which makes the politician wise,
And see through all things with his half-shut eyes)
Sent up in vapours to the baron's brain
New stratagems, the radiant lock to gain.   120
Ah cease, rash youth! desist ere 'tis too late,
Fear the just gods, and think of Scylla's fate!
Changed to a bird, and sent to flit in air,
She dearly pays for Nisus' injured hair!
But when to mischief mortals bend their will,   125
How soon they find fit instruments of ill!
Just then, Clarissa drew with tempting grace
A two-edged weapon from her shining case:
So ladies, in romance, assist their knight,
Present the spear, and arm him for the fight.   130
He takes the gift with reverence and extends
The little engine on his fingers' ends;
This just behind Belinda's neck he spread,
As o'er the fragrant steams she bends her head.
Swift to the lock a thousand sprites repair,   135
A thousand wings, by turns, blow back the hair;
And thrice they twitch'd the diamond in her ear;
Thrice she look'd back, and thrice the foe drew near.
Just in that instant, anxious Ariel sought
The close recesses of the virgin's thought: 140
As on the nosegay in her breast reclin'd,
He watch'd th' ideas rising in her mind,
Sudden he view'd, in spite of all her art,
An earthly lover lurking at her heart.
Amazed, confused, he found his power expired,   145
Resign'd to fate, and with a sigh retired.
The peer now spreads the glitt'ring forfex wide,
T' inclose the lock; now joins it, to divide.
Ev'n then, before the fatal engine closed,
A wretched sylph too fondly interposed;   150

122 *Scylla:* she was punished for cutting the one golden hair
from the head of her father, Nisus 127 *Clarissa:* a friend of
the Baron's 147 *forfex:* scissors

Fate urged the shears, and cut the sylph in twain,
(But airy substance soon unites again)
The meeting points the sacred hair dissever
From the fair head, for ever, and for ever!
  Then flash'd the living lightning from her eyes,   155
And screams of horror rend th' affrighted skies.
Not louder shrieks to pitying Heaven are cast,
When husbands or when lap-dogs breathe their last;
Or when rich China vessels, fall'n from high,
In glitt'ring dust and painted fragments lie!   160
  "Let wreaths of triumph now my temples twine,
(The victor cried) the glorious prize is mine!
While fish in streams, or birds delight in air,
Or in a coach and six the British fair,
As long as *Atalantis* shall be read,   165
Or the small pillow grace a lady's bed,
While visits shall be paid on solemn days,
When numerous wax-lights in bright order blaze,
While nymphs take treats, or assignations give,
So long my honour, name, and praise shall live!"   170
What Time would spare, from steel receives its date,
And monuments, like men, submit to fate!
Steel could the labour of the gods destroy,
And strike to dust th' imperial towers of Troy;
Steel could the works of mortal pride confound,   175
And hew triumphal arches to the ground.
What wonder then, fair nymph! thy hairs should feel
The conquering force of unresisted steel?

165 *Atalantis: The New Atalantis*, a popular book by Mrs.
Manley published in 1709

Canto IV

But anxious cares the pensive nymph oppress'd,
And secret passions labour'd in her breast.
Not youthful kings in battle seized alive,
Not scornful virgins who their charms survive,
Not ardent lovers robb'd of all their bliss,   5
Not ancient ladies when refused a kiss,
Not tyrants fierce that unrepenting die,

Not Cynthia when her manteau's pinn'd awry,
E'er felt such rage, resentment, and despair,
As thou, sad virgin! for thy ravish'd hair.   10
    For, that sad moment, when the sylphs withdrew,
And Ariel weeping from Belinda flew,
Umbriel, a dusky, melancholy sprite,
As ever sullied the fair face of light,
Down to the central earth, his proper scene,   15
Repair'd to search the gloomy Cave of Spleen.
    Swift on his sooty pinions flits the gnome,
And in a vapour reach'd the dismal dome.
No cheerful breeze this sullen region knows,
The dreaded east is all the wind that blows.   20
Here in a grotto, shelter'd close from air,
And screen'd in shades from day's detested glare,
She sighs for ever on her pensive bed,
Pain at her side, and Megrim at her head.
Two handmaids wait the throne: alike in place,   25
But diff'ring far in figure and in face.
Here stood Ill-nature like an ancient maid,
Her wrinkled form in black and white array'd;
With store of prayers, for mornings, nights, and noons,
Her hand is fill'd; her bosom with lampoons.   30
    There Affectation, with a sickly mien,
Shows in her cheek the roses of eighteen,
Practised to lisp, and hang the head aside,
Faints into airs, and languishes with pride,
On the rich quilt sinks with becoming woe,   35
Wrapp'd in a gown, for sickness, and for show.
The fair ones feel such maladies as these,
When each new night-dress gives a new disease.
    A constant vapour o'er the palace flies;
Strange phantoms rising as the mists arise;   40
Dreadful, as hermits' dreams in haunted shades,
Or bright, as visions of expiring maids.
Now glaring fiends, and snakes on rolling spires,

---

8 *manteau:* a loose upper garment 16 *Spleen:* a popular term
for a vague psychosomatic disorder whose symptoms included moodiness, anger, indigestion, and so on 24 *Megrim:*
or migraine, meaning headache 39 *vapour:* a disorder not
unlike "spleen"

Pale spectres, gaping tombs, and purple fires:
Now lakes of liquid gold, Elysian scenes,   45
And crystal domes, and angels in machines.
   Unnumber'd throngs on every side are seen
Of bodies changed to various forms by Spleen.
Here living tea-pots stand, one arm held out,
One bent; the handle this, and that the spout: 50
A pipkin there, like Homer's tripod walks;
Here sighs a jar, and there a goose-pie talks:
Men prove with child, as powerful fancy works,
And maids turn'd bottles call aloud for corks.
   Safe pass'd the gnome through this fantastic band,   55
A branch of healing spleen-wort in his hand.
Then thus address'd the power: "Hail, wayward Queen!
Who rule the sex to fifty from fifteen;
Parent of vapours, and of female wit,
Who give th' hysteric or poetic fit;   60
On various tempers act by various ways,
Make some take physic, others scribble plays;
Who cause the proud their visits to delay,
And send the godly in a pet to pray;
A nymph there is, that all thy power disdains,   65
And thousands more in equal mirth maintains.
But oh! if e'er thy gnome could spoil a grace,
Or raise a pimple on a beauteous face,
Like citron waters matrons' cheeks inflame,
Or change complexions at a losing game;   70
If e'er with airy horns I planted heads,
Or rumpled petticoats, or tumbled beds,
Or caused suspicion when no soul was rude,
Or discomposed the head-dress of a prude,
Or e'er to costive lap-dog gave disease,   75
Which not the tears of brightest eyes could ease;
Hear me, and touch Belinda with chagrin,
That single act gives half the world the spleen."
   The Goddess with a discontented air
Seems to reject him, though she grants his prayer.   80

51 *pipkin:* a small pot 71 *horns:* a man whose wife was unfaithful to him was said, metaphorically, to be wearing horns
74 *prude:* a woman who is overstrict about modesty or pro-
priety

A wondrous bag with both her hands she binds,
Like that where once Ulysses held the winds;
There she collects the force of female lungs,
Sighs, sobs, and passions, and the war of tongues.
A vial next she fills with fainting fears,   85
Soft sorrows, melting griefs, and flowing tears.
The gnome rejoicing bears her gifts away,
Spreads his black wings, and slowly mounts to day.
   Sunk in Thalestris' arms the nymph he found,
Her eyes dejected, and her hair unbound.   90
Full o'er their heads the swelling bag he rent,
And all the furies issued at the vent.
Belinda burns with more than mortal ire,
And fierce Thalestris fans the rising fire;
"O wretched maid!" she spread her hands, and cried,   95
(While Hampton's echoes, "Wretched maid!" replied)
"Was it for this you took such constant care
The bodkin, comb, and essence to prepare?
For this your locks in paper durance bound?
For this with torturing irons wreathed around?   100
For this with fillets strain'd your tender head,
And bravely bore the double loads of lead?
Gods! shall the ravisher display your hair,
While the fops envy and the ladies stare?
Honour forbid! at whose unrivall'd shrine   105
Ease, pleasure, virtue, all our sex resign.
Methinks already I your tears survey,
Already hear the horrid things they say,
Already see you a degraded toast,
And all your honour in a whisper lost!   110
How shall I then your helpless fame defend?
'Twill then be infamy to seem your friend!
And shall this prize, th' inestimable prize,
Exposed through crystal to the gazing eyes,

---

82 *Like that where once Ulysses:* in Book X of the *Odyssey,*
Aeolus, god of the winds, gave Ulysses a bag containing the
winds that might blow him off his course during his voyage
home 89 *Thalestris:* the name of an Amazon queen, used for
Belinda's friend 98 *bodkin:* here, a hairpin 102 *double loads of
lead:* the curl papers were weighted with lead 109 *a degraded
toast:* that is, she would be the subject of a mocking toast

And heighten'd by the diamond's circling rays,   115
On that rapacious hand for ever blaze?
Sooner shall grass in Hyde Park Circus grow,
And wits take lodgings in the sound of Bow;
Sooner let earth, air, sea, to Chaos fall,
Men, monkeys, lap-dogs, parrots, perish all!"   120
    She said; then raging to Sir Plume repairs,
And bids her beau demand the precious hairs:
(Sir Plume of amber snuff-box justly vain,
And the nice conduct of a clouded cane)
With earnest eyes, and round, unthinking face,   125
He first the snuff-box open'd, then the case,
And thus broke out—"My Lord, why, what the devil!
Z—ds! damn the lock! 'fore Gad, you must be civil!
Plague on't! 'tis past a jest—nay prithee, pox!
Give her the hair"—he spoke, and rapp'd his box.   130
"It grieves me much (replied the peer again)
Who speaks so well should ever speak in vain,
But by this lock, this sacred lock, I swear,
(Which never more shall join its parted hair;
Which never more its honours shall renew,   135
Clipp'd from the lovely head where late it grew)
That while my nostrils draw the vital air,
This hand, which won it, shall for ever wear."
He spoke, and speaking, in proud triumph spread
The long-contended honours of her head.   140
    But Umbriel, hateful gnome! forbears not so;
He breaks the vial whence the sorrows flow.
Then see! The nymph in beauteous grief appears,
Her eyes half-languishing, half-drowned in tears;
On her heaved bosom hung her drooping head,   145
Which, with a sigh, she raised; and thus she said:
    "For ever cursed be this detested day,
Which snatch'd my best, my fav'rite curl away!
Happy! ay ten times happy had I been,
If Hampton Court these eyes had never seen!   150
Yet am I not the first mistaken maid,
By love of courts to numerous ills betray'd,
Oh had I rather unadmired remain'd

118 *in the sound of Bow:* Bow bells were in the part of London frequented by serious men of business

In some lone isle, or distant northern land;
Where the gilt chariot never marks the way,   155
Where none learn ombre, none e'er taste bohea!
There kept my charms conceal'd from mortal eye,
Like roses that in deserts bloom and die.
What moved my mind with youthful lords to roam?
Oh had I stayed, and said my prayers at home!   160
'Twas this the morning omens seem'd to tell:
Trice from my trembling hand the patch-box fell;
The tott'ring china shook without a wind;
Nay, Poll sat mute, and Shock was most unkind!
A sylph too warn'd me of the threats of Fate,   165
In mystic visions, now believed too late!
See the poor remnants of these slighted hairs!
My hands shall rend what e'en thy rapine spares:
These in two sable ringlets taught to break,
Once gave new beauties to the snowy neck;   170
The sister-lock now sits uncouth, alone,
And in its fellow's fate foresees its own;
Uncurl'd it hangs, the fatal shears demands,
And tempts, once more, thy sacrilegious hands.
Oh hadst thou, cruel! been content to seize   175
Hairs less in sight, or any hairs but these!"

156 *bohea:* a kind of tea

Canto V

She said: the pitying audience melt in tears;
But Fate and Jove had stopp'd the baron's ears.
In vain Thalestris with reproach assails,
For who can move when fair Belinda fails?
Not half so fix'd the Trojan could remain,   5
While Anna begg'd and Dido raged in vain.
Then grave Clarissa graceful waved her fan;
Silence ensued, and thus the nymph began:
    "Say, why are beauties praised and honoured most,
The wise man's passion, and the vain man's toast?   10

5 *the Trojan:* in the *Aeneid*, Aeneas remains obdurate in his
decision to leave Carthage, in spite of the pleas of Dido and
her sister Anna

Why deck'd with all that land and sea afford,
Why angels call'd, and angel-like adored?
Why round our coaches crowd the white-gloved beaux?
Why bows the side-box from its inmost rows?
How vain are all these glories, all our pains,   15
Unless good sense preserve what beauty gains;
That men may say, when we the front-box grace,
'Behold the first in virtue as in face!'
Oh! if to dance all night, and dress all day,
Charm'd the small-pox, or chased old age away;   20
Who would not scorn what housewife's cares produce,
Or who would learn one earthly thing of use?
To patch, nay, ogle, might become a saint,
Nor could it sure be such a sin to paint.
But since, alas! frail beauty must decay,   25
Curl'd or uncurl'd, since locks will turn to grey;
Since painted, or not painted, all shall fade,
And she who scorns a man must die a maid;
What then remains, but well our power to use,
And keep good-humour still, whate'er we lose?   30
And trust me, dear, good-humour can prevail,
When airs, and flights, and screams, and scolding fail.
Beauties in vain their pretty eyes may roll;
Charms strike the sight, but merit wins the soul."
    So spoke the dame, but no applause ensued;   35
Belinda frown'd, Thalestris call'd her prude.
"To arms, to arms!" the fierce virago cries,
And swift as lightning to the combat flies.
All side in parties, and begin th' attack:
Fans clap, silks rustle, and tough whalebones crack;   40
Heroes' and heroines' shouts confusedly rise,
And bass and treble voices strike the skies.
No common weapons in their hands are found,
Like Gods they fight, nor dread a mortal wound.
    So when bold Homer makes the Gods engage,   45
And heavenly breasts with human passions rage;
'Gainst Pallas, Mars; Latona, Hermes arms;
And all Olympus rings with loud alarms;

14 *side-box:* a box at the side of the theater 40 *whalebones:*
used as a stiffening in corsets 47 *Pallas. . . . :* deities found
in Homer's epics

Jove's thunder roars, Heaven trembles all around,
Blue Neptune storms, the bellowing deeps resound: 50
Earth shakes her nodding towers, the ground gives way,
And the pale ghosts start at the flash of day!
  Triumphant Umbriel on a sconce's height
Clapp'd his glad wings, and sate to view the fight:
Propp'd on their bodkin spears, the sprites survey   55
The growing combat, or assist the fray.
  While through the press enraged Thalestris flies,
And scatters death around from both her eyes,
A beau and witling perish'd in the throng,
One died in metaphor, and one in song.   60
"O cruel nymph! a living death I bear,"
Cried Dapperwit, and sunk beside his chair.
A mournful glance Sir Fopling upwards cast,
"Those eyes are made so killing,"—was his last:
Thus on Mæander's flowery margin lies   65
Th' expiring swan, and as he sings he dies.
  When bold Sir Plume had drawn Clarissa down,
Chloe stepp'd in, and kill'd him with a frown;
She smiled to see the doughty hero slain,
But, at her smile, the beau revived again.   70
  Now Jove suspends his golden scales in air,
Weighs the men's wits against the lady's hair:
The doubtful beam long nods from side to side;
At length the wits mount up, the hairs subside.
  See fierce Belinda on the baron flies,   75
With more than usual lightning in her eyes:
Nor fear'd the chief th' unequal fight to try,
Who sought no more than on his foe to die.
But this bold lord with manly strength endued,
She with one finger and a thumb subdued: 80
Just where the breath of life his nostrils drew,
A charge of snuff the wily virgin threw;
The gnomes direct, to every atom just,
The pungent grains of titillating dust.

53 *sconce:* a support for candles set in the wall 64 *"Those eyes
are made so killing"*: the first words of a popular song of the
time 65 *Mæander:* a river of antiquity. These two lines are a
paraphrase of a passage in Ovid

Sudden, with starting tears each eye o'erflows,   85
And the high dome re-echoes to his nose,
  "Now meet thy fate," incensed Belinda cried,
And drew a deadly bodkin from her side.
(The same, his ancient personage to deck,
Her great-great-grandsire wore about his neck,   90
In three seal rings; which after, melted down,
Form'd a vast buckle for his widow's gown:
Her infant grandame's whistle next it grew,
The bells she jingled, and the whistle blew;
Then in a bodkin graced her mother's hairs,   95
Which long she wore, and now Belinda wears.)
  "Boast not my fall, (he cried) insulting foe!
Thou by some other shalt be laid as low.
Nor think, to die dejects my lofty mind:
All that I dread is leaving you behind!   100
Rather than so, ah let me still survive,
And burn in Cupid's flames—but burn alive."
  "Restore the lock!" she cries; and all around
"Restore the lock!" the vaulted roofs rebound.
Not fierce Othello in so loud a strain   105
Roar'd for the handkerchief that caused his pain.
But see how oft ambitious aims are cross'd,
And chiefs contend till all the prize is lost!
The lock, obtain'd with guilt, and kept with pain,
In every place is sought, but sought in vain: 110
With such a prize no mortal must be blest,
So Heaven decrees! with Heaven who can contest?
  Some thought it mounted to the lunar sphere,
Since all things lost on earth are treasured there.
There heroes' wits are kept in pond'rous vases,   115
And beaux' in snuff-boxes and tweezer-cases.
There broken vows, and death-bed alms are found,
And lovers' hearts with ends of riband bound,
The courtier's promises, and sick man's prayers,
The smiles of harlots, and the tears of heirs,   120
Cages for gnats, and chains to yoke a flea,
Dried butterflies, and tomes of casuistry.
  But trust the Muse—she saw it upward rise,
Though mark'd by none but quick, poetic eyes:
(So Rome's great founder to the heavens withdrew,   125

To Proculus alone confess'd in view)
A sudden star it shot through liquid air,
And drew behind a radiant trail of hair.
Not Berenice's lock first rose so bright,
The heavens bespangling with dishevell'd light.   130
The sylphs behold it kindling as it flies,
And pleased pursue its progress through the skies.
   This the beau-monde shall from the Mall survey,
And hail with music its propitious ray.
This the blest lover shall for Venus take,   135
And send up vows from Rosamonda's lake.
This Partridge soon shall view in cloudless skies,
When next he looks through Galileo's eyes;
And hence th' egregious wizard shall foredoom
The fate of Louis, and the fall of Rome.   140
   Then cease, bright nymph! to mourn thy ravish'd hair,
Which adds new glory to the shining sphere!
Not all the tresses that fair head can boast
Shall draw such envy as the lock you lost.
For, after all the murders of your eye,   145
When, after millions slain, yourself shall die;
When those fair suns shall set, as set they must,
And all those tresses shall be laid in dust;
This lock, the Muse shall consecrate to fame,
And 'midst the stars inscribe Belinda's name.   150

126 *Proculus:* a man who claimed that he had visions of
Romulus, the founder of Rome 129 *Berenice:* the queen of
Ptolemy III, of Egypt. She had her hair cut off and hung in a
temple as a thanks offering for the safe return of her husband.
It was supposed to have been raised to the sky as a constellation, *Coma Berenices.* 133 the *Mall:* an avenue in St. James's
Park frequented by people of fashion 136 *Rosamonda's lake:*
also in St. James's Park 136 *Partridge:* John Partridge, a well-
known London astrologer 140 *Louis:* the king of France

William Shenstone

(1714–1763)

WRITTEN AT AN INN AT HENLEY

To thee, fair freedom! I retire
　From flattery, cards, and dice, and din;
Nor art thou found in mansions higher
　Than the low cot, or humble inn.

'Tis here with boundless pow'r I reign;　　　　5
　And ev'ry health which I begin,
Converts dull port to bright champagne;
　Such freedom crowns it, at an inn.

I fly from pomp, I fly from plate!
　I fly from falsehood's specious grin!　　　　10
Freedom I love, and form I hate,
　And choose my lodgings at an inn.

Here, waiter! take my sordid ore,
　Which lackeys else might hope to win;
It buys, what courts have not in store;　　　　15
　It buys me freedom, at an inn.

Whoe'er has travell'd life's dull round,
　Where'er his stages may have been,
May sigh to think he still has found
　The warmest welcome, at an inn.　　　　20

Thomas Gray

(1716–1771)

ODE ON THE DEATH OF A FAVOURITE CAT, DROWNED IN A TUB OF GOLDFISHES

'Twas on a lofty vase's side,
Where China's gayest art had dyed
  The azure flowers that blow,
Demurest of the tabby kind,
The pensive Selima, reclined,   5
  Gazed on the lake below.

Her conscious tail her joy declared:
The fair round face, the snowy beard,
  The velvet of her paws,
Her coat that with the tortoise vies,   10
Her ears of jet, and emerald eyes,
  She saw; and purr'd applause.

Still had she gazed, but 'midst the tide
Two angel forms were seen to glide,
  The Genii of the stream: 15
Their scaly armour's Tyrian hue
Through richest purple to the view
  Betray'd a golden gleam.

The hapless Nymph with wonder saw:
A whisker first, and then a claw   20
  With many an ardent wish
She stretch'd, in vain, to reach the prize—
What female heart can gold despise?
  What Cat's averse to fish?

16 *Tyrian hue:* the famous purple dye of
antiquity

Presumptuous maid! with looks intent   25
Again she stretch'd, again she bent,
  Nor knew the gulf between—
Malignant Fate sat by and smiled—
The slippery verge her feet beguiled;
  She tumbled headlong in!   .   30

Eight times emerging from the flood
She mew'd to every watery God
  Some speedy aid to send:—
No Dolphin came, no Nereid stirr'd,
Nor cruel Tom nor Susan heard—   35
  A favourite has no friend!

From hence, ye Beauties, undeceived,
Know one false step is ne'er retrieved,
  And be with caution bold:
Not all that tempts your wandering eyes   40
And heedless hearts, is lawful prize,
  Nor all that glisters, gold.

34 *Nereid:* a sea nymph

William Cowper

(1731–1800)

THE CASTAWAY

Obscurest night involved the sky,
  The Atlantic billows roared,
When such a destined wretch as I,
  Washed headlong from on board,
Of friends, of hope, of all bereft,   5
His floating home forever left.

No braver chief could Albion boast
   Than he with whom he went,
Nor ever ship left Albion's coast,
   With warmer wishes sent.   10
He loved them both, but both in vain,
Nor him beheld, nor her again.

Not long beneath the whelming brine,
   Expert to swim, he lay;
Nor soon he felt his strength decline,   15
   Or courage die away;
But waged with death a lasting strife,
Supported by despair of life.

He shouted; nor his friends had failed
   To check the vessel's course,   20
But so the furious blast prevailed,
   That, pitiless perforce,
They left their outcast mate behind,
And scudded still before the wind.

Some succor yet they could afford;   25
   And, such as storms allow,
The cask, the coop, the floated cord,
   Delayed not to bestow.
But he (they knew) nor ship, nor shore,
Whate'er they gave, should visit more.   30

Nor, cruel as it seemed, could he
   Their haste himself condemn,
Aware that flight, in such a sea,
   Alone could rescue them;
Yet bitter felt it still to die   35
Deserted, and his friends so nigh.

He long survives, who lives an hour
   In ocean, self-upheld;
And so long he, with unspent power,
   His destiny repelled;   40
And ever, as the minutes flew,
Entreated help, or cried, "Adieu!"

7 *No braver chief:* the skipper was George
Lord Anson, mentioned by the name in line 52;
Albion: England

At length, his transient respite past,
  His comrades, who before
Had heard his voice in every blast,   45
  Could catch the sound no more.
For then, by toil subdued, he drank
The stifling wave, and then he sank.

No poet wept him: but the page
  Of narrative sincere,   50
That tells his name, his worth, his age,
  Is wet with Anson's tear.
And tears by bards or heroes shed
Alike immortalize the dead.

I therefore purpose not, or dream,   55
  Descanting on his fate,
To give the melancholy theme
  A more enduring date:
But misery still delights to trace
Its semblance in another's case.   60

No voice divine the storm allayed,
  No light propitious shone,
When, snatched from all effectual aid,
  We perished, each alone;
But I beneath a rougher sea,   65
And whelmed in a deeper gulfs than he.

VERSES

SUPPOSED TO BE WRITTEN BY ALEXANDER SELKIRK, DURING HIS SOLITARY ABODE IN THE ISLAND OF JUAN FERNANDEZ

I am monarch of all I survey,
  My right there is none to dispute;
From the centre all round to the sea,
  I am lord of the fowl and the brute.

Alexander Selkirk: the original of Defoe's
Robinson Crusoe

Oh, solitude! where are the charms   5
    That sages have seen in thy face?
Better dwell in the midst of alarms,
    Than reign in this horrible place.

I am out of humanity's reach,
    I must finish my journey alone,   10
Never hear the sweet music of speech;
    I start at the sound of my own.
The beasts, that roam over the plain,
    My form with indifference see;
They are so unacquainted with man,   15
    Their tameness is shocking to me.

Society, friendship, and love,
    Divinely bestow'd upon man,
Oh, had I the wings of a dove,
    How soon would I taste you again!   20
My sorrows I then might assuage
    In the ways of religion and truth,
Might learn from the wisdom of age,
    And be cheer'd by the sallies of youth.

Religion! what treasure untold   25
    Resides in that heavenly word!
More precious than silver and gold,
    Or all that this earth can afford.
But the sound of the church-going bell
    These vallies and rocks never heard,   30
Ne'er sigh'd at the sound of a knell,
    Or smil'd when a sabbath appear'd.

Ye winds, that have made me your sport,
    Convey to this desolate shore
Some cordial endearing report   35
    Of a land I shall visit no more.
My friends, do they now and then send
    A wish or a thought after me?
O tell me I yet have a friend,
    Though a friend I am never to see.   40

How fleet is a glance of the mind!
    Compar'd with the speed of its flight,
The tempest itself lags behind,

And the swift wing'd arrows of light.
When I think of my own native land,   45
  In a moment I seem to be there;
But alas! recollection at hand
  Soon hurries me back to despair.

But the sea-fowl is gone to her nest,
  The beast is laid down in his lair,   50
Ev'n here is a season of rest,
  And I to my cabin repair.
There's mercy in every place;
  And mercy, encouraging thought!
Gives even affliction a grace,   55
  And reconciles man to his lot.

William Blake

(1757–1827)

PREFACE TO MILTON

And did those feet in ancient time
Walk upon England's mountains green?
And was the holy Lamb of God
On England's pleasant pastures seen?

And did the Countenance Divine   5
Shine forth upon our clouded hills?
And was Jerusalem builded here
Among these dark Satanic Mills?

Bring me my Bow of burning gold:
Bring me my Arrows of desire: 10
Bring me my Spear: O clouds unfold!
Bring me my Chariot of fire.

I will not cease from Mental Fight,
Nor shall my Sword sleep in my hand
Till we have built Jerusalem   15
In England's green and pleasant Land.

A POISON TREE

I was angry with my friend:
I told my wrath, my wrath did end.
I was angry with my foe:
I told it not, my wrath did grow.

And I water'd it in fears,   5
Night and morning with my tears;
And I sunnèd it with smiles,
And with soft deceitful wiles.

And it grew both day and night,
Till it bore an apple bright;   10
And my foe beheld it shine,
And he knew that it was mine,

And into my garden stole
When the night had veil'd the pole:
In the morning glad I see   15
My foe outstretch'd beneath the tree.

THE TYGER

Tyger! Tyger! burning bright
In the forests of the night,
What immortal hand or eye
Could frame thy fearful symmetry?

In what distant deeps or skies   5
Burnt the fire of thine eyes?
On what wings dare he aspire?
What the hand dare seize the fire?

And what shoulder, and what art,
Could twist the sinews of thy heart?   10
And when thy heart began to beat,
What dread hand? and what dread feet?

What the hammer? what the chain?
In what furnace was thy brain?

What the anvil? what dread grasp   15
Dare its deadly terrors clasp?

When the stars threw down their spears,
And water'd heaven with their tears,
Did he smile his work to see?
Did he who made the Lamb make thee?   20

Tyger! Tyger! burning bright
In the forests of the night,
What immortal hand or eye,
Dare frame thy fearful symmetry?

William Wordsworth

(1770–1850)

COMPOSED UPON WESTMINSTER BRIDGE

Earth has not anything to show more fair:
Dull would he be of soul who could pass by
A sight so touching in its majesty:
This City now doth, like a garment, wear
The beauty of the morning; silent, bare,   5
Ships, towers, domes, theatres, and temples lie
Open unto the fields, and to the sky;
All bright and glittering in the smokeless air.
Never did sun more beautifully steep
In his first splendour, valley, rock, or hill;   10
Ne'er saw I, never felt, a calm so deep!
The river glideth at his own sweet will:
Dear God! the very houses seem asleep;
And all that mighty heart is lying still!

IT IS A BEAUTEOUS EVENING,
CALM AND FREE

It is a beauteous evening, calm and free,
The holy time is quiet as a Nun
Breathless with adoration; the broad sun
Is sinking down in its tranquillity;
The gentleness of heaven broods o'er the Sea: 5
Listen! the mighty Being is awake,
And doth with his eternal motion make
A sound like thunder—everlastingly.
Dear Child! dear Girl! that walkest with me here,
If thou appear untouched by solemn thought,   10
Thy nature is not therefore less divine:
Thou liest in Abraham's bosom all the year;
And worshipp'st at the Temple's inner shrine,
God being with thee when we know it not.

THE WORLD IS TOO MUCH WITH US;
LATE AND SOON

The world is too much with us; late and soon,
Getting and spending, we lay waste our powers:
Little we see in Nature that is ours;
We have given our hearts away, a sordid boon!
This Sea that bares her bosom to the moon;   5
The winds that will be howling at all hours,
And are up-gathered now like sleeping flowers;
For this, for everything, we are out of tune;
It moves us not.—Great God! I'd rather be
A Pagan suckled in a creed outworn;   10
So might I, standing on this pleasant lea,
Have glimpses that would make me less forlorn;
Have sight of Proteus rising from the sea;
Or hear old Triton blow his wreathèd horn.

13, 14: *Proteus, Triton:* pagan deities

THE SOLITARY REAPER

Behold her, single in the field,
Yon solitary Highland Lass!
Reaping and singing by herself;
Stop here, or gently pass!
Alone she cuts and binds the grain,   5
And sings a melancholy strain;
O listen! for the Vale profound
Is overflowing with the sound.

No Nightingale did ever chaunt
More welcome notes to weary bands   10
Of travellers in some shady haunt,
Among Arabian sands:
A voice so thrilling ne'er was heard
In spring-time from the Cuckoo-bird,
Breaking the silence of the seas   15
Among the farthest Hebrides.

Will no one tell me what she sings?—
Perhaps the plaintive numbers flow
For old, unhappy, far-off things,
And battles long ago: 20
Or is it some more humble lay,
Familiar matter of to-day?
Some natural sorrow, loss, or pain,
That has been, and may be again?

Whate'er the theme, the Maiden sang   25
As if her song could have no ending;
I saw her singing at her work,
And o'er the sickle bending;—
I listened, motionless and still;
And, as I mounted up the hill,   30
The music in my heart I bore,
Long after it was heard no more.

16 *Hebrides:* remote islands off northern
Scotland

FROM THE PRELUDE, BOOK I

Fair seed-time had my soul, and I grew up
Fostered alike by beauty and by fear:
Much favoured in my birth-place, and no less
In that belovèd Vale to which erelong
We were transplanted—there were we let loose   5
For sports of wider range. Ere I had told
Ten birth-days, when among the mountain slopes
Frost, and the breath of frosty wind, had snapped
The last autumnal crocus, 'twas my joy
With store of springes o'er my shoulder hung   10
To range the open heights where woodcocks run
Along the smooth green turf. Through half the night,
Scudding away from snare to snare, I plied
That anxious visitation;—moon and stars
Were shining o'er my head. I was alone,   15
And seemed to be a trouble to the peace
That dwelt among them. Sometimes it befell
In these night wanderings, that a strong desire
O'erpowered my better reason, and the bird
Which was the captive of another's toil   20
Became my prey; and when the deed was done
I heard among the solitary hills
Low breathing coming after me, and sounds
Of undistinguishable motion, steps
Almost as silent as turf they trod.   25

Nor less, when spring had warmed the cultured Vale,
Roved we as plunderers where the mother-bird
Had in high places built her lodge; though mean
Our object and inglorious, yet the end
Was not ignoble. Oh! when I have hung   30
Above the raven's nest, by knots of grass
And half-inch fissures in the slippery rock
But ill sustained, and almost (so it seemed)
Suspended by the blast that blew amain,
Shouldering the naked crag, oh, at that time   35
While on the perilous ridge I hung alone,
With what strange utterance did the loud dry wind

Blow through my ear! the sky seemed not a sky
Of earth—and with what motion moved the clouds!

Dust as we are, the immortal spirit grows   40
Like harmony in music; there is a dark
Inscrutable workmanship that reconciles
Discordant elements, makes them cling together
In one society. How strange, that all
The terrors, pains, and early miseries,   45
Regrets, vexations, lassitudes interfused
Within my mind, should e'er have borne a part,
And that a needful part, in making up
The calm existence that is mine when I
Am worthy of myself! Praise to the end!   50
Thanks to the means which Nature deigned to employ;
Whether her fearless visitings, or those
That came with soft alarm, like hurtless light
Opening the peaceful clouds; or she may use
Severer interventions, ministry   55
More palpable, as best might suit her aim.

One summer evening (led by her) I found
A little boat tied to a willow tree
Within a rocky cave, its usual home.
Straight I unloosed her chain, and stepping in   60
Pushed from the shore. It was an act of stealth
And troubled pleasure, nor without the voice
Of mountain-echoes did my boat move on;
Leaving behind her still, on either side,
Small circles glittering idly in the moon,   65
Until they melted all into one track
Of sparkling light. But now, like one who rows,
Proud of his skill, to reach a chosen point
With an unswerving line, I fixed my view
Upon the summit of a craggy ridge,   70
The horizon's utmost boundary; for above
Was nothing but the stars and the grey sky.
She was an elfin pinnace; lustily
I dipped my oars into the silent lake,
And as I rose upon the stroke, my boat   75
Went heaving through the water like a swan;
When, from behind that craggy steep till then

The horizon's bound, a huge peak, black and huge,
As if with voluntary power instinct,
Upreared its head. I struck and struck again,   80
And growing still in stature the grim shape
Towered up between me and the stars, and still,
For so it seemed, with purpose of its own
And measured motion like a living thing,
Strode after me. With trembling oars I turned,   85
And through the silent water stole my way
Back to the covert of the willow tree;
There in her mooring-place I left my bark,—
And through the meadows homeward went, in grave
And serious mood; but after I had seen   90
That spectacle, for many days, my brain
Worked with a dim and undetermined sense
Of unknown modes of being; o'er my thoughts
There hung a darkness, call it solitude
Or blank desertion. No familiar shapes   95
Remained, no pleasant images of trees,
Of sea or sky, no colours of green fields;
But huge and mighty forms, that do not live
Like living men, moved slowly through the mind
By day, and were a trouble to my dreams.   100

ODE: INTIMATIONS OF IMMORTALITY

I

There was a time when meadow, grove, and stream,
The earth, and every common sight,
    To me did seem
    Apparelled in celestial light,
The glory and the freshness of a dream.   5
It is not now as it hath been of yore;—
    Turn wheresoe'er I may,
      By night or day,
The things which I have seen I now can see no more.

II

    The Rainbow comes and goes,   10
    And lovely is the Rose,

The Moon doth with delight
Look round her when the heavens are bare,
  Waters on a starry night
  Are beautiful and fair;   15
The sunshine is a glorious birth;
But yet I know, where'er I go,
That there hath past away a glory from the earth.

III

Now, while the birds thus sing a joyous song,
  And while the young lambs bound   20
    As to the tabor's sound,
To me alone there came a thought of grief:
A timely utterance gave that thought relief,
  And I again am strong:
The cataracts blow their trumpets from the steep;   25
No more shall grief of mine the season wrong;
I hear the Echoes through the mountains throng,
The Winds come to me from the fields of sleep,
  And all the earth is gay;
      Land and sea   30
  Give themselves up to jollity,
    And with the heart of May
  Doth every Beast keep holiday;—
    Thou Child of Joy,
Shout round me, let me hear thy shouts, thou
    happy Shepherd-boy!   35

IV

Ye blessèd Creatures, I have heard the call
  Ye to each other make; I see
The heavens laugh with you in your jubilee;
  My heart is at your festival,
    My head hath its coronal,   40
The fulness of your bliss, I feel—I feel it all.
    Oh evil day! if I were sullen
    While Earth herself is adorning,
      This sweet May-morning,
    And the Children are culling   45

21 *tabor:* a small drum

On every side,
In a thousand valleys far and wide,
Fresh flowers; while the sun shines warm,
And the Babe leaps up on his Mother's arm:—
I hear, I hear, with joy I hear!   50
—But there's a Tree, of many, one,
A single Field which I have looked upon,
Both of them speak of something that is gone:
The Pansy at my feet
Doth the same tale repeat: 55
Whither is fled the visionary gleam?
Where is it now, the glory and the dream?

v

Our birth is but a sleep and a forgetting:
The Soul that rises with us, our life's Star,
Hath had elsewhere its setting,   60
And cometh from afar:
Not in entire forgetfulness,
And not in utter nakedness,
But trailing clouds of glory do we come
From God, who is our home: 65
Heaven lies about us in our infancy!
Shades of the prison-house begin to close
Upon the growing Boy,
But He beholds the light, and whence it flows,
He sees it in his joy;   70
The Youth, who daily farther from the east
Must travel, still is Nature's Priest,
And by the vision splendid
Is on his way attended;
At length the Man perceives it die away,   75
And fade into the light of common day.

vi

Earth fills her lap with pleasures of her own;
Yearnings she hath in her own natural kind,
And, even with something of a Mother's mind,
And no unworthy aim,   80
The homely Nurse doth all she can
To make her Foster-child, her Inmate Man,

Forget the glories he hath known,
And that imperial palace whence he came.

VII

Behold the Child among his new-born blisses,   85
A six years' Darling of a pigmy size!
See, where 'mid work of his own hand he lies,
Fretted by sallies of his mother's kisses,
With light upon him from his father's eyes!
See, at his feet, some little plan or chart,   90
Some fragment from his dream of human life,
Shaped by himself with newly-learned art;
    A wedding or a festival,
    A mourning or a funeral;
      And this hath now his heart,   95
    And unto this he frames his song:
      Then will he fit his tongue
To dialogues of business, love, or strife;
    But it will not be long
    Ere this be thrown aside,   100
    And with new joy and pride
The little Actor cons another part;
Filling from time to time his "humorous stage"
With all the Persons, down to palsied Age,
That Life brings with her in her equipage;   105
    As if his whole vocation
    Were endless imitation.

VIII

Thou whose exterior semblance doth belie
    Thy Soul's immensity;
Thou best Philosopher, who yet dost keep   110
Thy heritage, thou Eye among the blind,
That, deaf and silent, read'st the eternal deep,
Haunted for ever by the eternal mind,—
    Mighty Prophet! Seer blest!
    On whom those truths do rest,   115
Which we are toiling all our lives to find,
In darkness lost, the darkness of the grave;

84 *that Imperial palace:* his previous existence

Thou, over whom thy Immortality
Broods like the Day, a Master o'er a Slave,
A Presence which is not to be put by;   120
Thou little Child, yet glorious in the might
Of heaven-born freedom on thy being's height,
Why with such earnest pains dost thou provoke
The years to bring the inevitable yoke,
Thus blindly with thy blessedness at strife?   125
Full soon thy Soul shall have her earthly freight,
And custom lie upon thee with a weight,
Heavy as frost, and deep almost as life!

                                IX

        O joy! that in our embers
        Is something that doth live,   130
        That nature yet remembers
        What was so fugitive!
The thought of our past years in me doth breed
Perpetual benediction: not indeed
For that which is most worthy to be blest;   135
Delight and liberty, the simple creed
Of Childhood, whether busy or at rest,
With new-fledged hope still fluttering in his breast:—
        Not for these I raise
            The song of thanks and praise;   140
        But for those obstinate questionings
        Of sense and outward things,
        Fallings from us, vanishings;
        Blank misgivings of a Creature
Moving about in worlds not realised,   145
High instincts before which our mortal Nature
Did tremble like a guilty Thing surprised:
        But for those first affections,
        Those shadowy recollections,
        Which, be they what they may,   150
Are yet the fountain-light of all our day,
Are yet a master-light of all our seeing;
        Uphold us, cherish, and have power to make
Our noisy years seem moments in the being
Of the eternal Silence: truths that wake,   155
        To perish never:

Which neither listlessness, nor mad endeavour,
     Nor Man nor Boy,
Nor all that is at enmity with joy,
Can utterly abolish or destroy.   160
     Hence in a season of calm weather
      Though inland far we be,
Our Souls have sight of that immortal sea
      Which brought us hither,
     Can in a moment travel thither,   165
And see the Children sport upon the shore,
And hear the mighty waters rolling evermore.

X

Then sing, ye Birds, sing, sing a joyous song!
     And let the young Lambs bound
     As to the tabor's sound!   170
We in thought will join your throng,
     Ye that pipe and ye that play,
     Ye that through your hearts to-day
     Feel the gladness of the May!
What though the radiance which was once so bright   175
Be now for ever taken from my sight,
     Though nothing can bring back the hour
Of splendour in the grass, of glory in the flower;
     We will grieve not, rather find
     Strength in what remains behind;   180
     In the primal sympathy
     Which having been must ever be;
     In the soothing thoughts that spring
     Out of human suffering;
     In the faith that looks through death,   185
In years that bring the philosophic mind.

XI

And O, ye Fountains, Meadows, Hills, and Groves,
Forebode not any severing of our loves!
Yet in my heart of hearts I feel your might;
I only have relinquished one delight   190
To live beneath your more habitual sway.
I love the Brooks which down their channels fret,
Even more than when I tripped lightly as they;

The innocent brightness of a new-born Day
   Is lovely yet;   195
The Clouds that gather round the setting sun
Do take a sober colouring from an eye
That hath kept watch o'er man's mortality;
Another race hath been, and other palms are won.
Thanks to the human heart by which we live,   200
Thanks to its tenderness, its joys, and fears,
To me the meanest flower that blows can give
Thoughts that do often lie too deep for tears.

Sir Walter Scott

(1771–1832)

PROUD MAISIE

Proud Maisie is in the wood
   Walking so early;
Sweet Robin sits on the bush,
   Singing so rarely.

"Tell me, thou bonny bird,   5
   When shall I marry me?"—
"When six braw gentlemen
   Kirkwood shall carry ye."

"Who makes the bridal bed,
   Birdie, say truly?"—   10
"The gray-headed sexton
   That delves the grave duly.

The glowworm o'er grave and stone
   Shall light thee steady,
The owl from the steeple sing,   15
   'Welcome, proud lady.' "

Walter Savage Landor
(1775–1864)

PAST RUIN'D ILION HELEN LIVES

Past ruin'd Ilion Helen lives,
    Alcestis rises from the shades;
Verse calls them forth; 'tis verse that gives
    Immortal youth to mortal maids.

Soon shall Oblivion's deepening veil   5
    Hide all the peopled hills you see,
The gay, the proud, while lovers hail
    These many summers you and me.

Ilion: ancient Troy 2 *Alcestis:* a wife of Greek legend who sacrificed her life for her husband's

DIRCE

Stand close around, ye Stygian set,
    With Dirce in one boat conveyed,
Or Charon, seeing, may forget
    That he is old, and she a shade.

1 *Stygian set:* dead souls being transported to Hades over the river Styx 3 *Charon:* the legendary boatman 4 *a shade:* that is, a spirit

George Gordon, Lord Byron

(1788–1824)

THE DESTRUCTION OF SENNACHERIB

The Assyrian came down like the wolf on the fold,
And his cohorts were gleaming in purple and gold;
And the sheen of their spears was like stars on the sea,
When the blue wave rolls nightly on deep Galilee.

Like the leaves of the forest when Summer is green,   5
That host with their banners at sunset were seen:
Like the leaves of the forest when Autumn hath blown,
That host on the morrow lay wither'd and strown.

For the Angel of Death spread his wings on the blast,
And breathed in the face of the foe as he pass'd;   10
And the eyes of the sleepers wax'd deadly and chill,
And their hearts but once heaved, and for ever grew still!

And there lay the steed with his nostril all wide,
But through it there roll'd not the breath of his pride:
And the foam of his gasping lay white on the turf,   15
And cold as the spray of the rock-beating surf.

And there lay the rider distorted and pale,
With the dew on his brow and the rust on his mail;
And the tents were all silent, the banners alone,
The lances unlifted, the trumpet unblown.   20

And the widows of Ashur are loud in their wail,
And the idols are broke in the temple of Baal;
And the might of the Gentile, unsmote by the sword,
Hath melted like snow in the glance of the Lord!

Sennacherib: an Assyrian king who besieged Jerusalem about
701 B.C., but was miraculously defeated (See Isaiah, 37:36–38)
21, 22 *Ashur, Baal:* Assyrian deities

FROM DON JUAN

(*Canto I: A Digression*)

CXV

And Julia sate with Juan, half embraced
  And half retiring from the glowing arm,
Which trembled like the bosom where 'twas placed;
  Yet still she must have thought there was no harm,
Or else 'twere easy to withdraw her waist;   5
  But then the situation had its charm,
And then—God knows what next—I can't go on;
I'm almost sorry that I e'er begun.

CXVI

Oh Plato! Plato! you have paved the way,
  With your confounded fantasies, to more   10
Immoral conduct by the fancied sway
  Your system feigns o'er the controlless core
Of human hearts, than all the long array
  Of poets and romancers:—You're a bore,
A charlatan, a coxcomb—and have been,   15
At best, no better than a go-between.

CXVII

And Julia's voice was lost, except in sighs,
  Until too late for useful conversation;
The tears were gushing from her gentle eyes,
  I wish indeed they had not had occasion,   20
But who, alas! can love, and then be wise?
  Not that remorse did not oppose temptation;
A little still she strove, and much repented,
And whispering 'I will ne'er consent'—consented.

1 *Julia:* the married woman to whom Don Juan, the hero of
the poem, is making love 9 *Plato:* in his *Symposium* is found
the doctrine of the superiority of spiritual, or Platonic, love
16 *a go-between:* that is, a messenger between lovers

CXVIII

'Tis said that Xerxes offer'd a reward   25
    To those who could invent him a new pleasure:
Methinks the requisition's rather hard,
    And must have cost his majesty a treasure:
For my part, I'm a moderate-minded bard,
    Fond of a little love (which I call leisure);   30
I care not for new pleasures, as the old
Are quite enough for me, so they but hold.

CXIX

Oh Pleasure! you're indeed a pleasant thing,
    Although one must be damn'd for you, no doubt:
I make a resolution every spring   35
    Of reformation, ere the year run out,
But somehow, this my vestal vow takes wing,
    Yet still, I trust it may be kept throughout:
I'm very sorry, very much ashamed,
And mean, next winter, to be quite reclaim'd.   40

CXX

Here my chaste Muse a liberty must take—
    Start not! still chaster reader—she'll be nice hence-
Forward, and there is no great cause to quake;
    This liberty is a poetic licence,
Which some irregularity may make   45
    In the design, and as I have a high sense
Of Aristotle and the Rules, 't is fit
To beg his pardon when I err a bit.

CXXI

This licence is to hope the reader will
    Suppose from June the sixth (the fatal day,   50
Without whose epoch my poetic skill
    For want of facts would be all thrown away),
But keeping Julia and Don Juan still
    In sight, that several months have pass'd; we'll say
'T was in November, but I'm not so sure   55
About the day—the era's more obscure.

25 *Xerxes:* a king of ancient Persia

CXXII

We'll talk of that anon.—'Tis sweet to hear
　At midnight on the blue and moonlit deep
The song and oar of Adria's gondolier,
　By distance mellow'd, o'er the waters sweep;   60
'T is sweet to see the evening star appear;
　'T is sweet to listen as the night-winds creep
From leaf to leaf; 't is sweet to view on high
The rainbow, based on ocean, span the sky.

CXXIII

'T is sweet to hear the watch-dog's honest bark   65
　Bay deep-mouth'd welcome as we draw near home;
'T is sweet to know there is an eye will mark
　Our coming, and look brighter when we come;
'T is sweet to be awaken'd by the lark,
　Or lull'd by falling waters; sweet the hum   70
Of bees, the voice of girls, the song of birds,
The lisp of children, and their earliest words.

CXXIV

Sweet is the vintage, when the showering grapes
　In Bacchanal profusion reel to earth,
Purple and gushing: sweet are our escapes   75
　From civic revelry to rural mirth;
Sweet to the miser are his glittering heaps,
　Sweet to the father is his first-born's birth,
Sweet is revenge—especially to women,
Pillage to soldiers, prize-money to seamen.   80

CXXV

Sweet is a legacy, and passing sweet
　The unexpected death of some old lady
Or gentleman of seventy years complete,
　Who've made 'us youth' wait too—too long already
For an estate, or cash, or country seat,   85
　Still breaking, but with stamina so steady

59 *Adria:* a poetic name for Venice 74 *Bacchanal:* pertaining to Bacchus, the god of wine

That all the Israelites are fit to mob its
Next owner for their double-damn'd post-obits.

CXXVI

'Tis sweet to win, no matter how, one's laurels,
   By blood or ink; 't is sweet to put an end   90
To strife; 't is sometimes sweet to have our quarrels,
   Particularly with a tiresome friend:
Sweet is old wine in bottles, ale in barrels;
   Dear is the helpless creature we defend
Against the world; and dear the schoolboy spot   95
We ne'er forget, though there we are forgot.

CXXVII

But sweeter still than this, than these, than all,
   Is first and passionate love—it stands alone,
Like Adam's recollection of his fall;
   The tree of knowledge has been pluck'd—all's known—   100
And life yields nothing further to recall
   Worthy of this ambrosial sin, so shown,
No doubt in fable, as the unforgiven
Fire which Prometheus filch'd for us from heaven.

CXXVIII

Man's a strange animal, and makes strange use   105
   Of his own nature, and the various arts,
And likes particularly to produce
   Some new experiments to show his parts;
This is the age of oddities let loose,
   Where different talents find their different marts;   110
You'd best begin with truth, and when you've lost your
Labour, there's a sure market for imposture.

CXXIX

What opposite discoveries we have seen!
   (Signs of true genius, and of empty pockets.)
One makes new noses, one a guillotine,   115
   One breaks your bones, one sets them in their sockets;

87 *Israelites:* many of the money lenders were Jews 88 *post-obits:* loans payable after a person from whom the borrower expects to inherit money has died

But vaccination certainly has been
  A kind antithesis to Congreve's rockets,
With which the Doctor paid off an old pox,
By borrowing a new one from an ox.   120

CXXX

Bread has been made (indifferent) from potatoes;
  And galvanism has set some corpses grinning,
But has not answer'd like the apparatus
  Of the Humane Society's beginning
By which men are unsuffocated gratis: 125
  What wondrous new machines have late been spinning!
I said the small-pox has gone out of late;
Perhaps it may be follow'd by the great.

CXXXI

'T is said the great came from America;
  Perhaps it may set out on its return,—   130
The population there so spreads, they say
  'T is grown high time to thin it in its turn,
With war, or plague, or famine, any way,
  So that civilisation they may learn;
And which in ravage the more loathsome evil is— 135
Their real lues, or our pseudo-syphilis?

CXXXII

This is the patent-age of new inventions
  For killing bodies, and for saving souls,
All propagated with the best intentions;
  Sir Humphry Davy's lantern, by which coals   140
Are safely mined for in the mode he mentions,
  Tombuctoo travels, voyages to the Poles,
Are ways to benefit mankind, as true,
Perhaps, as shooting them at Waterloo.

118 *Congreve's rocket:* a primitive, but effective, weapon of
warfare 119 *paid off:* conquered; *pox:* smallpox 128 *the great:*
"the great pox" was a term for syphilis 136 *lues:* syphilis 140
Sir Humphry Davy's lantern: a safety lamp for miners invented in 1815 142 *Tombuctoo:* usually spelled Timbuctoo,
a remote city on the southwestern edge of the Sahara desert

CXXXIII

Man's a phenomenon, one knows not what,   145
   And wonderful beyond all wondrous measure;
'T is pity though, in this sublime world, that
   Pleasure's a sin, and sometimes sin's a pleasure;
Few mortals know what end they would be at,
   But whether glory, power, or love, or treasure,   150
The path is through perplexing ways, and when
The goal is gain'd, we die, you know—and then—

CXXXIV

What then?—I do not know, no more do you—
   And so good night.—Return we to our story . . . .

*P*ercy *B*ysshe *S*helley

(1792–1882)

TO _____

   Music, when soft voices die,
   Vibrates in the memory;
   Odors, when sweet violets sicken,
   Live within the sense they quicken.

   Rose leaves, when the rose is dead,   5
   Are heaped for the belovèd's bed;
   And so thy thoughts, when thou art gone,
   Love itself shall slumber on.

LINES: WHEN THE LAMP IS SHATTERED

   When the lamp is shattered,
  The light in the dust lies dead—
   When the cloud is scattered
  The rainbow's glory is shed.

When the lute is broken,   5
Sweet tones are remembered not;
    When the lips have spoken,
Loved accents are soon forgot.

    As music and splendor
Survive not the lamp and the lute,   10
    The heart's echoes render
No song when the spirit is mute:—
    No song but sad dirges,
Like the wind through a ruined cell,
    Or the mournful surges   15
That ring the dead seaman's knell.

When hearts have once mingled,
Love first leaves the well-built nest;
    The weak one is singled
To endure what it once possest.   20
    O, Love! who bewailest
The frailty of all things here,
    Why choose you the frailest
For your cradle, your home, and your bier?

    Its passions will rock thee,   25
As the storms rock the ravens on high:
    Bright reason will mock thee,
Like the sun from a wintry sky.
    From thy nest every rafter
Will rot, and thine eagle home   30
    Leave thee naked to laughter,
When leaves fall and cold winds come.

THE WORLD'S GREAT AGE BEGINS ANEW

(*Chorus from* Hellas)

The world's great age begins anew,
    The golden years return,
The earth doth like a snake renew
    Her winter weeds outworn:
Heaven smiles, and faiths and empires gleam,   5
Like wrecks of a dissolving dream.

4 *weeds:* clothing

A brighter Hellas rears its mountains
  From waves serener far;
A new Peneus rolls his fountains
  Against the morning star.   10
Where fairer Tempes bloom, there sleep
Young Cyclads on a sunnier deep.

A loftier Argo cleaves the main,
  Fraught with a later prize;
Another Orpheus sings again,   15
  And loves, and weeps, and dies.
A new Ulysses leaves once more
Calypso for his native shore.

Oh, write no more the tale of Troy,
  If earth Death's scroll must be!   20
Nor mix with Laian rage the joy
  Which dawns upon the free:
Although a subtler Sphinx renew
Riddles of death Thebes never knew.

Another Athens shall arise,   25
  And to remoter time
Bequeath, like sunset to the skies,
  The splendor of its prime;
And leave, if nought so bright may live,
All earth can take or Heaven can give.   30

Saturn and Love their long repose
  Shall burst, more bright and good

---

9 *Peneus:* the river of Tempe 11 *Tempes:*
Tempe is a valley in Thessaly known for its
beauty 12 *Cyclads:* the Cyclades, islands near
Greece 13 *Argo:* the ship in which Jason sailed
on his quest for the golden fleece 15 *Orpheus:*
musician of Greek legend who mourned for his
dead wife Eurydice 18 *Calypso:* the sea nymph
from whom Ulysses escaped after a captivity
of seven years 21 *Laian:* referring to Laius, King
of Thebes, who was killed by his unrecognized
son Oedipus in a quarrel 23, 24, *Sphinx, Thebes:*
in the Oedipus legend, the city of Thebes could
be delivered from suffering only if the riddle
of the sphinx were answered

Than all who fell, than One who rose,
  Than many unsubdued:
Not gold, not blood, their altar dowers,   35
But votive tears and symbol flowers.

Oh, cease! must hate and death return?
  Cease! must men kill and die?
Cease! drain not to its dregs the urn
  Of bitter prophecy.   40
The world is weary of the past,
Oh, might it die or rest at last!

33 *all who fall:* the pagan gods; *One:* Jesus 34
many unsubdued: idols still worshipped in
primitive cults

John Keats

(1795–1821)

ON SEEING THE ELGIN MARBLES
FOR THE FIRST TIME

My spirit is too weak; mortality
  Weighs heavily on me like unwilling sleep,
  And each imagined pinnacle and steep
Of godlike hardship tells me I must die
Like a sick eagle looking at the sky.   5
  Yet 'tis a gentle luxury to weep,
  That I have not the cloudy winds to keep
Fresh for the opening of the morning's eye.
Such dim-conceivéd glories of the brain
  Bring round the heart an indescribable feud;   10

The Elgin Marbles: a large collection of sculptures
from the Parthenon in Athens, which had recently
been brought to London by Lord Elgin

So do these wonders a most dizzy pain,
　That mingles Grecian grandeur with the rude
Wasting of old Time—with a billowy main,
　A sun, a shadow of a magnitude.

LA BELLE DAME SANS MERCI

O what can ail thee, Knight at arms,
　Alone and palely loitering?
The sedge has withered from the Lake
　And no birds sing!

O what can ail thee, Knight at arms,　　　　　5
　So haggard, and so woebegone?
The squirrel's granary is full
　And the harvest's done.

I see a lily on thy brow
　With anguish moist and fever dew,　　　　　10
And on thy cheeks a fading rose
　Fast withereth too.

I met a Lady in the Meads,
　Full beautiful, a faery's child,
Her hair was long, her foot was light　　　　　15
　And her eyes were wild.

I made a Garland for her head,
　And bracelets too, and fragrant Zone,
She looked at me as she did love
　And made sweet moan.　　　　　20

I set her on my pacing steed
　And nothing else saw all day long,
For sidelong would she bend and sing
　A faery's song.

She found me roots of relish sweet,　　　　　25
　And honey wild, and manna dew,

La Belle Dame Sans Merci: the title is from
a medieval French poem; it means "The
Beautiful Lady without Mercy" 18 *Zone:* a
belt

And sure in language strange she said
  "I love thee true."

She took me to her elfin grot
  And there she wept and sighed full sore,   30
And there I shut her wild wild eyes
  With kisses four.

And there she lulléd me asleep,
  And there I dreaméd, Ah Woe betide!
The latest dream I ever dreamt   35
  On the cold hill side.

I saw pale Kings, and Princes too,
  Pale warriors, death-pale were they all;
They cried, "La belle dame sans merci
  Thee hath in thrall!"   40

I saw their starved lips in the gloam
  With horrid warning gapéd wide,
And I awoke, and found me here
  On the cold hill's side.

And this is why I sojourn here,   45
  Alone and palely loitering;
Though the sedge has withered from the Lake
  And no birds sing.

ODE ON A GRECIAN URN

I

Thou still unravished bride of quietness,
  Thou foster child of silence and slow time,
Sylvan historian, who canst thus express
  A flowery tale more sweetly than our rhyme:
What leaf-fringed legend haunts about thy shape   5
  Of deities or mortals, or of both,
    In Tempe or the dales of Arcady?
  What men or gods are these? What maidens loath?
What mad pursuit? What struggle to escape?
    What pipes and timbrels? What wild ecstasy?   10

7 *Tempe:* a beautiful valley in Thessaly; *Arcady:* Arcadia,
supposedly the realm of a calm, pastoral way of life

2

Heard melodies are sweet, but those unheard
   Are sweeter; therefore, ye soft pipes, play on;
Not to the sensual ear, but, more endeared,
   Pipe to the spirit ditties of no tone:
Fair youth, beneath the trees, thou canst not leave   15
   Thy song, nor ever can those trees be bare;
     Bold Lover, never, never canst thou kiss,
Though winning near the goal—yet, do not grieve;
    She cannot fade, though thou hast not thy bliss,
    Forever wilt thou love, and she be fair!   20

3

Ah, happy, happy boughs! that cannot shed
   Your leaves, nor ever bid the Spring adieu;
And, happy melodist, unweariéd,
   Forever piping songs forever new;
More happy love! more happy, happy love!   25
   Forever warm and still to be enjoyed,
    Forever panting, and forever young;
All breathing human passion far above,
    That leaves a heart high-sorrowful and cloyed,
    A burning forehead, and a parching tongue.   30

4

Who are these coming to the sacrifice?
   To what green altar, O mysterious priest,
Lead'st thou that heifer lowing at the skies,
   And all her silken flanks with garlands dressed?
What little town by river or sea shore,   35
   Or mountain-built with peaceful citadel,
    Is emptied of this folk, this pious morn?
And, little town, thy streets forevermore
    Will silent be; and not a soul to tell
    Why thou art desolate, can e'er return.   40

5

O Attic shape! Fair attitude! with brede
   Of marble men and maidens overwrought,

14 note that the object of "pipe" is "ditties" 41 *Attic:*
referring to Attica, the region around Athens; *brede:*
a braided design

With forest branches and the trodden weed;
   Thou, silent form, dost tease us out of thought
As doth eternity: Cold Pastoral!   45
   When old age shall this generation waste,
     Thou shalt remain, in midst of other woe
Than ours, a friend to man, to whom thou say'st,
   "Beauty is truth, truth beauty,"—that is all
     Ye know on earth, and all ye need to know.   50

Henry Wadsworth Longfellow

(1807–1882)

THE JEWISH CEMETERY AT NEWPORT

How strange it seems! These Hebrews in their graves,
   Close by the street of this fair seaport town,
Silent beside the never-silent waves,
   At rest in all this moving up and down!

The trees are white with dust, that o'er their sleep   5
   Wave their broad curtains in the south-wind's breath,
While underneath such leafy tents they keep
   The long, mysterious Exodus of Death.

And these sepulchral stones, so old and brown,
   That pave with level flags their burial-place,   10
Seem like the tablets of the Law, thrown down
   And broken by Moses at the mountain's base.

The very names recorded here are strange,
   Of foreign accent, and of different climes;
Alvares and Rivera interchange   15
   With Abraham and Jacob of old times.

"Blessed be God! for he created Death!"
   The mourners said, "and Death is rest and peace";

8 *Exodus:* the literal meaning is "departure" (Latin)

Then added, in the certainty of faith,
  "And giveth Life that never more shall cease."   20

Closed are the portals of their Synagogue,
  No Psalms of David now the silence break,
No Rabbi reads the ancient Decalogue
  In the grand dialect the Prophets spake.

Gone are the living, but the dead remain,   25
  And not neglected; for a hand unseen,
Scattering its bounty, like a summer rain,
  Still keeps their graves and their remembrance green.

How came they here? What burst of Christian hate,
  What persecution, merciless and blind,   30
Drove o'er the sea—that desert desolate—
  These Ishmaels and Hagars of mankind?

They lived in narrow streets and lanes obscure,
  Ghetto and Judenstrass, in mirk and mire;
Taught in the school of patience to endure   35
  The life of anguish and the death of fire.

All their lives long, with the unleavened bread
  And bitter herbs of exile and its fears,
The wasting famine of the heart they fed,
  And slaked its thirst with marah of their tears.   40

Anathema maranatha! was the cry
  That ran from town to town, from street to street;
At every gate the accursed Mordecai
  Was mocked and jeered, and spurned by Christian feet.

Pride and humiliation hand in hand   45
  Walked with them through the world where'er they went;
Trampled and beaten were they as the sand,
  And yet unshaken as the continent.

For in the background figures vague and vast
  Of patriarchs and of prophets rose sublime,   50

23 *Decalogue:* the Ten Commandments 32 *Ishmael and Hagar:* a
son and his mother, Old Testament personages who were outcasts
34 *Judenstrass:* street of Jews (German) 41 *Anathema maranatha!*
St. Paul's curse on those who do not follow Jesus

And all the great traditions of the Past
  They saw reflected in the coming time.

And thus forever with reverted look
  The mystic volume of the world they read,
Spelling it backward, like a Hebrew book,   55
  Till life became a Legend of the Dead.

But ah! what once has been shall be no more!
  The groaning earth in travail and in pain
Brings forth its races, but does not restore,
  And the dead nations never rise again.   60

Edgar Allan Poe

(1809–1849)

ELDORADO

Gaily bedight,
A gallant knight,
In sunshine and in shadow,
Had journeyed long,
Singing a song,   5
In search of Eldorado.

But he grew old—
This knight so bold,—
And o'er his heart a shadow
Fell as he found   10
No spot of ground
That looked like Eldorado.

And, as his strength
Failed him at length,
He met a pilgrim shadow.   15
"Shadow," said he,
"Where can it be—
This land of Eldorado?"

"Over the mountains
   Of the Moon,   20
Down the Valley of the Shadow,
   Ride, boldly ride,"
The shade replied,
"If you seek for Eldorado!"

ISRAFEL

In Heaven a spirit doth dwell
   "Whose heart-strings are a lute":
None sing so wildly well
As the angel Israfel,
And the giddy stars (so legends tell),   5
Ceasing their hymns, attend the spell
   Of his voice, all mute.

Tottering above
   In her highest noon,
   The enamoured moon   10
Blushes with love,
   While, to listen, the red levin
   (With the rapid Pleiades, even,
   Which were seven)
   Pauses in Heaven.   15

And they say (the starry choir
   And the other listening things)
That Israfeli's fire
Is owing to that lyre
   By which he sits and sings—   20
The trembling living wire
   Of those unusual strings.

But the skies that angel trod,
   Where deep thoughts are a duty,
Where Love's a grown-up God,   25
   Where the Houri glances are
Imbued with all the beauty
   Which we worship in a star.

13 *levin:* lightning 14 *Pleiades:* the constellation known as the seven sisters 27 *Houri:*
a nymph of the Moslem paradise

Therefore thou art not wrong,
  Israfeli, who despisest   30
An unimpassioned song:
To thee the laurels belong,
  Best bard because the wisest;
Merrily live, and long!

The ecstasies above   •   35
  With thy burning measures suit—
Thy grief, thy joy, thy hate, thy love,
  With the fervour of thy lute:
  Well may the stars be mute!

Yes, Heaven is thine; but this   40
  Is a world of sweets and sours:
  Our flowers are merely—flowers,
And the shadow of thy perfect bliss
  Is the sunshine of ours.

If I could dwell   45
Where Israefel
  Hath dwelt, and he where I,
He might not sing so wildly well
  A mortal melody,
While a bolder note than this might swell   50
  From my lyre within the sky.

Alfred, Lord Tennyson

(1809–1892)

THE EAGLE: A FRAGMENT

He clasps the crag with crooked hands;
Close to the sun in lonely lands,
Ringed with the azure world, he stands.

The wrinkled sea beneath him crawls;
He watches from his mountain walls,   5
And like a thunderbolt he falls.

FLOWER IN THE CRANNIED WALL

Flower in the crannied wall,
I pluck you out of the crannies,
I hold you here, root and all, in my hand,
Little flower—but *if* I could understand
What you are, root and all, and all in all,   5
I should know what God and man is.

FROM IN MEMORIAM

XV

To-night the winds begin to rise
    And roar from yonder dropping day;
    The last red leaf is whirled away,
The rooks are blown about the skies;

The forest cracked, the waters curled,   5
    The cattle huddled on the lea;
    And wildly dashed on tower and tree
The sunbeam strikes along the world:

And but for fancies, which aver
    That all thy motions gently pass   10
    Athwart a plane of molten glass,
I scarce could brook the strain and stir

That makes the barren branches loud;
    And but for fear it is not so,
    The wild unrest that lives in woe   15
Would dote and pore on yonder cloud

That rises upward always higher
    And onward drags a laboring breast,
    And topples round the dreary west,
A looming bastion fringed with fire.   20

10 *thy motions:* the poem is addressed
to a dead friend who, he imagines, is
now at peace

LIV

O, yet we trust that somehow good
  Will be the final goal of ill,
  To pangs of nature, sins of will,
Defects of doubt, and taints of blood;

That nothing walks with aimless feet;   5
  That not one life shall be destroyed,
  Or cast as rubbish to the void,
When God hath made the pile complete;

That not a worm is cloven in vain;
  That not a moth with vain desire   10
  Is shrivelled in a fruitless fire,
Or but subserves another's gain.

Behold, we know not anything;
  I can but trust that good shall fall
  At last—far off—at last, to all,   15
And every winter change to spring.

So runs my dream; but what am I?
  An infant crying in the night;
  An infant crying for the light,
And with no language but a cry.   20

LXXXVI

Sweet after showers, ambrosial air,
  That rollest from the gorgeous gloom
  Of evening over brake and bloom
And meadow, slowly breathing bare

The round of space, and rapt below   5
  Thro' all the dewy-tasselled wood,
  And shadowing down the horned flood
In ripples, fan my brows and blow

The fever from my cheek, and sigh
  The full new life that feeds thy breath   10
  Throughout my frame, till Doubt and Death,
Ill brethren, let the fancy fly

From belt to belt of crimson seas
  On leagues of odor streaming far,
  To where in yonder orient star   15
A hundred spirits whisper "Peace."

CXVIII

Contemplate all this work of Time,
  The giant laboring in his youth;
  Nor dream of human love and truth,
As dying Nature's earth and lime;

But trust that those we call the dead   5
  Are breathers of an ampler day
  For ever nobler ends. They say,
The solid earth whereon we tread

In tracts of fluent heat began,
  And grew to seeming-random forms,   10
  The seeming prey of cyclic storms,
Till at the last arose the man;

Who throve and branched from clime to clime,
  The herald of a higher race,
  And of himself in higher place,   15
If so he type this work of time

Within himself, from more to more;
  Or, crowned with attributes of woe
  Like glories, move his course, and show
That life is not as idle ore,   20

But iron dug from central gloom,
  And heated hot with burning fears,
  And dipt in baths of hissing tears,
And battered with the shocks of doom

To shape and use. Arise and fly   25
  The reeling Faun, the sensual feast;
  Move upward, working out the beast,
And let the ape and tiger die.

16 *type:* characterize 26 *Faun:* a minor deity with
gross appetites and desires

FROM THE LOTOS-EATERS

"Courage!" he said, and pointed toward the land,
"This mounting wave will roll us shoreward soon."
In the afternoon they came unto a land,
In which it seemed always afternoon.
All round the coast the languid air did swoon,   5
Breathing like one that hath a weary dream.
Full-faced above the valley stood the moon;
And like a downward smoke, the slender stream
Along the cliff to fall and pause and fall did seem.

A land of streams! some, like a downward smoke,   10
Slow-dropping veils of thinnest lawn, did go;
And some through wavering lights and shadows broke,
Rolling a slumbrous sheet of foam below.
They saw the gleaming river seaward flow
From the inner land; far off, three mountain-tops,   15
Three silent pinnacles of aged snow,
Stood sunset-flush'd: and, dew'd with showery drops,
Up-clomb the shadowy pine above the woven copse.

The charmed sunset linger'd low adown
In the red West: through mountain clefts the dale   20
Was seen far inland, and the yellow down
Border'd with palm, and many a winding vale
And meadow, set with slender galingale;
A land where all things always seem'd the same!
And round about the keel with faces pale,   25
Dark faces pale against that rosy flame,
The mild-eyed melancholy Lotos-eaters came.

Branches they bore of that enchanted stem,
Laden with flower and fruit, whereof they gave
To each, but whoso did receive of them,   30
And taste, to him the gushing of the wave
Far far away did seem to mourn and rave
On alien shores; and if his fellow spake,
His voice was thin, as voices from the grave;
And deep-asleep he seem'd, yet all awake,   35
And music in his ears his beating heart did make.

They sat them down upon the yellow sand,
Between the sun and moon upon the shore;
And sweet it was to dream of Fatherland,
Of child, and wife, and slave; but evermore   40
Most weary seem'd the sea, weary the oar,
Weary the wandering fields of barren foam.
Then some one said, "We will return no more";
And all at once they sang, "Our island home
Is far beyond the wave; we will no longer roam."   45

TITHONUS

According to Greek legend, Tithonus was a mor-
tal who loved Aurora, the goddess of the dawn.
She gave him the gift of immortality, but not of
eternal youth, so that as he lived on he became
old and feeble.

The woods decay, the woods decay and fall,
The vapors weep their burthen to the ground,
Man comes and tills the field and lies beneath,
And after many a summer dies the swan.
Me only cruel immortality   5
Consumes; I wither slowly in thine arms,
Here at the quiet limit of the world,
A white-haired shadow roaming like a dream
The ever-silent spaces of the East,
Far-folded mists, and gleaming halls of morn.   10
    Alas! for this gray shadow, once a man—
So glorious in his beauty and thy choice,
Who madest him thy chosen, that he seemed
To his great heart none other than a God!
I asked thee, "Give me immortality."   15
Then didst thou grant mine asking with a smile,
Like wealthy men who care not how they give.
But thy strong Hours indignant worked their wills,
And beat me down and marred and wasted me,
And though they could not end me, left me maimed   20
To dwell in presence of immortal youth,
Immortal age beside immortal youth,

And all I was in ashes. Can thy love,
Thy beauty, make amends, though even now,
Close over us, the silver star, thy guide,   25
Shines in those tremulous eyes that fill with tears
To hear me? Let me go; take back thy gift.
Why should a man desire in any way
To vary from the kindly race of men,
Or pass beyond the goal of ordinance   30
Where all should pause, as is most meet for all?
     A soft air fans the cloud apart; there comes
A glimpse of that dark world where I was born.
Once more the old mysterious glimmer steals
From thy pure brows, and from thy shoulders pure,   35
And bosom beating with a heart renewed.
Thy cheek begins to redden through the gloom,
Thy sweet eyes brighten slowly close to mine,
Ere yet they blind the stars, and the wild team
Which love thee, yearning for thy yoke, arise,   40
And shake the darkness from their loosened manes,
And beat the twilight into flakes of fire.
     Lo! ever thus thou growest beautiful
In silence, then before thine answer given
Departest, and thy tears are on my cheek.   45
     Why wilt thou ever scare me with thy tears,
And make me tremble lest a saying learnt,
In days far-off, on that dark earth, be true?
"The Gods themselves cannot recall their gifts."
     Ay me! ay me! with what another heart   50
In days far-off, and with what other eyes
I used to watch—if I be he that watched—
The lucid outline forming round thee; saw
The dim curls kindle into sunny rings;
Changed with thy mystic change, and felt my blood   55
Glow with the glow that slowly crimsoned all
Thy presence and thy portals, while I lay,
Mouth, forehead, eyelids, growing dewy-warm
With kisses balmier than half-opening buds
Of April, and could hear the lips that kissed   60
Whispering I knew not what of wild and sweet,
Like that strange song I heard Apollo sing,
While Ilion like a mist rose into towers.

Yet hold me not forever in thine East;
How can my nature longer mix with thine?   65
Coldly thy rosy shadows bathe me, cold
Are all thy lights, and cold my wrinkled feet
Upon thy glimmering thresholds, when the steam
Floats up from those dim fields about the homes
Of happy men that have the power to die,   70
And grassy barrows of the happier dead.
Release me, and restore me to the ground.
Thou seest all things, thou wilt see my grave;
Thou wilt renew thy beauty morn by morn,
I earth in earth forget these empty courts,   75
And thee returning on thy silver wheels.

Robert Browning

(1812–1890)

MEMORABILIA

1

Ah, did you once see Shelley plain,
      And did he stop and speak to you
And did you speak to him again?
      How strange it seems and new!

2

But you were living before that,   5
      And also you are living after;
And the memory I started at—
      My starting moves your laughter.

Memorabilia: "Things to be remembered." This
poem was written after Browning had met a
man who had once known Shelley, a poet he
admired very much.

3

I crossed a moor, with a name of its own
    And a certain use in the world no doubt,   10
Yet a hand's-breadth of it shines alone
    'Mid the blank miles round about:

4

For there I picked up on the heather
    And there I put inside my breast
A molted feather, an eagle feather!   15
    Well, I forget the rest.

SOLILOQUY OF THE SPANISH CLOISTER

1

Gr-r-r—there go, my heart's abhorrence!
    Water your damned flowerpots, do!
If hate killed men, Brother Lawrence,
    God's blood, would not mine kill you!
What? your myrtle bush wants trimming?   5
    Oh, that rose has prior claims—
Needs its leaden vase filled brimming?
    Hell dry you up with its flames!

2

At the meal we sit together:
    Salve tibi! I must hear   10
Wise talk of the kind of weather,
    Sort of season, time of year:
Not a plenteous cork crop: scarcely
    Dare we hope oak-galls, I doubt:
What's the Latin name for "parsley"?   15
    What's the Greek name for Swine's Snout?

3

Whew! We'll have our platter burnished,
    Laid with care on our own shelf!

10 *Salve tibi!* "Hail to you," a Latin greeting

With a fire-new spoon we're furnished,
    And a goblet for ourself,   20
Rinsed like something sacrificial
    Ere 'tis fit to touch our chaps—
Marked with L. for our initial!
    (He-he! There his lily snaps!)

4

Saint, forsooth! While brown Dolores   25
    Squats outside the Convent bank
With Sanchicha, telling stories,
    Steeping tresses in the tank,
Blue-black, lustrous, thick like horsehairs,
    —Can't I see his dead eye glow,   30
Bright as 'twere a Barbary corsair's?
    (That is, if he'd let it show!)

5

When he finishes refection,
    Knife and fork he never lays
Cross-wise, to my recollection,   35
    As do I, in Jesu's praise.
I the Trinity illustrate,
    Drinking watered orange pulp—
In three sips the Arian frustrate;
    While he drains his at one gulp.   40

6

Oh, those melons? If he's able
    We're to have a feast! so nice!
One goes to the Abbot's table,
    All of us get each a slice.
How go on your flowers? None double?   45
    Not one fruit-sort can you spy?
Strange!—And I, too, at such trouble,
    Keep them close-nipped on the sly!

39 *Arian:* a member of a heretical sect which did
not accept the doctrine of the Trinity

7

There's a great text in Galatians,
    Once you trip on it, entails   50
Twenty-nine distinct damnations,
    One sure, if another fails:
If I trip him just a-dying,
    Sure of heaven as sure can be,
Spin him round and send him flying   55
    Off to hell, a Manichee?

8

Or, my scrofulous French novel
    On gray paper with blunt type!
Simply glance at it, you grovel
    Hand and foot in Belial's gripe: 60
If I double down its pages
    At the woeful sixteenth print,
When he gathers his greengages,
    Ope a sieve and slip it in't?

9

Or, there's Satan!—one might venture   65
    Pledge one's soul to him, yet leave
Such a flaw in the indenture
    As he'd miss till, past retrieve,
Blasted lay that rose-acacia
    We're so proud of! *Hy, Zy, Hine* . . .   70
'St, there's Vespers! *Plena gratia*
    Ave, Virgo! Gr-r-r—you swine!

49 *Galatians:* Paul's Epistle to the Galatians, one of the books of the New Testament, contains a list of sins 56 *Manichee:*
the Manicheans were another heretical sect
60 *Belial:* the devil 64 *sieve:* a kind of
basket 70 *Hy, Zy, Hine:* these words have
never been satisfactorily explained. Perhaps they
represent the sound of the vesper bells. 71
Plena gratia. . . : the first words of the evening
prayer

A TOCCATA OF GALUPPI'S

1

Oh, Galuppi, Baldassare, this is very sad to find!
I can hardly misconceive you; it would prove me deaf and blind;
But although I take your meaning, 'tis with such a heavy mind!

2

Here you come with your old music, and here's all the good it brings.
What, they lived once thus at Venice where the merchants were
    the kings,   5
Where Saint Mark's is, where the Doges used to wed the sea with
    rings?

3

Aye, because the sea's the street there; and 'tis arched by . . . what
    you call
. . . Shylock's bridge with houses on it, where they kept the carnival:
I was never out of England—it's as if I saw it all.

4

Did young people take their pleasure when the sea was warm in
    May?   10
Balls and masks begun at midnight, burning ever to midday,
When they made up fresh adventures for the morrow, do you say?

5

Was a lady such a lady, cheeks so round and lips so red—
On her neck the small face buoyant, like a bellflower on its bed,
O'er the breast's superb abundance where a man might base his
    head?   15

6

Well, and it was graceful of them—they'd break talk off and afford
—She, to bite her mask's black velvet—he, to finger on his sword,
While you sat and played toccatas, stately at the clavichord?

Galuppi: a Venetian composer of the eighteenth century 6 *Doges:* chief
magistrates of Venice. This line alludes to the custom of throwing a ring
into the sea as a symbol of alliance between Venice and the sea, upon
which she depended for her commerce. 8 *Shylock's bridge:* the Rialto, which
is associated with the character in Shakespeare's *Merchant of Venice.*

7

What? Those lesser thirds so plaintive, sixths diminished, sigh on
    sigh,
Told them something? Those suspensions, those solutions—"Must
    we die?"   20
Those commiserating sevenths—"Life might last! we can but try!"

8

"Were you happy?"—"Yes."—"And are you still as happy?"—"Yes.
    And you?"
—"Then, more kisses!"—"Did *I* stop them, when a million seemed
    so few?"
Hark, the dominant's persistence till it must be answered to!

9

So, an octave struck the answer. Oh, they praised you, I dare say! 25
"Brave Galuppi! that was music; good alike at grave and gay!
I can always leave off talking when I hear a master play!"

10

Then they left you for their pleasure: till in due time, one by one,
Some with lives that came to nothing, some with deeds as well un-
    done,
Death stepped tacitly and took them where they never see the sun. 30

11

But when I sit down to reason, think to take my stand nor swerve,
While I triumph o'er a secret wrung from nature's close reserve,
In you come with your cold music till I creep through every nerve.

12

Yes, you, like a ghostly cricket, creaking where a house was burned:
"Dust and ashes, dead and done with, Venice spent what Venice
    earned.   35
The soul, doubtless, is immortal—where a soul can be discerned.

13

"Yours for instance: you know physics, something of geology,
Mathematics are your pastime; souls shall rise in their degree;
Butterflies may dread extinction—you'll not die, it cannot be!

14

"As for Venice and her people, merely born to bloom and drop,   40
Here on earth they bore their fruitage, mirth and folly were the
    crop:
What of soul was left, I wonder, when the kissing had to stop?

15

"Dust and ashes!" So you creak it, and I want the heart to scold.
Dear dead women, with such hair, too—what's become of all the
    gold
Used to hang and brush their bosoms? I feel chilly and grown
    old.   45

THE BISHOP ORDERS HIS TOMB AT
SAINT PRAXED'S CHURCH

Rome, 15—

Vanity, saith the preacher, vanity!
Draw round my bed: is Anselm keeping back?
Nephews—sons mine . . . ah God, I know not! Well—
She, men would have to be your mother once,
Old Gandolf envied me, so fair she was!   5
What's done is done, and she is dead beside,
Dead long ago, and I am Bishop since,
And as she died so must we die ourselves,
And thence ye may perceive the world's a dream.
Life, how and what is it? As here I lie   10
In this state chamber, dying by degrees,
Hours and long hours in the dead night, I ask
"Do I live, am I dead?" Peace, peace seems all.
Saint Praxed's ever was the church for peace;
And so, about this tomb of mine. I fought   15
With tooth and nail to save my niche, ye know:
—Old Gandolf cozened me, despite my care;
Shrewd was that snatch from out the corner south
He graced his carrion with, God curse the same!

1 *Vanity*. . . : an allusion to Ecclesiastes, 1:2 17 *cozened:*
cheated

Yet still my niche is not so cramped but thence   20
One sees the pulpit o' the epistle side,
And somewhat of the choir, those silent seats,
And up into the aery dome where live
The angels, and a sunbeam's sure to lurk:
And I shall fill my slab of basalt there,   25
And 'neath my tabernacle take my rest,
With those nine columns round me, two and two,
The odd one at my feet where Anselm stands:
Peach-blossom marble all, the rare, the ripe
As fresh-poured red wine of a mighty pulse.   30
—Old Gandolf with his paltry onion-stone,
Put me where I may look at him! True peach,
Rosy and flawless: how I earned the prize!
Draw close: that conflagration of my church
—What then? So much was saved if aught were missed!   35
My sons, ye would not be my death? Go dig
The white-grape vineyard where the oil-press stood,
Drop water gently till the surface sink,
And if ye find . . . Ah God, I know not, I! . . .
Bedded in store of rotten fig leaves soft,   40
And corded up in a tight olive-frail,
Some lump, ah God, of *lapis lazuli,*
Big as a Jew's head cut off at the nape,
Blue as a vein o'er the Madonna's breast . . .
Sons, all have I bequeathed you, villas, all,   45
That brave Frascati villa with its bath,
So, let the blue lump poise between my knees,
Like God the Father's globe on both his hands
Ye worship in the Jesu Church so gay,
For Gandolf shall not choose but see and burst!   50
Swift as a weaver's shuttle fleet our years:
Man goeth to the grave, and where is he?
Did I say basalt for my slab, sons? Black—
'Twas ever antique-black I meant! How else
Shall ye contrast my frieze to come beneath?   55

30 *pulse:* the mash of grapes from which the wine is poured 31 *onion-stone:* inferior marble 41 *olive-frail:* olive basket 42 *lapis lazuli:* a semiprecious stone 51 This line is another Biblical allusion (See Job, 7:7) 55 *frieze:* of sculpture

The bas-relief in bronze ye promised me,
Those Pans and Nymphs ye wot of, and perchance
Some tripod, thyrsus, with a vase or so,
The Saviour at his sermon on the mount,
Saint Praxed in a glory, and one Pan   60
Ready to twitch the Nymph's last garment off,
And Moses with the tables . . . but I know
Ye mark me not! What do they whisper thee,
Child of my bowels, Anselm? Ah, ye hope
To revel down my villas while I gasp   65
Bricked o'er with beggar's moldy travertine
Which Gandolf from his tomb-top chuckles at!
Nay, boys, ye love me—all of jasper, then!
'Tis jasper ye stand pledged to, lest I grieve.
My bath must needs be left behind, alas!   70
One block, pure green as a pistachio nut,
There's plenty jasper somewhere in the world—
And have I not Saint Praxed's ear to pray
Horses for ye, and brown Greek manuscripts,
And mistresses with great smooth marbly limbs?   75
—That's if ye carve my epitaph aright,
Choice Latin, picked phrase, Tully's every word,
No gaudy ware like Gandolf's second line—
Tully, my masters? Ulpian serves his need!
And then how I shall lie through centuries,   80
And hear the blessed mutter of the mass,
And see God made and eaten all day long,
And feel the steady candle flame, and taste
Good strong thick stupefying incense-smoke!
For as I lie here, hours of the dead night,   85
Dying in state and by such slow degrees,
I fold my arms as if they clasped a crook,
And stretch my feet forth straight as stone can point,
And let the bedclothes, for a mortcloth, drop
Into great laps and folds of sculptor's-work: 90

57 *thyrsus:* a staff associated with Bacchus, the god of
wine 66 *travertine:* an inferior type of stone 76 *Tully:*
Marcus Tullius Cicero, the writer of Latin prose whose
style was classical 79 *Ulpian:* a later and inferior Latin
writer 82 *see God made. . . :* that is, see the mass cele-
brated

And as yon tapers dwindle, and strange thoughts
Grow, with a certain humming in my ears,
About the life before I lived this life,
And this life too, popes, cardinals, and priests,
Saint Praxed at his sermon on the mount,   95
Your tall pale mother with her talking eyes,
And new-found agate urns as fresh as day,
And marble's language, Latin pure, discreet
—Aha, ELUCESCEBAT quoth our friend?
No Tully, said I, Ulpian at the best!   100
Evil and brief hath been my pilgrimage.
All *lapis*, all, sons! Else I give the Pope
My villas! Will ye ever eat my heart?
Ever your eyes were as a lizard's quick,
They glitter like your mother's for my soul,   105
Or ye would heighten my impoverished frieze,
Piece out its starved design, and fill my vase
With grapes, and add a vizor and a Term,
And to the tripod ye would tie a lynx
That in his struggle throws the thyrsus down,   110
To comfort me on my entablature
Whereon I am to lie till I must ask
"Do I live, am I dead?" There, leave me, there!
For ye have stabbed me with ingratitude
To death—ye wish it—God, ye wish it! Stone—   115
Gritstone, a-crumble! Clammy squares which sweat
As if the corpse they keep were oozing through—
And no more *lapis* to delight the world!
Well go! I bless ye. Fewer tapers there,
But in a row: and, going, turn your backs   120
—Aye, like departing altar-ministrants,
And leave me in my church, the church for peace,
That I may watch at leisure if he leers—
Old Gandolf, at me, from his onion-stone,
As still he envied me, so fair she was!   125

99 *ELUCESEBAT:* apparently, a word from the inscription on Gandolf's tomb. It is a debased form not found in the best Latin texts. 108 *Term:* a pillar whose top is carved into a figure or bust 111 *entablature:* the base of a statue

Emily Brontë

(1818–1848)

REMEMBRANCE

Cold in the earth—and the deep snow piled above thee,
Far, far removed, cold in the dreary grave!
Have I forgot, my only love, to love thee,
Severed at last by Time's all-severing wave?

Now, when alone, do my thoughts no longer hover   5
Over the mountains, on that northern shore,
Resting their wings where heath and fern-leaves cover
The noble heart for ever, ever more?

Cold in the earth—and fifteen wild Decembers,
From those brown hills, have melted into spring: 10
Faithful, indeed, is the spirit that remembers
After such years of change and suffering!

Sweet Love of youth, forgive, if I forget thee,
While the world's tide is bearing me along;
Other desires and other hopes beset me,   15
Hopes which obscure, but cannot do thee wrong!

No later light has lightened up my heaven,
No second morn has ever shone for me;
All my life's bliss from thy dear life was given,
All my life's bliss is in the grave with thee.   20

But, when the days of golden dreams had perished,
And even Despair was powerless to destroy;
Then did I learn how existence could be cherished,
Strengthened and fed without the aid of joy.

Then did I check the tears of useless passion—   25
Weaned my young soul from yearning after thine;
Sternly denied its burning wish to hasten
Down to that tomb already more than mine.

And, even yet, I dare not let it languish,
Dare not indulge in memory's rapturous pain;   30
Once drinking deep of that divinest anguish,
How could I seek the empty world again?

Walt Whitman

(1819–1892)

THE DALLIANCE OF THE EAGLES

Skirting the river road, (my forenoon walk, my rest,)
Skyward in air a sudden muffled sound, the dalliance of the eagles,
The rushing amorous contact high in space together,
The clinching interlocking claws, a living, fierce, gyrating wheel,
Four beating wings, two beaks, a swirling mass tight grappling,   5
In tumbling turning clustering loops, straight downward falling,
Till o'er the river pois'd, the twain yet one, a moment's lull,
A motionless still balance in the air, then parting, talons loosing,
Upward again on slow-firm pinions slanting, their separate diverse
    flight,
She hers, he his, pursuing.   10

TO A LOCOMOTIVE IN WINTER

Thee for my recitative,
Thee in the driving storm even as now, the snow, the winter-day
    declining,
Thee in thy panoply, thy measur'd dual throbbing and thy beat
    convulsive,
Thy black cylindric body, golden brass and silvery steel,
Thy ponderous side-bars, parallel and connecting rods, gyrating,
    shuttling at thy sides,   5
Thy metrical, now swelling pant and roar, now tapering in the distance,
Thy great protruding head-light fix'd in front,

Thy long, pale, floating vapor-pennants, tinged with delicate purple,
The dense and murky clouds out-belching from thy smoke-stack,
Thy knitted frame, thy springs and valves, the tremulous twinkle of
    thy wheels,   10
Thy train of cars behind, obedient, merrily following,
Through gale or calm, now swift, now slack, yet steadily careering;
Type of the modern—emblem of motion and power—pulse of the
    continent,
For once come serve the Muse and merge in verse, even as here I
    see thee,
With storm and buffeting gusts of wind and falling snow,   15
By day thy warning ringing bell to sound its notes,
By night thy silent signal lamps to swing.

Fierce-throated beauty!
Roll through my chant with all thy lawless music, thy swinging lamps
    at night,
Thy madly-whistled laughter, echoing, rumbling like an earthquake,
    rousing all,   20
Law of thyself complete, thine own track firmly holding,
(No sweetness debonair of tearful harp or glib piano thine,)
Thy trills of shrieks by rocks and hills return'd,
Launch'd o'er the prairies wide, across the lakes,
To the free skies unpent and glad and strong.   25

I SAW IN LOUISIANA A LIVE-OAK GROWING

I saw in Louisiana a live-oak growing,
All alone stood it and the moss hung down from the branches,
Without any companion it grew there uttering joyous leaves of dark
    green,
And its look, rude, unbending, lusty, made me think of myself,
But I wonder'd how it could utter joyous leaves standing alone there
    without its friend, its lover near, for I knew I could not,   5
And I broke off a twig with a certain number of leaves upon it, and
    twined around it a little moss,
And brought it away, and I have placed it in sight in my room,
It is not needed to remind me as of my own dear friends,
(For I believe lately I think of little else than of them,)

Yet it remains to me a curious token, it makes me think of manly
    love;   10
For all that, and though the live-oak glistens there in Louisiana solitary
    in a wide flat space,
Uttering joyous leaves all its life without a friend, a lover near,
I know very well I could not.

GIVE ME THE SPLENDID SILENT SUN

I

Give me the splendid silent sun with all his beams full-dazzling,
Give me juicy autumnal fruit ripe and red from the orchard,
Give me a field where the unmow'd grass grows,
Give me an arbor, give me the trellis'd grape,
Give me fresh corn and wheat, give me serene-moving animals teach-
    ing content,   5
Give me nights perfectly quiet as on high plateaus west of the Mis-
    sissippi, and I looking up at the stars,
Give me odorous at sunrise a garden of beautiful flowers where I can
    walk undisturb'd,
Give me for marriage a sweet-breath'd woman of whom I should
    never tire,
Give me a perfect child, give me away aside from the noise of the
    world a rural domestic life,
Give me to warble spontaneous songs recluse by myself, for my own
    ears only,   10
Give me solitude, give me Nature, give me again O Nature your
    primal sanities!

These demanding to have them, (tired with ceaseless excitement, and
    rack'd by the war-strife,)
These to procure incessantly asking, rising in cries from my heart,
While yet incessantly asking still I adhere to my city,
Day upon day and year upon year O city, walking your streets,   15
Where you hold me enchain'd a certain time refusing to give me up,
Yet giving to make me glutted, enrich'd of soul, you give me forever
    faces;
(O I see what I sought to escape, confronting, reversing my cries,
I see my own soul trampling down what it ask'd for.)

2

Keep your splendid silent sun,   20
Keep your woods O Nature, and the quiet places by the woods,
Keep your fields of clover and timothy, and your corn-fields and
    orchards,
Keep the blossoming buckwheat fields where the Ninth-month bees
    hum;
Give me faces and streets—give me these phantoms incessant and
    endless along the trottoirs!
Give me interminable eyes—give me women—give me comrades and
    lovers by the thousand!   25
Let me see new ones every day—let me hold news ones by the hand
    every day!
Give me such shows—give me the streets of Manhattan!
Give me Broadway, with the soldiers marching—give me the sound
    of the trumpets and drums!
(The soldiers in companies or regiments—some starting away, flush'd
    and reckless,
Some, their time up, returning with thinn'd ranks, young, yet very
    old, worn, marching, noticing nothing;)   30
Give me the shores and wharves heavy-fringed with black ships!
O such for me! O an intense life, full to repletion and varied!
The life of the theatre, bar-room, huge hotel, for me!
The saloon of the steamer! the crowded excursion for me! the torch-
    light procession!
The dense brigade bound for the war, with high piled military wagons
    following;   35
People, endless, streaming, with strong voices, passions, pageants,
Manhattan streets with their powerful throbs, with beating drums as
    now,
The endless and noisy chorus, the rustle and clank of muskets, (even
    the sight of the wounded,)
Manhattan crowds, with their turbulent musical chorus!
Manhattan faces and eyes forever for me.   40

Matthew Arnold

(1822–1888)

DOVER BEACH

The sea is calm tonight,
The tide is full, the moon lies fair
Upon the straits—on the French coast the light
Gleams and is gone; the cliffs of England stand,
Glimmering and vast, out in the tranquil bay.   5
Come to the window, sweet is the night air!
Only, from the long line of spray
Where the sea meets the moon-blanched land,
Listen! you hear the grating roar
Of pebbles which the waves draw back, and fling,   10
At their return, up the high strand,
Begin, and cease, and then again begin,
With tremulous cadence slow, and bring
The eternal note of sadness in.

Sophocles long ago   15
Heard it on the Aegean, and it brought
Into his mind the turbid ebb and flow
Of human misery; we
Find also in the sound a thought,
Hearing it by this distant northern sea.   20

The Sea of Faith
Was once, too, at the full, and round earth's shore
Lay like the folds of a bright girdle furled.
But now I only hear
Its melancholy, long, withdrawing roar,   25
Retreating, to the breath
Of the night-wind, down the vast edges drear
And naked shingles of the world.

15 *Sophocles* . . . : an allusion to an image in
Sophocles' *Antigone* 28 *shingles:* rocky beaches

Ah, love, let us be true
To one another! for the world, which seems   30
To lie before us like a land of dreams,
So various, so beautiful, so new,
Hath really neither joy, nor love, nor light,
Nor certitude, nor peace, nor help for pain;
And we are here as on a darkling plain   35
Swept with confused alarms of struggle and flight,
Where ignorant armies clash by night.

George Meredith

(1828–1909)

FROM MODERN LOVE

*These two poems are from a sequence about a
husband and wife who have lost their love for
each other. The speaker is the husband.*

XXVI

Love ere he bleeds, an eagle in high skies,
Has earth beneath his wings: from reddened eve
He views the rosy dawn. In vain they weave
The fatal web below while far he flies.
But when the arrow strikes him, there's a change.   5
He moves but in the track of his spent pain,
Whose red drops are the links of a harsh chain,
Binding him to the ground, with narrow range.
A subtle serpent then has Love become.
I had the eagle in my bosom erst: 10
Henceforward with the serpent I am cursed.
I can interpret where the mouth is dumb.
Speak, and I see the side-lie of a truth.
Perchance my heart may pardon you this deed:

10 *erst:* formerly

But be no coward:—you that made Love bleed,   15
You must bear all the venom of his tooth!

XLVII

We saw the swallows gathering in the sky,
And in the osier-isle we heard them noise.
We had not to look back on summer joys,
Or forward to a summer of bright dye:
But in the largeness of the evening earth   5
Our spirits grew as we went side by side.
The hour became her husband and my bride.
Love, that had robbed us so, thus blessed our dearth!
The pilgrims of the year waxed very loud
In multitudinous chatterings, as the flood   10
Full brown came from the West, and like pale blood
Expanded to the upper crimson cloud.
Love, that had robbed us of immortal things,
This little moment mercifully gave,
Where I have seen across the twilight wave   15
The swan sail with her young beneath her wings.

2 *osier:* a kind of willow

WINTER HEAVENS

Sharp is the night, but stars with frost alive
Leap off the rim of earth across the dome.
It is a night to make the heavens our home
More than the nest whereto apace we strive.
Lengths down our road each fir-tree seems a hive,   5
In swarms outrushing from the golden comb.
They waken waves of thoughts that burst to foam:
The living throb in me, the dead revive.
Yon mantle clothes us: there, past mortal breath,
Life glistens on the river of the death.   10
It folds us, flesh and dust; and have we knelt,
Or never knelt, or eyed as kine the springs
Of radiance, the radiance enrings:
And this is the soul's haven to have felt.

12 *kine:* cows

Dante Gabriel Rossetti
(1828–1882)

FOR AN ALLEGORICAL DANCE OF WOMEN
BY ANDREA MANTEGNA
(IN THE LOUVRE)

Scarcely, I think; yet it indeed *may* be
  The meaning reached him, when this music rang
  Clear through his frame, a sweet possessive pang,
And he beheld these rocks and that ridged sea.
But I believe that, leaning tow'rds them, he   5
  Just felt their hair carried across his face
  As each girl passed him; nor gave ear to trace
How many feet; nor bent assuredly
His eyes from the blind fixedness of thought
  To know the dancers. It is bitter glad   10
    Even unto tears. Its meaning filleth it,
    A secret of the wells of Life; to wit:—
  The heart's each pulse shall keep the sense it had
With all, though the mind's labor run to nought.

Emily Dickinson
(1830–1886)

AFTER GREAT PAIN A FORMAL
FEELING COMES

After great pain a formal feeling comes—
The nerves sit ceremonious like tombs;
The stiff Heart questions—was it He that bore?
And yesterday—or centuries before?

The feet, mechanical, go round   5
A wooden way
Of ground, or air, or ought,
Regardless grown,
A quartz contentment, like a stone.

This is the hour of lead   10
Remembered if outlived,
As freezing persons recollect the snow—
First chill, then stupor, then the letting go.

A CERTAIN SLANT OF LIGHT

There's a certain slant of light,
On winter afternoons,
That oppresses, like the weight
Of cathedral tunes.

Heavenly hurt it gives us;   5
We can find no scar,
But internal difference
Where the meanings are.

None may teach it anything
'Tis the seal, despair,—   10
An imperial affliction
Sent us of the air.

When it comes, the landscape listens,
Shadows hold their breath;
When it goes, 'tis like the distance   15
On the look of death.

SUCCESS IS COUNTED SWEETEST

Success is counted sweetest
By those who ne'er succeed.
To comprehend a nectar
Requires sorest need.

Not one of all the purple host   5
Who took the flag to-day
Can tell the definition,
So clear, of victory,

As he, defeated, dying,
On whose forbidden ear　　　　　　　　　10
The distant strains of triumph
Burst agonized and clear!

I HEARD A FLY BUZZ WHEN I DIED

I heard a fly buzz when I died—
The stillness in the room
Was like the stillness in the air
Between the heaves of storm.

The eyes around had wrung them dry　　　5
And breaths were gathering firm
For that last onset when the King
Be witnessed in the room.

I willed my keepsakes, signed away
What portion of me be　　　　　　　　　10
Assignable—and then it was
There interposed a fly,

With blue, uncertain, stumbling buzz,
Between the light and me.
And then the windows failed, and then　　15
I could not see to see.

A. C. Swinburne

(1837–1909)

A LYKE-WAKE SONG

Fair of face, full of pride,
Sit ye down by a dead man's side.

Lyke-Wake Song: lament for the dead 7
gowd kells: gold nets

Ye sang songs a' the day;
Sit down at night in the red worm's way.

Proud ye were a' day long;   5
Ye'll be but lean at evensong.

Ye had gowd kells on your hair;
Nae man kens what ye were.

Ye set scorn by the silken stuff;
Now the grave is clean enough.   10

Ye set scorn by the rubis ring;
Now the worm is a saft sweet thing.

Fine gold and blithe fair face,
Ye are come to a grimly place.

Gold hair and glad grey een,   15
Nae man kens if ye have been.

THE GARDEN OF PROSERPINE

Here, where the world is quiet;
    Here, where all trouble seems
Dead winds' and spent waves' riot
    In doubtful dreams of dreams;
I watch the green field growing   5
For reaping folk and sowing,
For harvest-time and mowing,
    A sleepy world of streams.

I am tired of tears and laughter,
    And men that laugh and weep;   10
Of what may come hereafter
    For men that sow to reap:
I am weary of days and hours,
Blown buds of barren flowers,
Desires and dreams and powers   15
    And everything but sleep.

Proserpine: or Persephone, whose garden
was in the underworld, according to the
Greek myth, the realm of dead souls

Here life has death for neighbour,
   And far from eye or ear
Wan waves and wet winds labour,
   Weak ships and spirits steer;   20
They drive adrift, and whither
They wot not who make thither;
But no such winds blow hither,
   And no such things grow here.

No growth of moor or coppice,   25
   No heather-flower or vine,
But bloomless buds of poppies,
   Green grapes of Proserpine,
Pale beds of blowing rushes
Where no leaf blooms or blushes   30
Save this whereout she crushes
   For dead men deadly wine.

Pale, without name or number,
   In fruitless fields of corn,
They bow themselves and slumber   35
   All night till light is born;
And like a soul belated,
In hell and heaven unmated,
By cloud and mist abated
   Comes out of darkness morn.   40

Though one were strong as seven,
   He too with death shall dwell,
Nor wake with wings in heaven,
   Nor weep for pains in hell;
Though one were fair as roses,   45
His beauty clouds and closes;
And well though love reposes,
   In the end it is not well.

Pale, beyond porch and portal,
   Crowned with calm leaves, she stands   50
Who gathers all things mortal
   With cold immortal hands;
Her languid lips are sweeter
Than love's who fears to greet her
To men that mix and meet her   55
   From many times and lands.

She waits for each and other,
    She waits for all men born;
Forgets the earth her mother,
    The life of fruits and corn,   60
But spring and seed and swallow
Take wing for her and follow
Where summer song rings hollow
    And flowers are put to scorn.

There go the loves that wither,   65
    The old loves with wearier wings;
And all dead years draw thither,
    And all disastrous things;
Dead dreams of days forsaken,
Blind buds that snows have shaken,   70
Wild leaves that winds have taken,
    Red strays of ruined springs.

We are not sure of sorrow,
    And joy was never sure;
To-day will die to-morrow;   75
    Time stoops to no man's lure;
And love, grown faint and fretful,
With lips but half regretful
Sighs, and with eyes forgetful
    Weeps that no loves endure.   80

From too much love of living,
    From hope and fear set free,
We thank with brief thanksgiving
    Whatever gods may be
That no life lives for ever;   85
That dead men rise up never;
That even the weariest river
    Winds somewhere safe to sea.

Then star nor sun shall waken
    Nor any change of light: 90
Nor sound of water shaken,
    Nor any sound or sight:
Nor wintry leaves nor vernal,
Nor days nor things diurnal;
Only the sleep eternal   95
    In an eternal night.

Thomas Hardy

(1840–1928)

IN TIME OF "THE BREAKING OF NATIONS"

I

Only a man harrowing clods
  In a slow silent walk
With an old horse that stumbles and nods
  Half asleep as they stalk.

II

Only thin smoke without flame   5
  From the heaps of couch-grass;
Yet this will go onward the same
  Though Dynasties pass.

III

Yonder a maid and her wight
  Come whispering by: 10
War's annals will fade into night
  Ere their story die.

AFTERWARDS

When the Present has latched its postern behind my tremulous stay,
  And the May month flaps its glad green leaves like wings,
Delicate-filmed as new-spun silk, will the neighbours say,
  "He was a man who used to notice such things"?

If it be in the dusk when, like an eyelid's soundless blink,   5
  The dewfall-hawk comes crossing the shades to alight
Upon the wind-warped upland thorn, a gazer may think,
  "To him this must have been a familiar sight."

If I pass during some nocturnal blackness, mothy and warm,
  When the hedgehog travels furtively over the lawn,   10

One may say, "He strove that such innocent creatures should come to
    no harm,
    But he could do little for them; and now he is gone."

If, when hearing that I have been stilled at last, they stand at the door,
    Watching the full-starred heavens that winter sees,
Will this thought rise on those who will meet my face no more,   15
    "He was one who had an eye for such mysteries"?

And will any say when my bell of quittance is heard in the gloom,
    And a crossing breeze cuts a pause in its outrollings,
Till they rise again, as they were a new bell's boom,
    "He hears it not now, but used to notice such things"?   20

CHANNEL FIRING

That night your great guns, unawares,
Shook all our coffins as we lay,
And broke the chancel window-squares,
We thought it was the Judgment-day

And sat upright. While drearisome   5
Arose the howl of wakened hounds:
The mouse let fall the altar-crumb,
The worms drew back into the mounds,

The glebe cow drooled. Till God called, "No;
It's gunnery practice out at sea   10
Just as before you went below;
The world is as it used to be:

"All nations striving strong to make
Red war yet redder. Mad as hatters
They do no more for Christés sake   15
Than you who are helpless in such matters.

"That this is not the judgment-hour
For some of them's a blessed thing,
For if it were they'd have to scour
Hell's floor for so much threatening. . . .   20

3 *chancel:* the area of a church near the altar 9
glebe cow: a cow that feeds on the village's public land

"Ha, ha. It will be warmer when
I blow the trumpet (if indeed
I ever do; for you are men,
And rest eternal sorely need)."

So down we lay again. "I wonder,   25
Will the world ever saner be,"
Said one, "than when He sent us under
In our indifferent century!"

And many a skeleton shook his head.
"Instead of preaching forty year,"   30
My neighbour Parson Thirdly said,
"I wish I had stuck to pipes and beer."

Again the guns disturbed the hour,
Roaring their readiness to avenge,
As far inland as Stourton Tower,   35
And Camelot, and starlit Stonehenge.

April 1914

35 *Stourton Tower:* Alfred's Tower, so-called,
in Dorset 36 *Camelot:* the legendary city of King
Arthur; *Stonehenge:* a prehistoric stone circle
built as a place of worship

*R*obert *B*ridges

(1844–1930)

LOW BAROMETER

The south-wind strengthens to a gale,
Across the moon the clouds fly fast,
The house is smitten as with a flail,
The chimney shudders to the blast.

On such a night, when Air has loosed   5
Its guardian grasp on blood and brain,
Old terrors then of god or ghost
Creep from their caves to life again;

And Reason kens he herits in
A haunted house. Tenants unknown   10
Assert their squalid lease of sin
With earlier title than his own.

Unbodied presences, the pack'd
Pollution and remorse of Time,
Slipp'd from oblivion reënact   15
The horrors of unhouseld crime.

Some men would quell the thing with prayer
Whose sightless footsteps pad the floor,
Whose fearful trespass mounts the stair
Or bursts the lock'd forbidden door.   20

Some have seen corpses long interr'd
Escape from hallowing control,
Pale charnel forms—nay ev'n have heard
The shrilling of a troubled soul,

That wanders till the dawn hath cross'd   25
The dolorous dark, or Earth hath wound
Closer her storm-spredd cloke, and thrust
The baleful phantoms underground.

9 *kens:* knows; *herits in:* loosely, inhabits 16
unhouseld: unconsecrated

Gerard Manley Hopkins

(1845–1889)

THE WINDHOVER

To Christ Our Lord

I caught this morning morning's minion, king-
    dom of daylight's dauphin, dapple-dawn-drawn Falcon, in his
    riding
Of the rolling level underneath him steady air, and striding

High there, how he rung upon the rein of a wimpling wing
In his ecstasy! then off, off forth on swing, 5
   As a skate's heel sweeps smooth on a bow-bend: the hurl and
     gliding
   Rebuffed the big wind. My heart in hiding
Stirred for a bird,—the achieve of, the mastery of the thing!

Brute beauty and valour and act, oh, air, pride, plume, here
   Buckle! AND the fire that breaks from thee then, a billion 10
Times told lovelier, more dangerous, O my chevalier!

   No wonder of it: shéer plód makes plough down sillion
Shine, and blue-bleak embers, ah my dear,
   Fall, gall themselves, and gash gold-vermilion.

Windhover: a variety of falcon 12 *sillion:* furrow

PIED BEAUTY

Glory be to God for dappled things—
   For skies of couple-colour as a brinded cow;
     For rose-moles all in stipple upon trout that swim;
     Fresh-firecoal chestnut-falls; finches' wings;
   Landscape plotted and pieced—fold, fallow, and plough; 5
     And áll trádes, their gear and tackle and trim.

All things counter, original, spare, strange;
   Whatever is fickle, freckled (who knows how?)
     With swift, slow; sweet, sour; adazzle, dim;
He fathers-forth whose beauty is past change: 10
     Praise him.

GOD'S GRANDEUR

The world is charged with the grandeur of God.
   It will flame out, like shining from shook foil;
   It gathers to a greatness, like the ooze of oil
Crushed. Why do men then now not reck his rod?
Generations have trod, have trod, have trod; 5
   And all is seared with trade; bleared, smeared with toil;
   And wears man's smudge and shares man's smell: the soil
Is bare now, nor can foot feel, being shod.

And for all this, nature is never spent;
   There lives the dearest freshness deep down things;   10
And though the last lights off the black West went
   Oh, morning, at the brown brink eastward, springs—
Because the Holy Ghost over the bent
   World broods with warm breast and with ah! bright wings.

NO WORST, THERE IS NONE

No worst, there is none. Pitched past pitch of grief,
More pangs will, schooled at forepangs, wilder wring.
Comforter, where, where is your comforting?
Mary, mother of us, where is your relief?
My cries heave, herds-long; huddle in a main, a chief   5
Woe, world-sorrow; on an age-old anvil wince and sing—
Then lull, then leave off. Fury had shrieked "No ling-
ering! Let me be fell: force I must be brief."

O the mind, mind has mountains; cliffs of fall
Frightful, sheer, no-man-fathomed. Hold them cheap
May who ne'er hung there. Nor does long our small   10
Durance deal with that steep or deep. Here! creep,
Wretch, under a comfort serves in a whirlwind: all
Life death does end and each day dies with sleep.

8 *fell:* cruel 11 *Durance:* capacity to endure

A. E. Housman

(1860–1936)

ON WENLOCK EDGE

On Wenlock Edge the wood's in trouble;
   His forest fleece the Wrekin heaves;
The gale, it plies the saplings double,
   And thick on Severn snow the leaves.

1 *Wenlock Edge:* a ridge in the countryside near
Ludlow, in Shropshire 2 *the Wrekin:* a high hill 4
the Severn: a river

'Twould blow like this through holt and hanger   5
  When Uricon the city stood:
'Tis the old wind in the old anger,
  But then it threshed another wood.

Then, 'twas before my time, the Roman
  At yonder heaving hill would stare: 10
The blood that warms an English yeoman,
  The thoughts that hurt him, they were there.

There, like the wind through woods in riot,
  Through him the gale of life blew high;
The tree of man was never quiet: 15
  Then 'twas the Roman, now 'tis I.

The gale, it plies the saplings double,
  It blows so hard, 'twill soon be gone:
To-day the Roman and his trouble
  Are ashes under Uricon.   20

5 *holt:* grove; *hanger:* steep, wooded hillside 6
Uricon: ancient Roman town near present
Wroxeter

EPITAPH ON AN ARMY OF MERCENARIES

These, in the day when heaven was falling,
  The hour when earth's foundations fled,
Followed their mercenary calling
  And took their wages and are dead.

Their shoulders held the sky suspended;   5
  They stood, and earth's foundations stay;
What God abandoned, these defended,
  And saved the sum of things for pay.

TO AN ATHLETE DYING YOUNG

The time you won your town the race
We chaired you through the market-place;
Man and boy stood cheering by,
And home we brought you shoulder-high.

To-day, the road all runners come   5
Shoulder-high we bring you home,
And set you at your threshold down,
Townsman of a stiller town.

Smart lad, to slip betimes away
From fields where glory does not stay,   10
And early though the laurel grows
It withers quicker than the rose.

Eyes the shady night has shut
Cannot see the record cut,
And silence sounds no worse than cheers   15
After earth has stopped the ears.

Now you will not swell the rout
Of lads that wore their honors out,
Runners whom renown outran
And the name died before the man.   20

So set, before its echoes fade,
The fleet foot on the sill of shade,
And hold to the low lintel up
The still-defended challenge-cup.

And round that early-laurelled head   25
Will flock to gaze the strengthless dead,
And find unwithered on its curls
The garland briefer than a girl's.

THE IMMORTAL PART

When I meet the morning beam
Or lay me down at night to dream,
I hear my bones within me say,
'Another night, another day.

'When shall this slough of sense be cast,   5
This dust of thoughts be laid at last,
The man of flesh and soul be slain
And the man of bone remain?

5 *slough:* skin, of the kind cast off by some
animals

'This tongue that talks, these lungs that shout,
These thews that hustle us about,   10
This brain that fills the skull with schemes,
And its humming hives of dreams,—

'These to-day are proud in power
And lord it in their little hour:
The immortal bones obey control   15
Of dying flesh and dying soul.

' 'Tis long till eve and morn are gone:
Slow the endless night comes on,
And late to fulness grows the birth
That shall last as long as earth.   20

'Wanderers eastward, wanderers west,
Know you why you cannot rest?
'Tis that every mother's son
Travails with a skeleton.

'Lie down in the bed of dust;   25
Bear the fruit that bear you must;
Bring the eternal seed to light,
And morn is all the same as night.

'Rest you so from trouble sore,
Fear the heat o' the sun no more,   30
Nor the snowing winter wild,
Now you labour not with child.

'Empty vessel, garment cast,
We that wore you long shall last.
—Another night, another day.'   35
So my bones within me say.

Therefore they shall do my will
To-day while I am master still,
And flesh and soul, now both are strong,
Shall hale the sullen slaves along,   40

Before this fire of sense decay,
This smoke of thought blow clean away,
And leave with ancient night alone
The stedfast and enduring bone.

10 *thews:* muscles 24 *Travails:* labors 40 *hale:* pull

W. B. Yeats

(1865–1939)

TO A FRIEND WHOSE WORK HAS COME TO NOTHING

Now all the truth is out,
Be secret and take defeat
From any brazen throat,
For how can you compete,
Being honor bred, with one   5
Who, were it proved he lies,
Were neither shamed in his own
Nor in his neighbors' eyes?
Bred to a harder thing
Than Triumph, turn away   10
And like a laughing string
Whereon mad fingers play
Amid a place of stone,
Be secret and exult,
Because of all things known   15
That is most difficult.

SAILING TO BYZANTIUM

I

That is no country for old men. The young
In one another's arms, birds in the trees
—Those dying generations—at their song,
The salmon-falls, the mackerel-crowded seas,
Fish, flesh, or fowl, commend all summer long   5
Whatever is begotten, born, and dies.

Byzantium: used by Yeats as a symbol of the
realm of art

Caught in that sensual music all neglect
Monuments of unageing intellect.

II

An aged man is but a paltry thing,
A tattered coat upon a stick, unless   10
Soul clap its hands and sing, and louder sing
For every tatter in its mortal dress,
Nor is there singing school but studying
Monuments of its own magnificence;
And therefore I have sailed the seas and come   15
To the holy city of Byzantium.

III

O sages standing in God's holy fire
As in the gold mosaic of a wall,
Come from the holy fire, perne in a gyre,
And be the singing-masters of my soul.   20
Consume my heart away; sick with desire
And fastened to a dying animal
It knows not what it is; and gather me
Into the artifice of eternity.

IV

Once out of nature I shall never take   25
My bodily form from any natural thing,
But such a form as Grecian goldsmiths make
Of hammered gold and gold enamelling
To keep a drowsy Emperor awake;
Or set upon a golden bough to sing   30
To lords and ladies of Byzantium
Of what is past, or passing, or to come.

19 *perne in a gyre:* spin in a cycle which had
symbolic significance

Walter De La Mare

(1873–1956)

IN THE DOCK

Pallid, mis-shapen he stands. The world's
   grimed thumb,
Now hooked securely in his matted hair,
Has haled him struggling from his poisonous slum
And flung him mute as fish close-netted there.
His bloodless hands entalon that iron rail.   5
He gloats in beastlike trance. His settling eyes
From staring face to face rove on—and quail.
Justice for carrion pants; and these the flies.
Voice after voice in smooth impartial drone
Erects horrific in his darkening brain   10
A timber framework, where agape, alone
Bright life will kiss good-bye the cheek of Cain.
Sudden like wolf he cries; and sweats to see
When howls man's soul, it howls inaudibly.

Robert Frost

(1874–1963)

DESERT PLACES

Snow falling and night falling fast, oh, fast
In a field I looked into going past,
And the ground almost covered smooth in snow,
But a few weeds and stubble showing last.

The woods around it have it—it is theirs.   5
All animals are smothered in their lairs.

I am too absent-spirited to count;
The loneliness includes me unawares.

And lonely as it is that loneliness
Will be more lonely ere it will be less—   10
A blanker whiteness of benighted snow
With no expression, nothing to express.

They cannot scare me with their empty spaces
Between stars—on stars where no human race is.
I have it in me so much nearer home   15
To scare myself with my own desert places.

RELUCTANCE

Out through the fields and the woods
    And over the walls I have wended;
I have climbed the hills of view
    And looked at the world, and descended;
I have come by the highway home,   5
    And lo, it is ended.

The leaves are all dead on the ground,
    Save those that the oak is keeping
To ravel them one by one
    And let them go scraping and creeping   10
Out over the crusted snow,
    When others are sleeping.

And the dead leaves lie huddled and still,
    No longer blown hither and thither;
The last lone aster is gone;   15
    The flowers of the witch-hazel wither;
The heart is still aching to seek,
    But the feet question "Whither?"

Ah, when to the heart of man
    Was it ever less than a treason   20
To go with the drift of things
    To yield with a grace to reason,
And bow and accept the end
    Of a love or a season?

SAND DUNES

Sea waves are green and wet,
But up from where they die
Rise others vaster yet,
And those are brown and dry.

They are the sea made land   5
To come at the fisher town,
And bury in solid sand
The men she could not drown.

She may know cove and cape,
But she does not know mankind   10
If by any change of shape
She hopes to cut off mind.

Men left her a ship to sink:
They can leave her a hut as well;
And be but more free to think   15
For the one more cast-off shell.

TWO TRAMPS IN MUD TIME

Out of the mud two strangers came
And caught me splitting wood in the yard.
And one of them put me off my aim
By hailing cheerily 'Hit them hard!'
I knew pretty well why he dropped behind   5
And let the other go on a way.
I knew pretty well what he had in mind:
He wanted to take my job for pay.

Good blocks of oak it was I split,
As large around as the chopping block;   10
And every piece I squarely hit
Fell splinterless as a cloven rock.
The blows that a life of self-control
Spares to strike for the common good
That day, giving a loose to my soul,   15
I spent on the unimportant wood.

The sun was warm but the wind was chill.
You know how it is with an April day
When the sun is out and the wind is still,
You're one month on in the middle of May.   20
But if you so much as dare to speak,
A cloud comes over the sunlit arch,
A wind comes off a frozen peak,
And you're two months back in the middle of March.

A bluebird comes tenderly up to alight   25
And turns to the wind to unruffle a plume
His song so pitched as not to excite
A single flower as yet to bloom.
It is snowing a flake: and he half knew
Winter was only playing possum.   30
Except in color he isn't blue,
But he wouldn't advise a thing to blossom.

The water for which we may have to look
In summertime with a witching-wand,
In every wheelrut's now a brook,   35
In every print of a hoof a pond.
Be glad of water, but don't forget
The lurking frost in the earth beneath
That will steal forth after the sun is set
And show on the water its crystal teeth.   40

The time when most I loved my task
These two must make me love it more
By coming with what they came to ask.
You'd think I never had felt before
The weight of an ax-head poised aloft,   45
The grip on earth of outspread feet.
The life of muscles rocking soft
And smooth and moist in vernal heat.

Out of the woods two hulking tramps
(From sleeping God knows where last night,   50
But not long since in the lumber camps).
They thought all chopping was theirs of right
Men of the woods and lumberjacks,
They judged me by their appropriate tool.
Except as a fellow handled an ax,   55
They had no way of knowing a fool.

Nothing on either side was said.
They knew they had but to stay their stay
And all their logic would fill my head:
As that I had no right to play   60
With what was another man's work for gain.
My right might be love but theirs was need.
And where the two exist in twain
Theirs was the better right—agreed.

But yield who will to their separation,   65
My object in living is to unite
My avocation and my vocation
As my two eyes make one in sight.
Only where love and need are one,
And the work is play for mortal stakes,   70
Is the deed ever really done
For Heaven and the future's sakes.

Anonymous

(about 1910)

THE BIG ROCK CANDY MOUNTAINS

One evening when the sun was low
And the jungle fires were burning
Down the track came a hobo hamming
And he said, Boys, I'm not turning;
I'm headed for a land that's far away   5
Beside the crystal fountains.
So come with me, we'll go and see
The Big Rock Candy Mountains.

In the Big Rock Candy Mountains
There's a land that's fair and bright,   10
Where the handouts grow on bushes
And you sleep out every night,
Where the box-cars all are empty

And the sun shines every day
On the birds and the bees   15
And the cigarette trees,
The rock-and-rye springs
Where the whangdoodle sings,
In the Big Rock Candy Mountains.

In the Big Rock Candy Mountains   20
All the cops have wooden legs
And the bulldogs all have rubber teeth
And the hens lay hard-boiled eggs;
The farmers' trees are full of fruit
And the barns are full of hay: 25
O I'm bound to go
Where there ain't no snow,
And the rain don't fall,
The wind don't blow,
In the Big Rock Candy Mountains.   30

In the Big Rock Candy Mountains
You never change your socks
And the little streams of alkyhol
Come a-trickling down the rocks;
The shacks all have to tip their hats   35
And the railroad bulls are blind;
There's a lake of stew,
You can paddle all around
In a big canoe,
In the Big Rock Candy Mountains.   40

In the Big Rock Candy Mountains
The jails are made of tin
And you can bust right out again
As soon as they put you in;
There ain't no short-handled shovels,   45
No axes, saws or picks:
O I'm going to stay
Where you sleep all day,
Where they hung the Turk
That invented work,   50
In the Big Rock Candy Mountains.
I'll see you all
This coming fall
In the Big Rock Candy Mountains.

Edwin Arlington Robinson

(1869–1935)

THE SHEAVES

Where long the shadows of the wind had rolled,
Green wheat was yielding to the change assigned;
And as by some vast magic undivined
The world was turning slowly into gold.
Like nothing that was ever bought or sold.   5
It waited there, the body and the mind;
And with a mighty meaning of a kind
That tells the more the more it is not told.

So in a land where all days are not fair,
Fair days went on till on another day   10
A thousand golden sheaves were lying there,
Shining and still, but not for long to stay—
As if a thousand girls with golden hair
Might rise from where they slept and go away.

Wallace Stevens

(1879–1955)

THE SNOW MAN

One must have a mind of winter
To regard the frost and the boughs
Of the pine-trees crusted with snow;

And have been cold a long time
To behold the junipers shagged with ice,   5
The spruces rough in the distant glitter

Of the January sun; and not to think
Of any misery in the sound of the wind,
In the sound of a few leaves,

Which is the sound of the land   10
Full of the same wind
That is blowing in the same bare place

For the listener, who listens in the snow,
And, nothing himself, beholds
Nothing that is not there and the nothing that is.   15

ANECDOTE OF THE JAR

I placed a jar in Tennessee,
And round it was, upon a hill.
It made the slovenly wilderness
Surround that hill.

The wilderness rose up to it,
And sprawled around, no longer wild.
The jar was round upon the ground
And tall and of a port in air.

It took dominion everywhere.
The jar was gray and bare.
It did not give of bird or bush,
Like nothing else in Tennessee.

THIRTEEN WAYS OF LOOKING
AT A BLACKBIRD

I

Among twenty snowy mountains,
The only moving thing
Was the eye of the blackbird.

II

I was of three minds,
Like a tree   5
In which there are three blackbirds.

III

The blackbird whirled in the autumn winds.
It was a small part of the pantomime.

IV

A man and a woman
Are one.   10
A man and a woman and a blackbird
Are one.

V

I do not know which to prefer,
The beauty of inflections
Or the beauty of innuendoes,   15
The blackbird whistling
Or just after.

VI

Icicles filled the long window
With barbaric glass.
The shadow of the blackbird   20
Crossed it, to and fro.
The mood
Traced in the shadow
An indecipherable cause.

VII

O thin men of Haddam,   25
Why do you imagine golden birds?
Do you not see how the blackbird
Walks around the feet
Of the women about you?

VIII

I know noble accents   30
And lucid, inescapable rhythms;
But I know, too,
That the blackbird is involved
In what I know.

25 *Haddam:* a Connecticut town

IX

When the blackbird flew out of sight,   35
It marked the edge
Of one of many circles.

X

At the sight of blackbirds
Flying in a green light,
Even the bawds of euphony   40
Would cry out sharply.

XI

He rode over Connecticut
In a glass coach.
Once, a fear pierced him,
In that he mistook   45
The shadow of his equipage
For blackbirds.

XII

The river is moving.
The blackbird must be flying.

XIII

It was evening all afternoon.   50
It was snowing
And it was going to snow.
The blackbird sat
In the cedar-limbs.

PETER QUINCE AT THE CLAVIER

I

Just as my fingers on these keys
Make music, so the selfsame sounds
On my spirit make a music, too.

Peter Quince: the carpenter who amateurishly
directs a play in Shakespeare's *Midsummer
Night's Dream; clavier:* the family of musical
instruments to which the piano belongs

Music is feeling, then, not sound;
And thus it is that what I feel,   5
Here in this room, desiring you,

Thinking of your blue-shadowed silk,
Is music. It is like the strain
Waked in the elders by Susanna.

Of a green evening, clear and warm,   10
She bathed in her still garden, while
The red-eyed elders watching, felt

The basses of their beings throb
In witching chords, and her thin blood
Pulse pizzicati of Hosanna.   15

II

In the green water, clear and warm,
Susanna lay.
She searched
The touch of springs,
And found   20
Concealed imaginings.
She sighed,
For so much melody.

Upon the bank, she stood
In the cool   25
Of spent emotions.
She felt, among the leaves,
The dew
Of old devotions.

She walked upon the grass,   30
Still quavering.
The winds were like her maids,
On timid feet,
Fetching her woven scarves,
Yet wavering.   35

9 *Susanna:* the poem is based on the tale of
Susanna and the Elders from the Biblical
Apocrypha 15 *Hosanna:* a Hebrew exclama-
tion praising the Lord

A breath upon her hand
Muted the night.
She turned—
A cymbal crashed,
And roaring horns.   40

III

Soon, with a noise like tambourines,
Came her attendant Byzantines.

They wondered why Susanna cried
Against the elders by her side;

And as they whispered, the refrain   45
Was like a willow swept by rain.

Anon, their lamps' uplifted flame
Revealed Susanna and her shame.

And then, the simpering Byzantines
Fled, with a noise like tambourines.   50

IV

Beauty is momentary in the mind—
The fitful tracing of a portal;
But in the flesh it is immortal.
The body dies; the body's beauty lives.
So evenings die, in their green going,   55
A wave, interminably flowing.
So gardens die, their meek breath scenting
The cowl of winter, done repenting.
So maidens die, to the auroral
Celebration of a maiden's choral.   60
Susanna's music touched the bawdy strings
Of those white elders; but, escaping,
Left only Death's ironic scraping.
Now, in its immortality, it plays
On the clear viol of her memory,   65
And makes a constant sacrament of praise.

William Carlos Williams

(1883–1963)

THE POOR

It's the anarchy of poverty
delights me, the old
Yellow wooden house indented
among the new brick tenements

Or a cast-iron balcony   5
with panels showing oak branches
in full leaf. It fits
the dress of the children

reflecting every stage and
custom of necessity—   10
Chimneys, roofs, fences of
wood and metal in an unfenced

age and enclosing next to
nothing at all: the old man
in a sweater and soft black   15
hat who sweeps the sidewalk—

his own ten feet of it
in a wind that fitfully
turning his corner has
overwhelmed the entire city   20

Ezra Pound

(1885–   )

THE GARDEN

En robe de parade—Samain

Like a skein of loose silk blown against a wall
She walks by the railing of a path in Kensington Gardens,
And she is dying piece-meal
   of a sort of emotional anæmia.

And round about there is a rabble   5
Of the filthy, sturdy, unkillable infants of the very
   poor.
They shall inherit the earth.

In her is the end of breeding.
Her boredom is exquisite and excessive.
She would like some one to speak to her,   10
And is almost afraid that I
   will commit that indiscretion.

  En robe de parade: "in official dress"

LAMENT OF THE FRONTIER GUARD

By the North Gate, the wind blows full of sand,
Lonely from the beginning of time until now!
Trees fall, the grass goes yellow with autumn.
I climb the towers and towers
   to watch out the barbarous land:
Desolate castle, the sky, the wide desert.   5
There is no wall left to this village.
Bones white with a thousand frosts,
High heaps, covered with trees and grass;
Who brought this to pass?

Who has brought the flaming imperial anger?   10
Who has brought the army with drums and with kettle-drums?
Barbarous kings.
A gracious spring, turned to blood-ravenous autumn,
A turmoil of wars-men, spread over the middle kingdom,
Three hundred and sixty thousand,   15
And sorrow, sorrow like rain.
Sorrow to go, and sorrow, sorrow returning.
Desolate, desolate fields,
And no children of warfare upon them,
            No longer the men for offence and defence.   20
Ah, how shall you know the dreary sorrow at the North Gate,
With Rihaku's name forgotten,
And we guardsmen fed to the tigers.

By Rihaku

THE RIVER-MERCHANT'S WIFE:
A LETTER

While my hair was still cut straight across my forehead
I played about the front gate, pulling flowers.
You came by on bamboo stilts, playing horse,
You walked about my seat, playing with blue plums.
And we went on living in the village of Chokan: 5
Two small people, without dislike or suspicion.

At fourteen I married My Lord you.
I never laughed, being bashful.
Lowering my head, I looked at the wall.
Called to, a thousand times, I never looked back.   10

At fifteen I stopped scowling,
I desired my dust to be mingled with yours
Forever and forever and forever.
Why should I climb the look out?

At sixteen you departed,   15
You went into far Ku-to-yen, by the river of swirl-
      ing eddies,
And you have been gone five months.
The monkeys make sorrowful noise overhead.

You dragged your feet when you went out.
By the gate now, the moss is grown, the different
　　　mosses,　　　　　　　　　　　　　　　　　　　20
Too deep to clear them away!
The leaves fall early this autumn, in wind.
The paired butterflies are already yellow with August
Over the grass in the West garden;
They hurt me. I grow older.　　　　　　　　　　　25
If you are coming down through the narrows of
　　　the river Kiang,
Please let me know beforehand,
And I will come out to meet you
　　　　　　　As far as Cho-fu-Sa.

By Rihaku

FROM CANTO LXXXI

What thou lovest well remains,
　　　　　　　　　　　the rest is dross
What thou lov'st well shall not be reft from thee
What thou lov'st well is thy true heritage
Whose world, or mine or theirs　　　　　　　　　5
　　　　　　　or is it of none?
First came the seen, then thus the palpable
　　Elysium, though it were in the halls of hell,
What thou lovest well is thy true heritage

The ant's a centaur in his dragon world.　　　　10
Pull down thy vanity, it is not man
Made courage, or made order, or made grace,
　　Pull down thy vanity, I say pull down.
Learn of the green world what can be thy place
In scaled invention or true artistry,　　　　　　15
Pull down thy vanity,
　　　　　　　Paquin pull down!
The green casque has outdone your elegance.

2 *dross:* waste 8 *Elysium:* the Greek equivalent of heaven, the
Isles of the Blest 10 *centaur:* a mythical creature having the
head and trunk of a man and the body and legs of a horse 16
Paquin: a Paris dress designer 18 *The green casque:* the poet
has been watching a new born wasp putting its head out of
the nest

"Master thyself, then others shall thee beare"
    Pull down thy vanity   20
Thou art a beaten dog beneath the hail,
A swollen magpie in a fitful sun,
Half black half white
Nor knowst'ou wing from tail
Pull down thy vanity   25
    How mean thy hates
Fostered in falsity,
    Pull down thy vanity,
Rathe to destroy, niggard in charity,
Pull down thy vanity,   30
    I say pull down.

But to have done instead of not doing
    this is not vanity
To have, with decency, knocked
That a Blunt should open   35
    To have gathered from the air a live tradition
or from a fine old eye the unconquered flame
This is not vanity.
    Here error is all in the not done,
all in the diffidence that faltered   40

29 *rathe:* quick 35 *Blunt:* Wilfrid Scawen Blunt (1840–1922),
English poet

ℋ. D. (ℋilda Doolittle)

(1886–   )

GARDEN

I

You are clear,
O rose, cut in rock.

I could scrape the colour
From the petals,
Like spilt dye from a rock.   5

If I could break you
I could break a tree.

If I could stir
I could break a tree,
I could break you.   10

II

O wind, rend open the heat,
Cut apart the heat,
Slit it to tatters.

Fruit cannot drop
Through this thick air;   15
Fruit cannot fall into heat
That presses up and blunts
The points of pears,
And rounds grapes.

Cut the heat: 20
Plough through it,
Turning it on either side
Of your path.

Robinson Jeffers
(1887–   )

HURT HAWKS

I

The broken pillar of the wing jags from the clotted shoulder,
The wing trails like a banner in defeat,
No more to use the sky forever but live with famine
And pain a few days: cat nor coyote
Will shorten the week of waiting for death, there is game without
    talons.   5

He stands under the oak-bush and waits
The lame feet of salvation; at night he remembers freedom
And flies in a dream, the dawns ruin it.
He is strong and pain is worse to the strong, incapacity is worse.
The curs of the day come and torment him   10
At distance, no one but death the redeemer will humble that head,
The intrepid readiness, the terrible eyes.
The wild God of the world is sometimes merciful to those
That ask mercy, not often to the arrogant.
You do not know him, you communal people, or you have forgotten
     him;   15
Intemperate and savage, the hawk remembers him;
Beautiful and wild, the hawks, and men that are dying, remember him.

                                    II

I'd sooner, except the penalties, kill a man than a hawk; but the great
     redtail
Had nothing left but unable misery
From the bone too shattered for mending, the wing that trailed under
     his talons when he moved.   20
We had fed him six weeks, I gave him freedom,
He wandered over the foreland hill and returned in the evening,
     asking for death,
Not like a beggar, still eyed with the old
Implacable arrogance. I gave him the lead gift in the twilight.
     What fell was relaxed,   25
Owl-downy, soft feminine feathers; but what
Soared: the fierce rush: the night-herons by the flooded river cried
     fear at its rising
Before it was quite unsheathed from reality.

                        BOATS IN A FOG

Sports and gallantries, the stage, the arts, the antics of dancers,
The exuberant voices of music,
Have charm for children but lack nobility; it is bitter earnestness
That makes beauty; the mind
Knows, grown adult.
                              A sudden fog-drift muffled the ocean,   5
A throbbing of engines moved in it,

At length, a stone's throw out, between the rocks and the vapor,
One by one moved shadows
Out of the mystery, shadows, fishing-boats, trailing each other
Following the cliff for guidance,   10
Holding a difficult path between the peril of the sea-fog
And the foam on the shore granite.
One by one, trailing their leader, six crept by me,
Out of the vapor and into it,
The throb of their engines subdued by the fog, patient and cautious, 15
Coasting all round the peninsula
Back to the buoys in Monterey harbor. A flight of pelicans
Is nothing lovelier to look at;
The flight of the planets is nothing nobler; all the arts lose virtue
Against the essential reality   20
Of creatures going about their business among the equally
Earnest elements of nature.

John Masefield

(1887–   )

THE DOWNLAND

Night is on the downland, on the lonely moorland,
On the hills where the wind goes over sheep-bitten turf,
Where the bent grass beats upon the unplowed poorland
And the pine-woods roar like the surf.

Here the Roman lived on the wind-barren lonely,   5
Dark now and haunted by the moorland fowl;
None comes here now but the peewit only,
And moth-like death in the owl.

Beauty was here on this beetle-droning downland;
The thought of a Caesar in the purple came   10
From the palace by the Tiber in the Roman townland
To this wind-swept hill with no name.

Lonely Beauty came here and was here in sadness,
Brave as a thought on the frontier of the mind,
In the camp of the wild upon the march of madness,   15
The bright-eyed Queen of the blind.

Now where Beauty was are the wind-withered gorses,
Moaning like old men in the hill-wind's blast;
The flying sky is dark with running horses,
And the night is full of the past.   20

Marianne Moore

(1887–   )

CRITICS AND CONNOISSEURS

There is a great amount of poety in unconscious
    fastidiousness. Certain Ming
        products, imperial floor-coverings of coach-
wheel yellow, are well enough in their way but I have
            seen something
    that I like better—a   5
        mere childish attempt to make an imperfectly bal-
        lasted animal stand up,
        similar determination to make a pup
        eat his meat from the plate.

I remember a swan under the willows in Oxford,   10
    with flamingo-coloured, maple-
        leaflike feet. It reconnoitred like a battle-
ship. Disbelief and conscious fastidiousness were the
            staple
    ingredients in its
        disinclination to move. Finally its hardihood was
        not proof against its   15
        proclivity to more fully appraise such bits
        of food as the stream

bore counter to it; it made away with what I gave it
    to eat. I have seen this swan and
        I have seen you; I have seen ambition without   20
    understanding in a variety of forms. Happening to stand
           by an ant-hill, I have
           seen a fastidious ant carrying a stick north, south,
               east, west, till it turned on
        itself, struck out from the flower-bed into the
           lawn,   25
           and returned to the point

from which it had started. Then abandoning the stick as
    useless and overtaxing its
        jaws with a particle of whitewash—pill-like but
heavy, it again went through the same course of pro-
           cedure.
           What is   30
      there in being able
        to say that one has dominated the stream in an
           attitude of self-defence;
      in proving that one has had the experience
        of carrying a stick?   35

A GRAVE

Man looking into the sea,
taking the view from those who have as much right to it as you have
    to it yourself,
it is human nature to stand in the middle of a thing,
but you cannot stand in the middle of this;
the sea has nothing to give but a well excavated grave.   5
The firs stand in a procession, each with an emerald turkey-foot at
    the top,
reserved as their contours, saying nothing;
repression, however, is not the most obvious characteristic of the sea;
the sea is a collector, quick to return a rapacious look.
There are others besides you who have worn that look—   10
whose expression is no longer a protest; the fish no longer investigate
    them
for their bones have not lasted:

men lower nets, unconscious of the fact that they are desecrating a
    grave,
and row quickly away—the blades of the oars
moving together like the feet of water-spiders as if there were no such
    thing as death.   15
The wrinkles progress among themselves in a phalanx—beautiful under
    networks of foam,
and fade breathlessly while the sea rustles in and out of the seaweed;
the birds swim through the air at top speed, emitting catcalls as
    heretofore—
the tortoise-shell scourges about the feet of the cliffs, in motion
    beneath them;
and the ocean, under the pulsation of lighthouses and noise of bell-
    buoys,   20
advances as usual, looking as if it were not that ocean in which dropped
    things are bound to sink—
in which if they turn and twist, it is neither with volition nor con-
    sciousness.

Edwin Muir

(1887–1958)

THE ENCHANTED KNIGHT

Lulled by La Belle Dame Sans Merci he lies
    In the bare wood below the blackening hill.
The plough drives nearer now, the shadow flies
    Past him across the plain, but he lies still.

Long since the rust its gardens here has planned,   5
    Flowering his armour like an autumn field.
From his sharp breast-plate to his iron hand
    A spider's web is stretched, a phantom shield.

1 *La Belle Dame Sans Merci:* the beautiful lady without
mercy. An allusion to the figure in Keats's poem; see
page 262.

When footsteps pound the turf besides his ear
  Armies pass through his dream in endless line,   10
And one by one his ancient friends appear;
  They pass all day, but he can make no sign.

When a bird cries within the silent grove
  The long-lost voice goes by, he makes to rise
And follow, but his cold limbs never move,   15
  And on the turf unstirred his shadow lies.

But if a withered leaf should drift
  Across his face and rest, the dread drops start
Chill on his forehead. Now he tries to lift
  The insulting weight that stays and breaks his heart.   20

THE WINDOW

    Within the great wall's perfect round
    Bird, beast and child serenely grew
    In endless change on changeless ground
    That in a single pattern bound
    The old perfection and the new.   5

    There was a tower set in the wall
    And a great window in the tower,
    And if one looked, beyond recall
    The twisting glass kept him in thrall
    With changing marvels hour by hour.   10
    And there one day we looked and saw
    Marsh, mere and mount in anger shaken,
    The world's great side, the giant flaw,
    And watched the stately forests fall,
    The white ships sinking in the sea,   15
    The tower run toppling in the field,
    The last left stronghold sacked and taken,
    And earth and heaven in jeopardy.
    Then turning towards you I beheld
    The wrinkle writhe across your brow,   20
    And felt time's cap clapped on my head,

    9 *in thrall:* in slavery 12 *mere:* pool of water

And all within the enclosure now,
Light leaf and smiling flower, was false,
The great wall breached, the garden dead.

Across the towering window fled   25
Disasters, victories, festivals.

T. S. Eliot

(1888–1965)

PRELUDES

I

The winter evening settles down
With smell of steaks in passageways.
Six o'clock.
The burnt-out ends of smoky days.
And now a gusty shower wraps   5
The grimy scraps
Of withered leaves about your feet
And newspapers from vacant lots;
The showers beat
On broken blinds and chimney-pots,   10
And at the corner of the street
A lonely cab-horse steams and stamps.
And then the lighting of the lamps.

II

The morning comes to consciousness
Of faint stale smells of beer   15
From the sawdust-trampled street
With all its muddy feet that press
To early coffee-stands.
With the other masquerades

That time resumes,   20
One thinks of all the hands
That are raising dingy shades
In a thousand furnished rooms.

III

You tossed a blanket from the bed,
You lay upon your back, and waited;   25
You dozed, and watched the night revealing
The thousand sordid images
Of which your soul was constituted;
They flickered against the ceiling.
And when all the world came back   30
And the light crept up between the shutters
And you heard the sparrows in the gutters,
You had such a vision of the street
As the street hardly understands;
Sitting along the bed's edge, where   35
You curled the papers from your hair,
Or clasped the yellow soles of feet
In the palms of both soiled hands.

IV

His soul stretched tight across the skies
That fade behind a city block,   40
Or trampled by insistent feet
At four and five and six o'clock;
And short square fingers stuffing pipes,
And evening newspapers, and eyes
Assured of certain certainties,   45
The conscience of a blackened street
Impatient to assume the world.
I am moved by fancies that are curled
Around these images, and cling:
The notion of some infinitely gentle   50
Infinitely suffering thing.

Wipe your hand across your mouth, and laugh;
The worlds revolve like ancient women
Gathering fuel in vacant lots.

GERONTION

Thou hast nor youth nor age
But as it were an after dinner sleep
Dreaming on both.

Here I am, an old man in a dry month,
Being read to by a boy, waiting for rain.
I was neither at the hot gates
Nor fought in the warm rain
Nor knee deep in the salt marsh, heaving a cutlass,   5
Bitten by flies, fought.
My house is a decayed house,
And the jew squats on the window sill, the owner,
Spawned in some estaminet of Antwerp,
Blistered in Brussels, patched and peeled in London.   10
The goat coughs at night in the field overhead;
Rocks, moss, stonecrop, iron, merds.
The woman keeps the kitchen, makes tea,
Sneezes at evening, poking the peevish gutter.
        I an old man,   15
A dull head among windy spaces.

Signs are taken for wonders. 'We would see a sign!'
The word within a word, unable to speak a word,
Swaddled with darkness. In the juvescence of the year
Came Christ the tiger   20
In depraved May, dogwood and chestnut, flowering judas,
To be eaten, to be divided, to be drunk
Among whispers; by Mr. Silvero
With caressing hands, at Limoges
Who walked all night in the next room;   25
By Hakagawa, bowing among the Titians;
By Madame de Tornquist, in the dark room
Shifting the candles; Fräulein von Kulp

12 *stonecrop:* a plant that often grows out of walls and rocks;
merds: dung 19 *juvescence:* juvenescence, that is, the period of
youth 23 *Mr. Silvero:* denotes a fictional character, like the other
personal names in this poem 26 *Titians:* paintings by the great
Italian Renaissance painter Tiziano Vecellio

Who turned in the hall, one hand on the door. Vacant shuttles
Weave the wind. I have no ghosts,   30
An old man in a draughty house
Under a windy knob.

After such knowledge, what forgiveness? Think now
History has many cunning passages, contrived corridors
And issues, deceives with whispering ambitions,   35
Guides us by vanities. Think now
She gives when our attention is distracted
And what she gives, gives with such supple confusions
That the giving famishes the craving. Gives too late
What's not believed in, or if still believed,   40
In memory only, reconsidered passion. Gives too soon
Into weak hands, what's thought can be dispensed with
Till the refusal propagates a fear. Think
Neither fear nor courage saves us. Unnatural vices
Are fathered by our heroism. Virtues   45
Are forced upon us by our impudent crimes.
These tears are shaken from the wrath-bearing tree.

The tiger springs in the new year. Us he devours.
      Think at last
We have not reached conclusion, when I
Stiffen in a rented house. Think at last   50
I have not made this show purposelessly
And it is not by any concitation
Of the backward devils.
I would meet you upon this honestly.
I that was near your heart was removed therefrom   55
To lose beauty in terror, terror in inquisition.
I have lost my passion: why should I need to keep it
Since what is kept must be adulterated?
I have lost my sight, smell, hearing, taste, and touch:
How should I use them for your closer contact?   60

These with a thousand small deliberations
Protract the profit of their chilled delirium,
Excite the membrane, when the sense has cooled,
With pungent sauces, multiply variety
In a wilderness of mirrors. What will the spider do,   65

52 *concitation:* stirring up

Suspend its operations, will the weevil
Delay? De Bailhache, Fresca, Mrs. Cammel, whirled
Beyond the circuit of the shuddering Bear
In fractured atoms. Gull against the wind, in the windy straits
Of Belle Isle, or running on the Horn,   70
White feathers in the snow, the Gulf claims,
And an old man driven by the Trades
To a sleepy corner.
                Tenants of the house,
Thoughts of a dry brain in a dry season.   75

68 *the Bear:* the constellation Ursa Major (or Minor) 70 *Belle Isle:* straits between Labrador and Newfoundland; *Horn:* Cape Horn 71 *Gulf:* of Mexico 72 *Trades:* the transatlantic winds

THE LOVE SONG OF J. ALFRED PRUFROCK

Let us go then, you and I,
When the evening is spread out against the sky
Like a patient etherised upon a table;
Let us go, through certain half-deserted streets,
The muttering retreats   5
Of restless nights in one-night cheap hotels
And sawdust restaurants with oyster-shells:
Streets that follow like a tedious argument
Of insidious intent
To lead you to an overwhelming question. . . .   10
Oh, do not ask, 'What is it?'
Let us go and make our visit.

In the room the women come and go
Talking of Michelangelo.

The yellow fog that rubs its back upon the window-
    panes,   15
The yellow smoke that rubs its muzzle on the window-
    panes
Licked its tongue into the corners of the evening,
Lingered upon the pools that stand in drains,
Let fall upon its back the soot that falls from chimneys,

Slipped by the terrace, made a sudden leap,   20
And seeing that it was a soft October night,
Curled once about the house, and fell asleep.

And indeed there will be time
For the yellow smoke that slides along the street
Rubbing its back upon the window-panes;   25
There will be time, there will be time
To prepare a face to meet the faces that you meet;
There will be time to murder and create,
And time for all the works and days of hands
That lift and drop a question on your plate;   30
Time for you and time for me,
And time yet for a hundred indecisions,
And for a hundred visions and revisions,
Before the taking of a toast and tea.

In the room the women come and go   35
Talking of Michelangelo.

And indeed there will be time
To wonder, 'Do I dare?' and, 'Do I dare?'
Time to turn back and descend the stair,
With a bald spot in the middle of my hair—   40
[They will say: 'How his hair is growing thin!']
My morning coat, my collar mounting firmly to the chin,
My necktie rich and modest, but asserted by a simple pin—
[They will say: 'But how his arms and legs are thin!']
Do I dare   45
Disturb the universe?
In a minute there is time
For decisions and revisions which a minute will reverse.

For I have know them all already, know them all—
Have known the evenings, mornings, afternoons,   50
I have measured out my life with coffee spoons;
I know the voices dying with a dying fall
Beneath the music from a farther room.
   So how should I presume?

And I have known the eyes already, known them all—   55
The eyes that fix you in a formulated phrase,
And when I am formulated, sprawling on a pin,

When I am pinned and wriggling on the wall,
Then how should I begin
To spit out all the butt-ends of my days and ways?   60
   And how should I presume?

And I have known the arms already, known them all—
Arms that are braceleted and white and bare
[But in the lamplight, downed with light brown hair!]
Is it perfume from a dress   65
That makes me so digress?
Arms that lie along a table, or wrap about a shawl.
   And should I then presume?
   And how should I begin?

Shall I say, I have gone at dusk through narrow streets   70
And watched the smoke that rises from the pipes
Of lonely men in shirt-sleeves, leaning out of windows? . . .

I should have been a pair of ragged claws
Scuttling across the floors of silent seas.

And the afternoon, the evening, sleeps so peacefully!   75
Smoothed by long fingers,
Asleep . . . tired . . . or it malingers,
Stretched on the floor, here beside you and me.
Should I, after tea and cakes and ices,
Have the strength to force the moment to its crisis?   80
But though I have wept and fasted, wept and prayed,
Though I have seen my head [grown slightly bald]
   brought in upon a platter,
I am no prophet—and here's no great matter;
I have seen the moment of my greatness flicker,   85
And I have seen the eternal Footman hold my coat,
   and snicker,
And in short, I was afraid.
And would it have been worth it, after all,
After the cups, the marmalade, the tea,
Among the porcelain, among some talk of you and me,   90
Would it have been worth while,
To have bitten off the matter with a smile,
To have squeezed the universe into a ball
To roll it toward some overwhelming question,
To say: 'I am Lazarus, come from the dead,   95

Come back to tell you all, I shall tell you all'—
If one, settling a pillow by her head,
   Should say: 'That is not what I meant at all.
   That is not it, at all.'

And would it have been worth it, after all,   100
Would it have been worth while,
After the sunsets and the dooryards and the sprinkled
   streets,
After the novels, after the teacups, after the skirts that
   trail along the floor—
And this, and so much more?—   105
It is impossible to say just what I mean!
But as if a magic lantern threw the nerves in patterns
   on a screen:
Would it have been worth while
If one, settling a pillow or throwing off a shawl,
And turning toward the window, should say: 110
   'That is not it at all,
   That is not what I meant, at all.'

No! I am not Prince Hamlet, nor was meant to be;
Am an attendant lord, one that will do
To swell a progress, start a scene or two,   115
Advise the prince; no doubt, an easy tool,
Deferential, glad to be of use,
Politic, cautious, and meticulous;
Full of high sentence, but a bit obtuse;
At times, indeed, almost ridiculous—   120
Almost, at times, the Fool.

I grow old . . . I grow old . . .
I shall wear the bottoms of my trousers rolled.

Shall I part my hair behind? Do I dare to eat a peach?
I shall wear white flannel trousers, and walk upon the
   beach.
I have heard the mermaids singing, each to each.   125

I do not think that they will sing to me.

I have seen them riding seaward on the waves
Combing the white hair of the waves blown back
When the wind blows the water white and black.   130

We have lingered in the chambers of the sea
By sea-girls wreathed with seaweed red and brown
Till human voices wake us, and we drown.

A COOKING EGG

En l'an trentiesme de mon aage
Que toutes mes hontes j'ay beues . . .

Pipit sate upright in her chair
  Some distance from where I was sitting;
Views of the Oxford Colleges
  Lay on the table, with the knitting.

Daguerreotypes and silhouettes,   5
  Her grandfather and great great aunts,
Supported on the mantelpiece
  An *Invitation to the Dance.*

    .   .   .   .   .

I shall not want Honour in Heaven
  For I shall meet Sir Philip Sidney   10
And have talk with Coriolanus
  And other heroes of that kidney.

I shall not want Capital in Heaven
  For I shall meet Sir Alfred Mond.
We two shall lie together, lapt   15
  In a five per cent. Exchequer Bond.

I shall not want Society in Heaven,
  Lucretia Borgia shall be my Bride;

A Cooking Egg: that is, an egg suitable only for making other dishes in which it is mixed; *En l'an trentiesme* . . . : the epigraph consists of the first two lines of François Villon's "Le Testament." It means, "In my thirtieth year, having drunk all my shames . . ." 1 *Pipit:* a fictional character 10 *Sir Philip Sidney:* the English poet 11 *Coriolanus:* a Roman hero, famed for valor 12 *kidney:* temperament 14 *Sir Alfred Mond:* prominent English industrialist and financier 18 *Lucretia Borgia:* a cultivated Italian noblewoman of the Renaissance

344 *An Anthology of English and American Poems*

Her anecdotes will be more amusing
   Than Pipit's experience could provide.   20

I shall not want Pipit in Heaven:
   Madame Blavatsky will instruct me
In the Seven Sacred Trances;
   Piccarda de Donati will conduct me.

. . . . . .

But where is the penny world I bought   25
   To eat with Pipit behind the screen?
The red-eyed scavengers are creeping
   From Kentish Town and Golder's Green;

Where are the eagles and the trumpets?

   Buried beneath some snow-deep Alps.   30
Over buttered scones and crumpets
   Weeping, weeping multitudes
Droop in a hundred A.B.C.'s

22 *Madame Blavatsky:* practitioner of occult doctrines and leader of the Theosophist Movement 24 *Piccarda de Donati:* the sister of a friend of Dante; she appears in Canto 3 of Dante's *Paradiso,* where she explains that the souls are content with the places they occupy in heaven 28 *Kentish Town* and *Golder's Green:* suburbs of London 29 *A.B.C.'s:* inexpensive tea shops managed by the Aerated Bread Company

John Crowe Ransom

(1888–   )

PARTING, WITHOUT A SEQUEL

She has finished and sealed the letter
At last, which he so richly has deserved,
With characters venomous and hatefully curved,
And nothing could be better.

But even as she gave it   5
Saying to the blue-capped functioner of doom,
'Into his hands,' she hoped the leering groom
Might somewhere lose and leave it.

Then all the blood
Forsook the face. She was too pale for tears,   10
Observing the ruin of her younger years.
She went and stood

Under her father's vaunting oak
Who kept his peace in wind and sun, and glistened
Stoical in the rain; to whom she listened   15
If he spoke.

And now the agitation of the rain
Rasped his sere leaves, and he talked low and gentle
Reproaching the wan daughter by the lintel;
Ceasing and beginning again.   20

Away went the messenger's bicycle,
His serpent's track went up the hill forever,
And all the time she stood there hot as fever
And cold as any icicle.

Archibald MacLeish

(1892–   )

YOU, ANDREW MARVELL

And here face down beneath the sun
And here upon earth's noonward height
To feel the always coming on
The always rising of the night:

You, Andrew Marvell: in "To His Coy
Mistress" Marvell refers to "Time's winged
chariot"

To feel creep up the curving east   5
The earthy chill of dusk and slow
Upon those under lands the vast
And ever climbing shadow grow

And strange at Ecbatan the trees
Take leaf by leaf the evening strange   10
The flooding dark about their knees
The mountains over Persia change

And now at Kermanshah the gate
Dark empty and the withered grass
And through the twilight now the late   15
Few travelers in the westward pass

And Baghdad darken and the bridge
Across the silent river gone
And through Arabia the edge
Of evening widen and steal on   20

And deepen on Palmyra's street
The wheel rut in the ruined stone
And Lebanon fade out and Crete
High through the clouds and overblown

And over Sicily the air   25
Still flashing with the landward gulls
And loom and slowly disappear
The sails above the shadowy hulls

And Spain go under and the shore
Of Africa the gilded sand   30
And evening vanish and no more
The low pale light across that land

Nor now the long light on the sea:

And here face downward in the sun
To feel how swift how secretly   35
The shadows of the night comes on . . .

9 *Ecbatan:* the modern Hamadan, in northwest Iran 13 *Kermanshah:* a province of
Iran 21 *Palmyra:* a town in central Syria

Wilfred Owen

(1893–1918)

ANTHEM FOR DOOMED YOUTH

What passing-bells for these who die as cattle?
Only the monstrous anger of the guns.
Only the stuttering rifles' rapid rattle
Can patter out their hasty orisons.
No mockeries for them from prayers or bells,   5
Nor any voice of mourning save the choirs,—
The shrill, demented choirs of wailing shells;
And bugles calling for them from sad shires.

What candles may be held to speed them all?
Not in the hands of boys, but in their eyes   10
Shall shine the holy glimmers of good-byes.
The pallor of girls' brows shall be their pall;
Their flowers the tenderness of patient minds,
And each slow dusk a drawing-down of blinds.

1 *passing-bells:* the passing-bell is rung at the time
of death 4 *orisons:* prayers

ARMS AND THE BOY

Let the boy try along this bayonet-blade
How cold steel is, and keen with hunger of blood;
Blue with all malice, like a madman's flash;
And thinly drawn with famishing for flesh.

Lend him to stroke these blind, blunt bullet-heads   5
Which long to nuzzle in the hearts of lads,
Or give him cartridges of fine zinc teeth,
Sharp with the sharpness of grief and death.

For his teeth seem for laughing round an apple.
There lurk no claws behind his fingers supple;   10
And God will grow no talons at his heels,
Nor antlers through the thickness of his curls.

E. E. Cummings

(1894–1962)

SINCE FEELING IS FIRST

since feeling is first
who pays any attention
to the syntax of things
will never wholly kiss you;

wholly to be a fool   5
while Spring is in the world

my blood approves,
and kisses are a better fate
than wisdom
lady i swear by all flowers. Don't cry   10
—the best gesture of my brain is less than
your eyelids' flutter which says

we are for each other: then
laugh, leaning back in my arms
for life's not a paragraph   15

And death i think is no parenthesis

I THANK YOU GOD FOR MOST THIS AMAZING

i thank You God for most this amazing
day:for the leaping greenly spirits of trees
and a blue true dream of sky;and for everything
which is natural which is infinite which is yes

(i who have died am alive again today,   5
and this is the sun's birthday;this is the birth
day of life and of love and wings:and of the gay
great happening illimitably earth)

how should tasting touching hearing seeing
breathing any—lifted from the no   10
of all nothing—human merely being
doubt unimaginable You?

(now the ears of my ears awake and
now the eyes of my eyes are opened)

SOMEWHERE I HAVE NEVER TRAVELLED, GLADLY BEYOND

somewhere i have never travelled,gladly beyond
any experience,your eyes have their silence:
in your most frail gesture are things which enclose me,
or which i cannot touch because they are too near

your slightest look easily will unclose me   5
though i have closed myself as fingers,
you open always petal by petal myself as Spring opens
(touching skilfully,mysteriously)her first rose

or if your wish be to close me,i and
my life will shut very beautifully,suddenly,   10
as when the heart of this flower imagines
the snow carefully everywhere descending;

nothing which we are to perceive in this world equals
the power of your intense fragility:whose texture
compels me with the colour of its countries,   15
rendering death and forever with each breathing

(i do not know what it is about you that closes
and opens;only something in me understands
the voice of your eyes is deeper than all roses)
nobody,not even the rain,has such small hands   20

ANYONE LIVED IN A PRETTY HOW TOWN

anyone lived in a pretty how town
(with up so floating many bells down)
spring summer autumn winter
he sang his didn't he danced his did.

Women and men (both little and small)   5
cared for anyone not at all
they sowed their isn't they reaped their same
sun moon stars rain

children guessed (but only a few
and down they forgot as up they grew   10
autumn winter spring summer)
that noone loved him more by more

when by now and tree by leaf
she laughed his joy she cried his grief
bird by snow and stir by still   15
anyone's any was all to her

someones married their everyones
laughed their cryings and did their dance
(sleep wake hope and then) they
said their nevers they slept their dream   20

stars rain sun moon
(and only the snow can begin to explain
how children are apt to forget to remember
with up so floating many bells down)

one day anyone died i guess   25
(and noone stooped to kiss his face)
busy folk buried them side by side
little by little and was by was

all by all and deep by deep
and more by more they dream their sleep   30
noone and anyone earth by april
wish by spirit and if by yes.

Women and men (both dong and ding)
summer autumn winter spring
reaped their sowing and went their came   35
sun moon stars rain

Robert Graves

(1895–   )

THE WORMS OF HISTORY

On the eighth day God died; his bearded mouth
That had been shut so long flew open.
So Adam's too in a dismay like death—
But the world still rolled on around him,
Instinct with all those lesser powers of life   5
That God had groaned against but not annulled.

'All-excellent', Adam had titled God,
And in his mourning now demeaned himself
As if all excellence, not God, had died;
Chose to be governed by those lesser powers,   10
More than inferior to excellence—
The worms astir in God's corrupt flesh.

God died, not excellence his name:
Excellence lived, but only was not God.
It was those lesser powers who played at God,   15
Bloated with Adam's deferential sighs
In mourning for expired divinity;
They reigned as royal monsters upon earth.

Adam grew lean, and wore perpetual black;
He made no reaching after excellence.   20
Eve gave him sorry comfort for his grief
With birth of sons, and mourning still he died.
Adam was buried in one grave with God
And the worms ranged and ravaged in between.

Into their white maws fell abundance   25
Of all things rotten. They were greedy-nosed
To smell the taint out and go scavenging,
Yet over excellence held no domain.
Excellence lives; they are already dead—
The ages of a putrefying corpse.   30

C. Day Lewis

(1904–   )

AS ONE WHO WANDERS INTO OLD WORKINGS

As one who wanders into old workings
Dazed by the noonday, desiring coolness,
Has found retreat barred by fall of rockface;
Gropes through galleries where granite bruises
Taut palm and panic patters close at heel;   5
Must move forward as tide to the moon's nod,
As mouth to breast in blindness is beckoned.
Nightmare nags at his elbow and narrows
Horizon to pinpoint, hope to hand's breadth.
Slow drip the seconds, time is stalactite,   10
For nothing intrudes here to tell the time,
Sun marches not, nor moon with muffled step.
He wants an opening,—only to break out,
To see the dark glass cut by day's diamond,
To relax again in the lap of light.   15

But we seek a new world through old workings,
Whose hope lies like seed in the loins of earth,
Whose dawn draws gold from the roots of darkness.
Not shy of light nor shrinking from shadow
Like Jesuits in jungle we journey   20
Deliberately bearing to brutish tribes
Christ's assurance, arts of agriculture.
As a train that travels underground track
Feels current flashed from far-off dynamos,
Our wheels whirling with impetus elsewhere   25
Generated we run, are ruled by rails.
Train shall spring from tunnel to terminus,
Out on to plain shall the pioneer plunge,
Earth reveal what veins fed, what hill covered.
Lovely the leap, explosion into light.   30

Old Workings: that is, an old mine

Hart Crane

(1899–1932)

THE AIR PLANT

Grand Cayman

This tuft that thrives on saline nothingness,
Inverted octopus with heavenward arms
Thrust parching from a palm-bole hard by the cove—
A bird almost—of almost bird alarms,

Is pulmonary to the wind that jars   5
Its tentacles, horrific in their lurch.
The lizard's throat, held bloated for a fly,
Balloons but warily from this throbbing perch.

The needles and hack-saws of cactus bleed
A milk of earth when stricken off the stalk;   10
But this,—defenseless, thornless, sheds no blood,
Almost no shadow—but the air's thin talk.

Angelic Dynamo! Ventriloquist of the Blue!
While beachward creeps the shark-swept Spanish Main
By what conjunctions do the winds appoint   15
Its apotheosis, at last—the hurricane!

The Air Plant: a plant that derives all its nourishment
from the air, although it usually grows on another plant.

O CARIB ISLE!

The tarantula rattling at the lily's foot
Across the feet of the dead, laid in white sand
Near the coral beach—nor zigzag fiddler crabs
Side-stilting from the path (that shift, subvert

And anagrammatize your name)—No, nothing here   5
Below the palsy that one eucalyptus lifts
In wrinkled shadows—mourns.

                              And yet suppose
I count these nacreous frames of tropic death,
Brutal necklaces of shells around each grave   10
Squared off so carefully. Then

To the white sand I may speak a name, fertile
Albeit in a stranger tongue. Tree names, flower names
Deliberate, gainsay death's brittle crypt. Meanwhile
The wind that knots itself in one great death—   15
Coils and withdraws. So syllables want breath.

But where is the Captain of the doubloon isle
Without a turnstile? Who but catchword crabs
Patrols the dry groins of the underbrush?
What man, or What   20
Is Commissioner of the mildew throughout the am-
        bushed senses?
His Carib mathematics web the eyes' baked lenses!

Under the poinciana, of a noon or afternoon
Let fiery blossoms clot the light, render my ghost
Sieved upward, white and black along the air   25
Until it meets the blue's comedian host.

Let not the pilgrim see himself again
For slow evisceration bound like those huge terrapin
Each daybreak on the wharf, their brine-caked eyes;
—Spiked, overturned; such thunder in their strain!   30

Slagged on the hurricane—I, cast within its flow,
Congeal by afternoons here, satin and vacant.
You have given me the shell, Satan,—carbonic amulet
Sere of the sun exploded in the sea.

Richard Eberhart

(1904–   )

THE GROUNDHOG

In June, amid the golden fields,
I saw a groundhog lying dead.
Dead lay he; my senses shook,
And mind outshot our naked frailty.
There lowly in the vigorous summer   5
His form began its senseless change,
And made my senses waver dim
Seeing nature ferocious in him.
Inspecting close his maggots' might
And seething cauldron of his being,   10
Half with loathing, half with a strange love,
I poked him with an angry stick.
The fever arose, became a flame
And Vigour circumscribed the skies,
Immense energy in the sun,   15
And through my frame a sunless trembling.
My stick had done nor good nor harm.
Then stood I silent in the day
Watching the object, as before;
And kept my reverence for knowledge   20
Trying for control, to be still,
To quell the passion of the blood;
Until I had bent down on my knees
Praying for joy in the sight of decay.
And so I left; and I returned   25
In Autumn strict of eye, to see
The sap gone out of the groundhog,
But the bony sodden hulk remained.
But the year had lost its meaning,
And in intellectual chains   30

I lost both love and loathing,
Mured up in the wall of wisdom.

Another summer took the fields again
Massive and burning, full of life,
But when I chanced upon the spot   35
There was only a little hair left,
And bones bleaching in the sunlight
Beautiful as architecture;
I watched them like a geometer,
And cut a walking stick from a birch.   40
It has been three years, now.
There is no sign of the groundhog.
I stood there in the whirling summer,
My hand capped a withered heart,
And thought of China and of Greece,   45
Of Alexander in his tent;
Of Montaigne in his tower,
Of Saint Theresa in her wild lament.

*S*tanley *K*unitz

(1905–   )

END OF SUMMER

An agitation of the air,
A perturbation of the light
Admonished me the unloved year
Would turn on its hinge that night.

I stood in the disenchanted field   5
Amid the stubble and the stones,
Amazed, while a small worm lisped to me
The song of my marrow-bones.

Blue poured into summer blue,
A hawk broke from his cloudless tower,   10

The roof of the silo blazed, and I knew
That part of my life was over.

Already the iron door of the north
Clangs open: birds, leaves, snows
Order their populations forth,   15
And a cruel wind blows.

APPROACH OF AUTUMN

The early violets we saw together,
Lifting their delicate swift heads
As if to dip them in the water, now wither,
Arching no more like thoroughbreds.

Slender and pale, they flee the rime   5
Of death: the ghosts of violets
Are running in a dream. Heart-flowering time
Decays, green goes, and the eye forgets.

Forgets? But what spring-blooded stock
Sprouts deathless violets in the skull   10
That, pawing on the hard and bitter rock
Of reason, make thinking beautiful?

Robert Penn Warren

(1905–   )

BEARDED OAKS

The oaks, how subtle and marine,
Bearded, and all the layered light
Above them swims; and thus the scene,
Recessed, awaits the positive night.

So, waiting, we in the grass now lie   5
Beneath the languorous tread of light:
The grasses, kelp-like, satisfy
The nameless motions of the air.

Upon the floor of light, and time,
Unmurmuring, of polyp made,   10
We rest; we are, as light withdraws,
Twin atolls on a shelf of shade.

Ages to our construction went,
Dim architecture, hour by hour:
And violence, forgot now, lent   15
The present stillness all its power.

The storm of noon above us rolled,
Of light the fury, furious gold,
The long drag troubling us, the depth:
Dark is unrocking, unrippling, still.   20

Passion and slaughter, ruth, decay
Descend, minutely whispering down,
Silted down swaying streams, to lay
Foundation for our voicelessness.

All our debate is voiceless here,   25
As all our rage, the rage of stone;
If hope is hopeless, then fearless fear,
And history is thus undone.

Our feet once wrought the hollow street
With echo when the lamps were dead   30
At windows, once our headlight glare
Disturbed the doe that, leaping, fled.

I do not love you less that now
The caged heart makes iron stroke,
Or less that all that light once gave   35
The graduate dark should now revoke.

We live in time so little time
And we learn all so painfully,
That we may spare this hour's term
To practice for eternity.   40

Vernon Watkins

(1906–   )

THE MUMMY

His eyes are closed. They are closed. His eyes are closed.
His hands are clenched. They are clenched. His hands are clenched.
The messenger comes. The letters are disciplined; they are disposed.
The black light quivers. Earth on Earth is avenged.

What has left music fast in the sockets of bone?   5
Had all been pattern, images sight had seen,
Blood would lie quiet, but something strokes the light, and a groan
Of great-rooted calm repels those images: nothing they mean.

Nothing here lives but the music in the eyes.
Hunting-scene, warriors, chariot, palm and wing   10
Bid the blood rest, thought perch where the time-bird sings or flies,
Year chasing year, following and following.

But tears wash these bones where parchments whisper to sand.
Here a laid vase offers the flying stream.
Sand darkening wakes a harp-string hidden, plucked by a blind
    hand,   15
Crying this theme to the world, this world-surrounding theme:

Valiant, alive, his voice pursued the lands,
Ruled the white sea, held mountains in his keep.
Leave him with delicate instruments formed for delicate hands;
In this locked room of treasures let him who chose them sleep.   20

I lean down, crying: 'Touch me, lay hold on my Spring,
Reach up, for I have loosened, tearing your skies,
Fountains of light, ages of listening!'
But the bound hands are folded, the fold its word denies.

What shudder of music unfulfilled vibrates?   25
What draws to a dust-grain's fall most distant stars?

In the last taper's light what shadow meditates?
What single, athletic shape never cast on wall or vase?

What shudder of birth and death? What shakes me most?
Job his Maker answering, the Stricken exclaiming 'Rejoice!'   30
Gripping late in the shifting moment giant Earth, making Earth a
    ghost,
Who heard a great friend's death without a change of voice.

THE HERON

The cloud-backed heron will not move:
He stares into the stream.
He stands unfaltering while the gulls
And oyster-catchers scream.
He does not hear, he cannot see   5
The great white horses of the sea,
But fixes eyes on stillness
Below their flying team.

How long will he remain, how long
Have the grey woods been green?   10
The sky and the reflected sky,
Their glass he has not seen,
But silent as a speck of sand
Interpreting the sea and land,
His fall pulls down the fabric   15
Of all that windy scene.

Sailing with clouds and woods behind,
Pausing in leisured flight,
He stepped, alighting on a stone,
Dropped from the stars of night.   20
He stood there unconcerned with day,
Deaf to the tumult of the bay,
Watching a stone in water,
A fish's hidden light.

Sharp rocks drive back the breaking waves,   25
Confusing sea with air.
Bundles of spray blown mountain-high
Have left the shingle bare.
A shipwrecked anchor wedged by rocks,

Loosed by the thundering equinox,   30
Divides the herded waters,
The stallion and his mare.

Yet no distraction breaks the watch
Of that time-killing bird.
He stands unmoving on the stone;   35
Since dawn he has not stirred.
Calamity about him cries,
But he has fixed his golden eyes
On water's crooked tablet,
On light's reflected word.   40

W. H. Auden

(1907–   )

MUSÉE DES BEAUX ARTS

About suffering they were never wrong,
The Old Masters: how well they understood
Its human position; how it takes place
While someone else is eating or opening a window or just walking
    dully along;
How, when the aged are reverently, passionately waiting   5
For the miraculous birth, there always must be
Children who did not specially want it to happen, skating
On a pond at the edge of the wood:
They never forgot
That even the dreadful martryrdom must run its course   10
Anyhow in a corner, some untidy spot
Where the dogs go on with their doggy life and the torturer's horse
Scratches its innocent behind on a tree.

In Brueghel's *Icarus*, for instance: how everything turns away
Quite leisurely from the disaster; the ploughman may   15

14 *Brueghel's Icarus:* a painting by Pieter Brueghel the Elder, a Dutch painter
of the sixteenth century

Have heard the splash, the forsaken cry,
But for him it was not an important failure; the sun shone
As it had to on the white legs disappearing into the green
Water; and the expensive delicate ship that must have seen
Something amazing, a boy falling out of the sky,   20
Had somewhere to get to and sailed calmly on.

VOLTAIRE AT FERNEY

Almost happy now, he looked at his estate.
An exile making watches glanced up as he passed
And went on working; where a hospital was rising fast,
A joiner touched his cap; an agent came to tell
Some of the trees he'd planted were progressing well.   5
The white alps glittered. It was summer. He was very great.

Far off in Paris where his enemies
Whispered that he was wicked, in an upright chair
A blind old woman longed for death and letters. He would write,
"Nothing is better than life." But was it? Yes, the fight   10
Against the false and the unfair
Was always worth it. So was gardening. Civilize.

Cajoling, scolding, scheming, cleverest of them all,
He'd had the other children in a holy war
Against the infamous grown-ups; and, like a child, been sly   15
And humble, when there was occasion for
The two-faced answer or the plain protective lie,
But patient like a peasant, waited for their fall.

And never doubted, like D'Alembert, he would win:
Only Pascal was a great enemy, the rest   20
Were rats already poisoned; there was much, though, to be done,
And only himself to count upon.
Dear Diderot was dull but did his best;
Rousseau, he'd always known, would blubber and give in.

Ferney: the estate to which Voltaire retired in old age 9 *a blind old
woman:* the Marquise Marie du Deffand, a cultivated woman who ex-
changed letters with Voltaire 14 *the other children:* that is, besides
Voltaire himself 19 ff. *D'Alembert, Pascal, Diderot, Rousseau:* leaders
of thought among Voltaire's contemporaries

So, like a sentinel, he could not sleep. The night was full
    of wrong,   25
Earthquakes and executions: Soon he would be dead,
And still all over Europe stood the horrible nurses
Itching to boil their children. Only his verses
Perhaps could stop them: He must go on working. Overhead
The uncomplaining stars composed their lucid song.   30

HERMAN MELVILLE

Towards the end he sailed into an extraordinary mildness,
And anchored in his home and reached his wife
And rode within the harbour of her hand,
And went across each morning to an office
As though his occupation were another island.   5

Goodness existed: that was the new knowledge
His terror had to blow itself quite out
To let him see it; but it was the gale had blown him
Past the Cape Horn of sensible success
Which cries: "This rock is Eden. Shipwreck here."   10

But deafened him with thunder and confused with lightning:
—The maniac hero hunting like a jewel
The rare ambiguous monster that had maimed his sex,
Hatred for hatred ending in a scream,
The unexplained survivor breaking off the nightmare—   15
All that was intricate and false; the truth was simple.

Evil is unspectacular and always human,
And shares our bed and eats at our own table,
And we are introduced to Goodness every day,
Even in drawing-rooms among a crowd of faults;   20
He has a name like Billy and is almost perfect
But wears a stammer like a decoration:
And every time they meet the same thing has to happen;
It is the Evil that is helpless like a lover
And has to pick a quarrel and succeeds,   25
And both are openly destroyed before our eyes.

12 *The maniac hero:* Ahab, the protagonist of Melville's novel
Moby Dick

For now he was awake and knew
No one is ever spared except in dreams;
But there was something else the nightmare had distorted—
Even the punishment was human and a form of love: 30
The howling storm had been his father's presence
And all the time he had been carried on his father's breast.

Who now had set him gently down and left him.
He stood upon the narrow balcony and listened:
And all the stars above him sang as in his childhood   35
"All, all is vanity," but it was not the same;
For now the words descended like the calm of mountains—
—Nathaniel had been shy because his love was selfish—
But now he cried in exultation and surrender
"The Godhead is broken like bread. We are the pieces."   40

And sat down at his desk and wrote a story.

38 *Nathaniel:* Hawthorne, a friend of Melville's, who lived near
him while he was writing *Moby Dick*

Louis MacNeice

(1907–   )

SCHIZOPHRENE

Hearing offstage the taps filling the bath
The set dissolves to childhood—in her cot
Hearing that ominous relentless noise
Which the grown-ups have started, who are not
She knows, aware of what it means; it means   5
The Dark, the Flood, the Malice. It destroys
All other meanings—dolls or gingerbread;
It means a Will that wills all children dead.

Hearing the gasfire breathe monotonously
She waits for words but no words come, she lifts   10

A soapstone hand to smooth her hair and feels
The hand is someone else's—the scene shifts
To a cold desert where the wind has dropped
And the earth's movement stopped and something steals
Up from the grit through nerve and bone and vein   15
To flaunt its iron tendrils in her brain.

Hearing again the telegraph wires again
Humming again and always, she must lean
Against the humming post and search her mind
For what it is they say; in some latrine   20
She knows she wrote it first upon the wall
In self-incrimination, duly signed;
And, unrevoked since then, that signature
Runs round the world on wires, accusing her.

Hearing the church-bells too, she knows at once   25
That only she can hear them for it is no
Church or even belfry where they hang,
There are no ropes attached or ringers down below,
These bells are disembodied, they express
The claims of frozen Chaos and will clang   30
Till this and every other world shall melt
And Chaos be Itself and nothing felt.

Lastly, hearing the cock in the grey dawn
Crow once, crow twice, she shivers and dissolves
To someone else who in the hour of trial   35
Denied his Master and his guilt devolves
On her head only. If she could speak up,
She might even now atone for that denial
But the grey cock still crows and she knows why;
For she must still deny, deny, deny.   40

35 *someone else:* an allusion to the denial of Christ by Peter

DEATH OF AN ACTRESS

I see from the paper that Florrie Forde is dead—
Collapsed after singing to wounded soldiers,
At the age of sixty-five. The American notice
Says no doubt all that need be said

About this one-time chorus girl; whose rôle   5
For more than forty stifling years was giving
Sexual, sentimental, or comic entertainment,
A gaudy posy for the popular soul.

Plush and cigars: she waddled into the lights,
Old and huge and painted, in velvet and tiara,   10
Her voice gone but around her head an aura
Of all her vanilla-sweet forgotten vaudeville nights.

With an elephantine shimmy and a sugared wink
She threw a trellis of Dorothy Perkins roses
Around an audience come from slum and suburb   15
And weary of the tea-leaves in the sink;

Who found her songs a rainbow leading west
To the home they never had, to the chocolate Sunday
Of boy and girl, to cowslip time, to the never-
Ending weekend Islands of the Blest.   20

In the Isle of Man before the war before
The present one she made a ragtime favourite
Of 'Tipperary', which became the swan-song
Of troop-ships on a darkened shore;

And during Munich sang her ancient quiz   25
Of *Where's Bill Bailey?* and the chorus answered,
Muddling through and glad to have no answer:
Where's Bill Bailey? How do *we* know where he is!

Now on a late and bandaged April day
In a military hospital Miss Florrie   30
Forde has made her positively last appearance
And taken her bow and gone correctly away.

Correctly. For she stood
For an older England, for children toddling
Hand in hand while the day was bright. Let the wren and robin   35
Gently with leaves cover the Babes in the Wood.

Theodore Roethke

(1908–1963)

THE ADAMANT

Thought does not crush to stone.
The great sledge drops in vain.
Truth never is undone;
Its shafts remain.

The teeth of knitted gears   5
Turn slowly through the night,
But the true substance bears
The hammer's weight.

Compression cannot break
A center so congealed;   10
The tool can chip no flake:
The core lies sealed.

EPIDERMAL MACABRE

Indelicate is he who loathes
The aspect of his fleshy clothes,—
The flying fabric stitched on bone,
The vesture of the skeleton,
The garment neither fur nor hair,   5
The cloak of evil and despair,
The veil long violated by
Caresses of the hand and eye.
Yet such is my unseemliness:
I hate my epidermal dress,   10
The savage blood's obscenity,
The rags of my anatomy,
And willingly would I dispense
With false accouterments of sense,
To sleep immodestly, a most   15
Incarnadine and carnal ghost.

DOLOR

I have known the inexorable sadness of pencils,
Neat in their boxes, dolor of pad and paper-weight,
All the misery of manilla folders and mucilage,
Desolation in immaculate public places,
Lonely reception room, lavatory, switchboard,   5
The unalterable pathos of basin and pitcher,
Ritual of multigraph, paper-clip, comma,
Endless duplication of lives and objects.
And I have seen dust from the walls of institutions,
Finer than flour, alive, more dangerous than silica,   10
Sift, almost invisible, through long afternoons of tedium,
Dropping a fine film on nails and delicate eyebrows,
Glazing the pale hair, the duplicate gray standard faces.

THE WAKING

I wake to sleep, and take my waking slow.
I feel my fate in what I cannot fear.
I learn by going where I have to go.

We think by feeling. What is there to know?
I hear my being dance from ear to ear.   5
I wake to sleep, and take my waking slow.

Of those so close beside me, which are you?
God bless the Ground! I shall walk softly there,
And learn by going where I have to go.

Light takes the Tree; but who can tell us how?   10
The lowly worm climbs up a winding stair;
I wake to sleep, and take my waking slow.

Great Nature has another thing to do
To you and me; so take the lively air,
And, lovely, learn by going where to go.   15

This shaking keeps me steady. I should know.
What falls away is always. And is near.
I wake to sleep, and take my waking slow.
I learn by going where I have to go.

Stephen Spender

(1909–   )

AN ELEMENTARY SCHOOL CLASSROOM
IN A SLUM

Far far from gusty waves these children's faces.
Like rootless weeds, the hair torn round their pallor.
The tall girl with her weighed-down head. The paper-
seeming boy, with rat's eyes. The stunted, unlucky heir
Of twisted bones, reciting a father's gnarled disease,   5
His lesson from his desk. At back of the dim class
One unnoted, sweet and young. His eyes live in a dream
Of squirrel's game, in tree room, other than this.

On sour cream walls, donations. Shakespeare's head,
Cloudless at dawn, civilized dome riding all cities.   10
Belled, flowery, Tyrolese valley. Open-handed map
Awarding the world its world. And yet, for these
Children, these windows, not this world, are world,
Where all their future's painted with a fog,
A narrow street sealed in with a lead sky,   15
Far far from rivers, capes, and stars of words.

Surely, Shakespeare is wicked, the map a bad example
With ships and sun and love tempting them to steal—
For lives that slyly turn in their cramped holes
From fog to endless night? On their slag heap, these children   20
Wear skins peeped through by bones and spectacles of steel
With mended glass, like bottle bits on stones.
All of their time and space are foggy slum.
So blot their maps with slums as big as doom.

Unless, governor, teacher, inspector, visitor,   25
This map becomes their window and these windows
That shut upon their lives like catacombs,
Break O break open till they break the town

And show the children to green fields, and make their world
Run azure on gold sands, and let their tongues   30
Run naked into books, the white and green leaves open
History theirs whose language is the sun.

TWO ARMIES

Deep in the winter plain, two armies
Dig their machinery, to destroy each other.
Men freeze and hunger. No one is given leave
On either side, except the dead, and wounded.
These have their leave; while new battalions wait   5
On time at last to bring them violent peace.

All have become so nervous and so cold
That each man hates the cause and distant words
That brought him here, more terribly than bullets.
Once a boy hummed a popular marching song,   10
Once a novice hand flapped their salute;
The voice was choked, the lifted hand fell,
Shot through the wrist by those of his own side.

From their numb harvest, all would flee, except
For discipline drilled once in an iron school   15
Which holds them at the point of the revolver.
Yet when they sleep, the images of home
Ride wishing horses of escape
Which herd the plain in a mass unspoken poem.

Finally, they cease to hate: for although hate   20
Bursts from the air and whips the earth with hail
Or shoots it up in fountains to marvel at,
And although hundreds fall, who can connect
The inexhaustible anger of the guns
With the dumb patience of those tormented animals?   25

Clean silence drops at night, when a little walk
Divides the sleeping armies, each
Huddled in linen woven by remote hands.
When the machines are stilled, a common suffering
Whitens the air with breath and makes both one   30
As though these enemies slept in each other's arms.

Only the lucid friend to aerial raiders,
The brilliant pilot moon, stares down
Upon this plain she makes a shining bone
Cut by the shadows of many thousand bones.   35
Where amber clouds scatter on No-Man's-Land
She regards death and time throw up
The furious words and minerals which destroy.

PORT BOU

As a child holds a pet
Arms clutching but with hands that do not join
And the coiled animal looks through the gap
To outer freedom animal air,
So the earth-and-rock arms of this small harbour   5
Embrace but do not encircle the sea
Which, through a gap, vibrates into the ocean,
Where dolphins swim and liners throb.
In the bright winter sunlight I sit on the parapet
Of a bridge; my circling arms rest on a newspaper   10
And my mind is empty as the glittering stone
While I search for an image
(The one written above) and the words (written above)
To set down the childish headlands of Port Bou.
A lorry halts beside me with creaking brakes   15
And I look up at warm downwards-looking faces
Of militia men staring at my (French) newspaper.
'How do they write of our struggle over the frontier?'
I hold out the paper, but they cannot read it,
They want speech and to offer cigarettes.   20
In their waving flag-like faces the war finds peace. The famished
      mouths
Of rusted carbines lean against their knees,
Like leaning, rust-coloured, fragile reeds.
Wrapped in cloth—old granny in a shawl—
The stuttering machine-gun rests.   25
They shout—salute back as the truck jerks forward
Over the vigorous hill, beyond the headland.
An old man passes, his mouth dribbling,
From three rusted teeth, he shoots out: 'pom-pom-pom'.

The children run after; and, more slowly, the women;   30
Clutching their skirts, trail over the horizon.
Now Port Bou is empty, for the firing practice.
I am left alone on the parapet at the exact centre
Above the river trickling through the gulley, like that old man's
    saliva.
The exact centre, solitary as the bull's eye in a target.   35
Nothing moves against the background of stage-scenery houses
Save the skirring mongrels. The firing now begins
Across the harbour mouth, from headland to headland,
White flecks of foam whipped by lead from the sea.
An echo spreads its cat-o'-nine tails   40
Thrashing the flanks of neighbour hills.
My circling arms rest on the newspaper,
My mind is paper on which dust and words sift,
I assure myself the shooting is only for practice
But I am the coward of cowards. The machine-gun stitches   45
My intestines with a needle, back and forth;
The solitary, spasmodic, white puffs from the carbines
Draw fear in white threads back and forth through my body.

$\mathcal{E}$lizabeth $\mathcal{B}$ishop

(1911–   )

THE FISH

I caught a tremendous fish
and held him beside the boat
half out of water, with my hook
fast in a corner of his mouth.
He didn't fight.   5
He hadn't fought at all.
He hung a grunting weight,
battered and venerable
and homely. Here and there
his brown skin hung in strips   10

like ancient wall-paper,
and its pattern of darker brown
was like wall-paper:
shapes like full-blown roses
stained and lost through age.   15
He was speckled with barnacles,
fine rosettes of lime,
and infested
with tiny white sea-lice,
and underneath two or three   20
rags of green weed hung down.
While his gills were breathing in
the terrible oxygen
—the frightening gills
fresh and crisp with blood,   25
that can cut so badly—
I thought of the coarse white flesh
packed in like feathers,
the big bones and the little bones,
the dramatic reds and blacks   30
of his shiny entrails,
and the pink swim-bladder
like a big peony.
I looked into his eyes
which were far larger than mine   35
but shallower, and yellowed,
the irises backed and packed
with tarnished tinfoil
seen through the lenses
of old scratched isinglass.   40
They shifted a little, but not
to return my stare.
—It was more like the tipping
of an object toward the light.
I admired his sullen face,   45
the mechanism of his jaw,
and then I saw
that from his lower lip
—if you could call it a lip—
grim, wet, and weapon-like,   50
hung five old pieces of fish-line,
or four and a wire leader

with the swivel still attached,
with all their five big hooks
grown firmly in his mouth.   55
A green line, frayed at the end
where he broke it, two heavier lines,
and a fine black thread
still crimped from the strain and snap
when it broke and he got away.   60
Like medals with their ribbons
frayed and wavering,
a five-haired beard of wisdom
trailing from his aching jaw.
I stared and stared   65
and victory filled up
the little rented boat,
from the pool of bilge
where oil had spread a rainbow
around the rusted engine   70
to the bailer rusted orange,
the sun-cracked thwarts,
the oarlocks on their strings,
the gunnels—until everything
was rainbow, rainbow, rainbow!   75
And I let the fish go.

Josephine Miles

(1911–   )

MONKEY

God, a man at Yale, adopted a monkey
In order to raise him up in his own image,
But only in some respects could the monk identify,
Could learn manners, but not the word of God.

1 *God, a man at Yale:* an allusion to a book by William
F. Buckley, *God and Man at Yale*

Ah, always it was so, meditated the monkey dazzled
        and befuddled,   5
Out of my tree I fell in the forest of Eden,
Or if I mannerly ate, it was the wrong apple,
Or if I climbed I died.

And this is all, I guess, a semantical series
Of my ascent and fall.   10
His tree is not my tree, His word, my word;
His Yale, my Yale.

Karl Shapiro

(1913–   )

BUICK

As a sloop with a sweep of immaculate wing on her delicate spine
And a keel as steel as a root that holds in the sea as she leans,
Leaning and laughing, my warm-hearted beauty, you ride, you ride,
You tack on the curves with parabola speed and a kiss of goodbye,
Like a thoroughbred sloop, my new high-spirited spirit, my kiss.   5

As my foot suggests that you leap in the air with your hips of a girl,
My finger that praises your wheel and announces your voices of song,
Flouncing your skirts, you blueness of joy, you flirt of politeness,
You leap, you intelligence, essence of wheelness with silvery nose,
And your platinum clocks of excitement stir like the hairs of a fern.   10

But how alien you are from the blooming belts of your birth and the
        smoke
Where you turned on the stinging lathes of Detroit and Lansing
        at night
And shrieked at the torch in your secret parts and the amorous tests,
But now with your eyes that enter the future of roads you forget;
You are all instinct with your phosphorous glow and your streaking
        hair.   15

And now when we stop it is not as the bird from the shell that I leave
Or the leathery pilot who steps from his bird with a sneer of delight,
And not as the ignorant beast do you squat and watch me depart,
But with exquisite breathing you smile, with satisfaction of love,
And I touch you again as you tick in the silence and settle in sleep. 20

Lawrence Durrell

(1914–   )

'JE EST UN AUTRE'
—Rimbaud

He is the man who makes notes,
The observer in the tall black hat,
Face hidden in the brim:
In three European cities
He has watched me watching him.   5

The street-corner in Buda and after
By the post-office a glimpse
Of the disappearing tails of his coat,
Gave the same illumination, spied upon,
The tightness in the throat.   10

Once too meeting by the Seine
The waters a moving floor of stars,
He had vanished when I reached the door,
But there on the pavement burning
Lay one of his familiar black cigars.   15

The meeting on the dark stairway
Where the tide ran clean as a loom:
The betrayal of her, her kisses

"Je Est Un Autre": a deliberately ungrammatical
sentence from a letter by the French poet Arthur
Rimbaud. Its translation would be "I is another
person."

He has witnessed them all: often
I hear him laughing in the other room.   20

He watches me now, working late,
Bringing a poem to life, his eyes
Reflect the malady of De Nerval:
O useless in this old house to question
The mirrors, his impenetrable disguise.   25

23 *De Nerval:* Gérard de Nerval (1808–1855),
a highly original and eccentric French poet

*R*andall *J*arrell

(1914–1965)

THE ORIENT EXPRESS

One looks from the train
Almost as one looked as a child. In the sunlight
What I see still seems to me plain,
I am safe; but at evening
As the lands darken, a questioning   5
Precariousness comes over everything.

Once after a day of rain
I lay longing to be cold; and after a while
I was cold again, and hunched shivering
Under the quilt's many colors, gray   10
With the dull ending of the winter day.
Outside me there were a few shapes
Of chairs and tables, things from a primer;
Outside the window
There were the chairs and tables of the world. . . .   15
I saw that the world
That had seemed to me the plain
Gray mask of all that was strange
Behind it—of all that *was*—was all   20

But it is beyond belief.
One thinks, "Behind everything
An unforced joy, an unwilling

Sadness (a willing sadness, a forced joy)
Moves changelessly"; one looks from the train   25
And there is something, the same thing
Behind everything: all these little villages,
A passing woman, a field of grain,
The man who says good-bye to his wife—
A path through a wood all full of lives, and the train   30
Passing, after all unchangeable
And not now ever to stop, like a heart—

It is like any other work of art.
It is and never can be changed.
Behind everything there is always   35
The unknown unwanted life.

THE LONELY MAN

A cat sits on the pavement by the house.
It lets itself be touched, then slides away.
A girl goes by in a hood; the winter noon's
Long shadows lengthen. The cat is gray,
It sits there. It sits there all day, every day.   5

A collie bounds into my arms: he is a dog
And, therefore, finds nothing human alien.
He lives at the preacher's with a pair of cats.
The soft half-Persian sidles to me;
Indoors, the old white one watches blindly.   10

How cold it is! Some snow slides from a roof
When a squirrel jumps off it to a squirrel-proof
Feeding-station; and, a lot and two yards down,
A fat spaniel snuffles out to me
And sobers me with his untrusting frown.   15

He worries about his yard: past it, it's my affair
If I halt Earth in her track—his duty's done.
And the cat and the collie worry about the old one:
They come, when she's out too, so uncertainly. . . .
It's my block; I know them, just as they know me.   20

As for the others, those who wake up every day
And feed these, keep the houses, ride away
To work—I don't know them, they don't know me.
Are we friends or enemies? Why, who can say?
We nod to each other sometimes, in humanity,   25

Or search one another's faces with a yearning
Remnant of faith that's almost animal. . . .
The gray cat that just sits there: surely it is learning
To be a man; will find, soon, *some especial*
Opening in a good firm for a former cat.   30

Henry Reed

(1914–   )

JUDGING DISTANCES

Not only how far away, but the way that you say it
Is very important. Perhaps you may never get
The knack of judging a distance, but at least you know
How to report on a landscape: the central sector,
The right of arc and that, which we had last Tuesday,   5
    And at least you know

That maps are of time, not place, so far as the army
Happens to be concerned—the reason being,
Is one which need not delay us. Again, you know
There are three kinds of tree, three only, the fir and the poplar   10
And those which have bushy tops too; and lastly
    That things only seem to be things.

A barn is not called a barn, to put it more plainly,
Or a field in the distance, where sheep may be safely grazing.
You must never be over-sure. You must say, when reporting: 15
At five o'clock in the central sector is a dozen
Of what appear to be animals; whatever you do,
    Don't call the bleeders *sheep.*

I am sure that's quite clear; and suppose, for the sake of
  example,
The one at the end, asleep, endeavours to tell us   20
What he sees over there to the west, and how far away,
After first having come to attention. There to the west,
On the fields of summer the sun and the shadows bestow
  Vestments of purple and gold.

The still white dwellings are like a mirage in the heat,   25
And under the swaying elms a man and a woman
Lie gently together. Which is, perhaps, only to say
That there is a row of houses to the left of arc,
And that under some poplars a pair of what appear to be humans
  Appear to be loving.   30

Well that, for an answer, is what we might rightly call
Moderately satisfactory only, the reason being,
Is that two things have been omitted, and those are important.
The human beings, now: in what direction are they,
And how far away, would you say? And do not forget   35
  There may be dead ground in between.

There may be dead ground in between; and I may not have got
The knack of judging a distance; I will only venture
A guess that perhaps between me and the apparent lovers,
(Who, incidentally, appear by now to have finished,)   40
At seven o'clock from the houses, is roughly a distance
  Of about one year and a half.

Dylan Thomas

(1914–1953)

THE FORCE THAT THROUGH THE GREEN FUSE DRIVES THE FLOWER

The force that through the green fuse drives the flower
Drives my green age; that blasts the roots of trees
Is my destroyer.

And I am dumb to tell the crooked rose
My youth is bent by the same wintry fever. 5

The force that drives the water through the rocks
Drives my red blood; that dries the mouthing streams
Turns mine to wax.
And I am dumb to mouth unto my veins
How at the mountain spring the same mouth sucks. 10

The hand that whirls the water in the pool
Stirs the quicksand; that ropes the blowing wind
Hauls my shroud sail.
And I am dumb to tell the hanging man
How of my clay is made the hangman's lime. 15

The lips of time leech to the fountain head;
Love drips and gathers, but the fallen blood
Shall calm her sores.
And I am dumb to tell a weather's wind
How time has ticked a heaven round the stars. 20

And I am dumb to tell the lover's tomb
How at my sheet goes the same crooked worm.

THE HUNCHBACK IN THE PARK

The hunchback in the park
A solitary mister
Propped between trees and water
From the opening of the garden lock
That lets the trees and water enter 5
Until the Sunday sombre bell at dark

Eating bread from a newspaper
Drinking water from the chained cup
That the children filled with gravel
In the fountain basin where I sailed my ship 10
Slept at night in a dog kennel
But nobody chained him up.

Like the park birds he came early
Like the water he sat down
And Mister they called Hey mister 15
The truant boys from the town

Running when he had heard them clearly
On out of sound

Past lake and rockery
Laughing when he shook his paper   20
Hunchbacked in mockery
Through the loud zoo of the willow groves
Dodging the park keeper
With his stick that picked up leaves.

And the old dog sleeper   25
Alone between nurses and swans
While the boys among willows
Made the tigers jump out of their eyes
To roar on the rockery stones
And the groves were blue with sailors   30

Made all day until bell time
A woman figure without fault
Straight as a young elm
Straight and tall from his crooked bones
That she might stand in the night   35
After the locks and chains

All night in the unmade park
After the railings and shrubberies
The birds the grass the trees the lake
And the wild boys innocent as strawberries   40
Had followed the hunchback
To his kennel in the dark.

A REFUSAL TO MOURN THE DEATH,
BY FIRE, OF A CHILD IN LONDON

Never until the mankind making
Bird beast and flower
Fathering and all humbling darkness
Tells with silence the last light breaking
And the still hour   5
Is come of the sea tumbling in harness

And I must enter again the round
Zion of the water bead
And the synagogue of the ear of corn
Shall I let pray the shadow of a sound   10
Or sow my salt seed
In the least valley of sackcloth to mourn

The majesty and burning of the child's death.
I shall not murder
The mankind of her going with a grave truth   15
Nor blaspheme down the stations of the breath
With any further
Elegy of innocence and youth.

Deep with the first dead lies London's daughter,
Robed in the long friends,   20
The grains beyond age, the dark veins of her mother,
Secret by the unmourning water
Of the riding Thames.
After the first death, there is no other.

POEM IN OCTOBER

It was my thirtieth year to heaven
Woke to my hearing from harbour and neighbour wood
And the mussel pooled and the heron
Priested shore
The morning beckon   5
With water praying and call of seagull and rook
And the knock of sailing boats on the net-webbed wall
Myself to set foot
That second
In the still sleeping town and set forth.   10

My birthday began with the water—
Birds and the birds of the winged trees flying my name
Above the farms and the white horses
And I rose
In rainy autumn   15
And walked abroad in a shower of all my days.

High tide and the heron dived when I took the road
        Over the border
          And the gates
    Of the town closed as the town awoke.   20

    A springful of larks in a rolling
Cloud and the roadside bushes brimming with whistling
    Blackbirds and the sun of October
        Summery
       On the hill's shoulder,   25
Here were fond climates and sweet singers suddenly
Come in the morning where I wandered and listened
      To the rain wringing
       Wind blow cold
    In the wood faraway under me.   30

    Pale rain over the dwindling harbour
And over the sea wet church the size of a snail
    With its horns through mist and the castle
       Brown as owls
      But all the gardens   35
Of spring and summer were blooming in the tall tales
Beyond the border and under the lark full cloud.
      There could I marvel
       My birthday
    Away but the weather turned around.   40

    It turned away from the blithe country
And down the other air and the blue altered sky
    Streamed again a wonder of summer
       With apples
      Pears and red currants,   45
And I saw in the turning so clearly a child's
Forgotten mornings when he walked with his mother
      Through the parables
       Of sun light
    And the legends of the green chapels   50

    And the twice told fields of infancy
That his tears burned my cheeks and his heart moved in
    mine.
      These were the woods the river and sea
       Where a boy

                    In the listening   55
        Summertime of the dead whispered the truth of his joy
        To the trees and the stones and the fish in the tide.
                    And the mystery
                        Sang alive
            Still in the water and singing birds.   60

                And there could I marvel my birthday
        Away but the weather turned around. And the true
                Joy of the long dead child sang burning
                        In the sun.
                It was my thirtieth   65
        Year to heaven stood there then in the summer noon
        Though the town below lay leaved with October blood.
                O may my heart's truth
                        Still be sung
            On this high hill in a year's turning.

ON THE MARRIAGE OF A VIRGIN

Waking alone in a multitude of loves when morning's light
Surprised in the opening of her nightlong eyes
His golden yesterday asleep upon the iris
And this day's sun leapt up the sky out of her thighs
Was miraculous virginity old as loaves and fishes,   5
Though the moment of a miracle is unending lightning
And the shipyards of Galilee's footprints hide a navy of doves.

No longer will the vibrations of the sun desire on
Her deepsea pillow where once she married alone,
Her heart all ears and eyes, lips catching the avalanche   10
Of the golden ghost who ringed with his streams her mercury bone,
Who under the lids of her windows hoisted his golden luggage,
For a man sleeps where fire leapt down and she learns through his arm
That other sun, the jealous coursing of the unrivalled blood.

John Manifold
(1915–   )

FIFE TUNE

(6/8) for Sixth Platoon, 308th I.T.C.

One morning in spring
We marched from Devizes
All shapes and all sizes
Like beads on a string,
But yet with a swing   5
We trod the bluemetal
And full of high fettle
We started to sing.

She ran down the stair
A twelve-year-old darling   10
And laughing and calling
She tossed her bright hair;
Then silent to stare
At the men flowing past her—
There were all she could master   15
Adoring her there.

It's seldom I'll see
A sweeter or prettier;
I doubt we'll forget her
In two years or three.   20
And lucky he'll be
She takes for a lover
While we are far over
The treacherous sea.

2 *Devizes:* a town in Wiltshire,
England

John Betjeman

(1916–   )

IN WESTMINSTER ABBEY

Let me take this other glove off
  As the *vox humana* swells,
And the beauteous fields of Eden
  Bask beneath the Abbey bells.
Here, where England's statesmen lie,   5
Listen to a lady's cry.

Gracious Lord, oh bomb the Germans.
  Spare their women for Thy Sake,
And if that is not too easy
  We will pardon Thy Mistake.   10
But, gracious Lord, whate'er shall be,
Don't let anyone bomb me.

Keep our Empire undismembered
  Guide our Forces by Thy Hand,
Gallant blacks from far Jamaica,   15
    Honduras and Togoland;
Protect them Lord in all their fights,
And, even more, protect the whites.

Think of what our Nation stands for,
  Books from Boots' and country lanes,   20
Free speech, free passes, class distinction,
  Democracy and proper drains.
Lord, put beneath Thy special care
One-eighty-nine Cadogan Square.

Although dear Lord I am a sinner,   25
  I have done no major crime;
Now I'll come to Evening Service

20 *Boots'*: a chain of drugstores in Britain

Whensoever I have the time.
So, Lord, reserve for me a crown,
And do not let my shares go down.   30

I will labour for Thy Kingdom,
  Help our lads to win the war,
Send white feathers to the cowards
  Join the Women's Army Corps,
Then wash the Steps around Thy Throne   35
In the Eternal Safety Zone.

Now I feel a little better,
  What a treat to hear Thy Word,
Where the bones of leading statesmen,
  Have so often been interr'd.   40
And now, dear Lord, I cannot wait
Because I have a luncheon date.

*R*obert *L*owell

(1917–   )

THE CRUCIFIX

How dry time screaks in its fat axle-grease,
As spare November strikes us through the ice
And the Leviathan breaks water in the rice
Fields, at the poles, at the hot gates to Greece;
It's time: the old unmastered lion roars   5
And ramps like a mad dog outside the doors,
Snapping at gobbets in my thumbless hand.
The seaways lurch through Sodom's knees of sand
Tomorrow. We are sinking. "Run, rat, run,"

3 *Leviathan:* a sea monster mentioned in the Bible 4 *at the
hot gates:* Thermopylae, where a small, heroic force of
Spartans met an army of invading Persians

The prophets thunder, and I run upon   10
My father, Adam. Adam, if our land
Become the desolation of a hand
That shakes the Temple back to clay, how can
War ever change my old into new man?
Get out from under my feet, old man. Let me pass;   15
On Ninth Street, through the Hallowe'en's soaped glass,
I picked at an old bone on two crossed sticks
And found, to *Via et Vita et Veritas*
A stray dog's signpost is a crucifix.

18 *Via et Vita et Veritas:* the Way, the Life, and the Truth

AS A PLANE TREE BY THE WATER

Darkness has called to darkness, and disgrace
Elbows about our windows in this planned
Babel of Boston where our money talks
And multiplies the darkness of a land
Of preparation where the Virgin walks   5
And roses spiral her enamelled face
Or fall to splinters on unwatered streets.
Our Lady of Babylon, go by, go by,
I was once the apple of your eye;
Flies, flies are on the plane tree, on the streets.   10

The flies, the flies, the flies of Babylon
Buzz in my ear-drums while the devil's long
Dirge of the people detonates the hour
For floating cities where his golden tongue
Enchants the masons of the Babel Tower   15
To raise tomorrow's city to the sun
That never sets upon these hell-fire streets
Of Boston, where the sunlight is a sword
Striking at the withholder of the Lord:
Flies, flies are on the plane tree, on the streets.   20

Flies strike the miraculous waters of the iced
Atlantic and the eyes of Bernadette

22 *Bernadette:* St. Bernadette, who had a vision of
the Virgin

Who saw Our Lady standing in the cave
At Massabielle, saw her so squarely that
Her vision put out reason's eyes. The grave   25
Is open-mouthed and swallowed up in Christ.
O walls of Jericho! And all the streets
To our Atlantic wall are singing: "Sing,
Sing for the resurrection of the King."
Flies, flies are on the plane tree, on the streets.   30

Howard Nemerov

(1920–   )

THE SNOW GLOBE

A long time ago, when I was a child,
They left my light on while I went to sleep,
As though they would have wanted me beguiled
By brightness if at all; dark was too deep.

And they left me one toy, a village white   5
With the fresh snow and silently in glass
Frozen forever. But if you shook it,
The snow would rise up in the rounded space

And from the limits of the universe
Snow itself down again. O world of white,   10
First home of dreams! Now that I have my dead,
I want so cold an emblem to rehearse
How many of them have gone from the world's light,
As I have gone, too, from my snowy bed.

WRITING

The cursive crawl, the squared-off characters,
these by themselves delight, even without
a meaning, in a foreign language, in
Chinese, for instance, or when skaters curve

all day across the lake, scoring their white   5
records in ice. Being intelligible,
these winding ways with their audacities
and delicate hesitations, they become
miraculous, so intimately, out there
at the pen's point or brush's tip, do world   10
and spirit wed. The small bones of the wrist
balance against great skeletons of stars
exactly; the blind bat surveys his way
by echo alone. Still, the point of style
is character. The universe induces   15
a different tremor in every hand, from the
check-forger's to that of the Emperor
Hui Tsung, who called his own calligraphy
the 'Slender Gold.' A nervous man
writes nervously of a nervous world, and so on.   20

Miraculous. It is as though the world
were a great writing. Having said so much,
let us allow there is more to the world
than writing; continental faults are not
bare convoluted fissures in the brain.   25
Not only must the skaters soon go home;
also the hard inscription of their skates
is scored across the open water, which long
remembers nothing, neither wind nor wake.

*R*ichard *W*ilbur
(1921–   )

MIND

Mind in its purest play is like some bat
That beats about in caverns all alone,
Contriving by a kind of senseless wit
Not to conclude against a wall of stone.

It has no need to falter or explore;   5
Darkly it knows what obstacles are there,
And so may weave and flitter, dip and soar
In perfect courses through the blackest air.

And has this simile a like perfection?
The mind is like a bat. Precisely. Save   10
That in the very happiest intellection
A graceful error may correct the cave.

THE PARDON

My dog lay dead five days without a grave
In the thick of summer, hid in a clump of pine
And a jungle of grass and honeysuckle-vine.
I who had loved him while he kept alive

Went only close enough to where he was   5
To sniff the heavy honeysuckle-smell
Twined with another odor heavier still
And hear the flies' intolerable buzz.

Well, I was ten and very much afraid.
In my kind world the dead were out of range   10
And I could not forgive the sad or strange
In beast or man. My father took the spade

And buried him. Last night I saw the grass
Slowly divide (it was the same scene
But now it glowed a fierce and mortal green)   15
And saw the dog emerging. I confess

I felt afraid again, but still he came
In the carnal sun, clothed in a hymn of flies,
And death was breeding in his lively eyes.
I started in to cry and call his name,   20

Asking forgiveness of his tongueless head.
. . . I dreamt the past was never past redeeming:
But whether this was false or honest dreaming
I beg death's pardon now. And mourn the dead.

W. D. Snodgrass

(1926–   )

APRIL INVENTORY

The green catalpa tree has turned
All white; the cherry blooms once more.
In one whole year I haven't learned
A blessed thing they pay you for.
The blossoms snow down in my hair;   5
The trees and I will soon be bare.

The trees have more than I to spare.
The sleek, expensive girls I teach,
Younger and pinker every year,
Bloom gradually out of reach.   10
The pear tree lets its petals drop
Like dandruff on a tabletop.

The girls have grown so young by now
I have to nudge myself to stare.
This year they smile and mind me how   15
My teeth are falling with my hair.
In thirty years I may not get
Younger, shrewder, or out of debt.

The tenth time, just a year ago,
I made myself a little list   20
Of all the things I'd ought to know,
Then told my parents, analyst,
And everyone who's trusted me
I'd be substantial, presently.

I haven't read one book about   25
A book or memorized one plot.
Or found a mind I did not doubt.
I learned one date. And then forgot.

And one by one the solid scholars
Get the degrees, the jobs, the dollars.   30

And smile above their starchy collars.
I taught my classes Whitehead's notions;
One lovely girl, a song of Mahler's.
Lacking a source-book or promotions,
I showed one child the colors of   35
A luna moth and how to love.

I taught myself to name my name,
To bark back, loosen love and crying;
To ease my woman so she came,
To ease an old man who was dying.   40
I have not learned how often I
Can win, can love, but choose to die.

I have not learned there is a lie
Love shall be blonder, slimmer, younger;
That my equivocating eye   45
Loves only by my body's hunger;
That I have forces, true to feel,
Or that the lovely world is real.

While scholars speak authority
And wear their ulcers on their sleeves,   50
My eyes in spectacles shall see
These trees procure and spend their leaves.
There is a value underneath
The gold and silver in my teeth.

Though trees turn bare and girls turn wives,   55
We shall afford our costly seasons;
There is a gentleness survives
That will outspeak and has its reasons.
There is a loveliness exists,
Preserves us, not for specialists.   60

Donald Hall
(1928–   )

THE MORNING PORCHES

Even the morning is formal. A coughing dog
  scatters the birds, whose quick hysteria
Becomes a lady's fan against the fog.

I sit upon a changing porch, and think
  ideas about the insubstantial wood,   5
That I may make real porches out of ink.

This is a crazy morning. There are times
  when it seems highly serious to catch
The indeterminate between two rhymes.

Yet such a catch is fond, for in the act   10
  analogy becomes the thing itself.
Porches are made of wood. This is a fact.

So look again, and deeper. I have heard
  that though the animal is singular,
Two billion particles make up a bird.   15

GLOSSARY

Glossary

ALEXANDRINE. A line of verse in iambic hexameter. An alexandrine is sometimes used in a poem written prevailingly in pentameter in order to gain emphasis or some other effect by means of the extra foot. The last line of the *Spenserian stanza* is an alexandrine.

ALLITERATION. The effect achieved by repeating consonant sounds at the beginnings of words. Example: "*W*aste *w*ater *w*ashes, and tall ships founder, and *d*eep *d*eath *w*aits."

AMBIGUITY. The use of a word in more senses than one at the same time. This may be a source of confusion when it is unintended, but it is used as a deliberate expressive resource in poetry.

ANALOGY. A comparison between two unlike things, usually emphasizing some similarity of structure or effect for expository or argumentative purposes. In poetry it usually appears as an extended comparison, not unlike an *extended metaphor*.

ANTITHESIS. A balancing of opposites in a sentence, line of verse, couplet, stanza, or poem as a whole, emphasized by parallelism of grammatical structure.

ANAPEST. A three-syllable *foot* or unit of poetic rhythm. It consists of two unstressed syllables followed by a single stressed one: ˘ ˘ ‒ .

ASSONANCE. The effect achieved by repeating vowel sounds within a line of verse. Example: "Unwept and welter to the parching wind."

BALLAD. A narrative poem intended to be sung, usually composed and transmitted orally. English ballads are often written in the *ballad stanza* and may have a *refrain*. Typical of nonliterate societies, ballads generally reflect the interests and attitudes of the common people. Traditional ballads are anonymous, but the form has often been imitated by later poets.

Ballade. A prescribed form consisting of three eight-line stanzas and a four-line *envoi* with a refrain at the end of each stanza. Examples: "The Complaint of Chaucer to his Purse" and "Ballade of a Toyokuni Colour-Print."

BLANK VERSE. Unrhymed verse in iambic pentameter. This is the medium of most verse plays, including Shakespeare's.

CAESURA. The main pause in a line of verse.

CONCEIT. A particularly elaborate and ingenious image, which usually exploits numerous points of resemblance between two unlike things. The Petrarchan conceit, a Renaissance convention, uses traditional comparisons; it is illustrated in the image of the ship in Wyatt's "My Galley Charged with Forgetfullness." The metaphysical conceit gains its effect through startling and unexpected parallels and by stressing resemblances that are incidental, far-fetched, or highly abstract. John Donne's "A Valediction: Forbidding Mourning" has several metaphysical images, including the ones involving earthquakes, beaten gold, and compasses.

CONNOTATION. The implied emotional meaning of a word, as opposed to its overt meaning, or denotation.

CONSONANCE. A variant of rhyme which matches consonants rather than vowels, with each other.

COUPLET. A pair of lines rhyming with each other. See *heroic couplet*.

DACTYL. A three-syllable *foot* or unit of poetic rhythm. It consists of a stressed syllable followed by two unstressed ones: $- \cup \cup$

DIDACTIC POETRY. Poetry whose main purpose is that of teaching a doctrine. "Pope's Essay on Man" is a well-known example.

DRAMATIC MONOLOGUE. A poem spoken by an imaginary personage, which usually reveals character, depicts a dramatic situation, and suggests some conclusion. Examples are Tennyson's "Tithonus" and Browning's "The Bishop Orders His Tomb."

ELEGY. A poem of mourning for the dead. It may be about the death of a particular person (Milton's "Lycidas") or about a more general situation that inspires melancholy. Sometimes the two types will blend with each other, as the poet's thoughts about the dead person lead to general reflections. Among the great elegies in English are Gray's "Elegy Written in a Country Churchyard" and Shelley's "Adonais." See *pastoral elegy*.

END-STOPPED LINE. A line of verse with a pause at the end, usually indicated by some mark of punctuation.

Enjambment. See *run-on line*.

EPIC. A long and substantial narrative poem of ambitious scope and lofty style. Epics usually have a heroic figure at their center and involve gods as well as men. Typically, their themes are the origins or traditions of a nation. The older or "primary" form of epic was composed for oral recitation and differs in style from literary epics, which have a single author and are produced in written form. Examples of the primary, or folk-epic form are the *Iliad* and the *Odyssey* and the Old English *Beowulf*. The best-known literary epics are Virgil's *Aeneid* and Milton's *Paradise Lost*.

EXTENDED METAPHOR. A metaphor which develops numerous resemblances between the two terms being compared.

FIGURE OF SPEECH. Strictly, any deviation from literal language for rhetorical purposes, including such effects as irony, climax, and hyperbole. But the term is ordinarily used to mean an *image*, such as simile, metaphor, personification, and so on.

FOOT. The basic unit of rhythm in poetry. It may consist of either two or three syllables. The metric feet ordinarily used in English are the iamb ⌣ −, the trochee − ⌣, the dactyl − ⌣ ⌣, and the anapest ⌣ ⌣ −. Substitutive feet are the spondee − − and the pyrrhic ⌣ ⌣.

FREE VERSE or *vers libre*. Unrhymed verse without any regular rhythm. The length of the line is variable, and the rhythm is usually loose and flexible. Most of the poems of Walt Whitman are in free verse.

HEROIC COUPLET. The unrhymed iambic pentameter couplet. In neoclassic verse, both lines are usually end-stopped, and a complete thought is contained within the couplet. The two lines are also sometimes unified with each other by parallelism, contrast, or some other effect.

HYPERBOLE. A figure of speech using exaggeration to emphasize the statement being made.

> Not marble nor the gilded monuments
> Of princes shall outlive this powerful rhyme
>
> —SHAKESPEARE, "Sonnet 45"

IAMB. The commonest *foot* or unit of rhythm in English poetry. It consists of an unstressed syllable followed by a stressed one: ˘ –.

IAMBIC PENTAMETER. See *blank verse*.

IMAGERY or IMAGES. Generally, these terms are used as if they were synonymous with *figures of speech* to mean such comparisons as simile, metaphor, personification, and so on but they also mean any vivid descriptive representation of experiences, usually visible ones.

IMPLIED METAPHOR. See *submerged metaphor*.

INCREMENTAL REPETITION. The device of repeating a stanza or refrain with some significant change or addition. It is often found in ballads. See "Edward" and "Lord Randal."

IRONY or IRONIC STRUCTURE. Strictly, the use of language in such a way that it implies the opposite of its literal meaning. A dramatic plot or sequence of thought in poetry or other forms has ironic structure when it arrives at a conclusion that seems inconsistent with its beginning.

ITALIAN, or PETRARCHAN SONNET. A poem in iambic pentameter having fourteen lines; it is divided into two sections, a first one of eight lines called an *octave*, and a second one of six lines called a *sestet*. The rhyme scheme of the octave is abbabba. That of the sestet is variable, but it must have only two rhymes.

LYRIC POEM. A poem giving direct and spontaneous expression to an emotion. Most lyrics are short and well unified, but they may express a modulation of feeling as well as a single feeling, and so become fairly complex. Songs and sonnets are typical lyric poems. Among the many examples of lyric poems in this book are Blake's "The Tyger" and Robert Frost's "Desert Places."

METAPHOR. A figure of speech which identifies the two terms being compared with each other. See *figures of speech, extended metaphor, submerged metaphor*.

METER. The pattern of rhythm in a poem. There are four basic meters in English poetry, two "rising" meters, the iambic and the anapestic, and two "falling" ones, the trochaic and the dactylic. See *foot* and pp. 88–93 for a detailed account of these meters and their combinations.

METONYMY. A figure of speech consisting of the substitution of something related to the subject being described for the subject itself. "The pen is mightier than the sword" means that ideas are more powerful than force. The use of "pen" and "sword" instead of the literal terms illustrates metonymy.

OCCASIONAL POEM. A poem written to celebrate or commemorate some event or date. Richard Lovelace's "To Lucasta, Going to the Wars" and Thomas Gray's "Ode on the Death of a Favourite Cat" are examples.

OCTAVE. The first division of an Italian sonnet. See *Italian sonnet*.

ODE. A long and dignified lyric poem on a particular theme. Originally, Greek odes consisted of sets of three stanzas sung by a chorus, but this structure is seldom found in English odes.

OFF-RHYME. An imperfect rhyme, whose vowels are similar but not identical. Some off-rhymes are due to historical shifts in pronunciation; others are deliberate.

ONOMATOPOEIA. The device of making words imitate the sounds they refer to. Words that perform this trick are "snap," "boom," "chug," and so on. Poets will occasionally compose lines with a similar effect, like Keats's "The murmurous haunt of flies on summer eves."

Ottava rima. An eight-line stanza with the rhyme scheme abababcc. Byron's "Don Juan" is in this stanza form.

PARADOX. An apparently self-contradictory statement which turns out, on closer examination, to be true.

PASTORAL ELEGY. A type of elegy invented by Greek poets and often used in English. It involves the convention that the dead man and the mourner are shepherds living in a simple country environment and includes an invocation to a muse, allusions to the world of nature in which the dead man lived, and an optimistic conclusion. Milton's "Lycidas" is an example.

PERSONIFICATION. A variety of metaphor that compares its subject to a human figure, attributing human qualities to it.

PYRRHIC. A two-syllable *foot* or unit of poetic rhythm. It consists of two unstressed syllables. Pyrrhics cannot serve as the basis of a poetic rhythm, but they occur as substitutes for other feet.

QUATRAIN. A group of four lines, usually rhyming alternately, but also having, as possible rhyme patterns, abba and axax.

REFRAIN. A line or group of words repeated in a poem at regular intervals.

RHYME. The effect achieved by matching sounds at the ends of lines of verse. A rhyme must have similarity of vowel sounds. If there is a consonant after the vowel, it must be identical in both cases. The consonant before the matching vowel need not be identical. See *off-rhyme.*

RHYME ROYAL. A seven-line stanza with the rhyme scheme ababbcc. Its lines are usually in iambic pentameter; it is often used in narrative poetry.

RUN-ON LINE or *enjambment*. A line of verse whose speech pattern does not call for a pause at the end.

SHAKESPEAREAN SONNET. A poem in iambic pentameter having fourteen lines with the following rhyme scheme: abab cdcd efef gg.

SIMILE. A figure of speech overtly expressing a comparison between its terms through the use of "as," "like," or a similar word.

SONNET. A poem in iambic pentameter having fourteen lines and one of two rhyme schemes; see *Shakespearean* and *Italian sonnet*.

SPRUNG RHYTHM or SPRUNG VERSE. The system of scansion devised by Gerard Manley Hopkins, in which the rhythm is determined by the number of stresses, rather than metric feet, in a line of verse.

SPENSERIAN STANZA. A nine-line stanza used by Spenser in *The Faerie Queen*. It has the rhyme scheme ababbcbcc. The first eight lines are iambic pentameter, and the final one is an *alexandrine*.

SPONDEE. A two-syllable *foot*, or unit of poetic rhythm. It consists of two stressed syllables. Spondees cannot serve as the basis of a poetic rhythm, but they occur as substitutes for other feet.

SUBMERGED or IMPLIED METAPHOR. A metaphor in which one of the terms being compared is unstated. The term that is stated implies both the other term and the relationship between them.

SYMBOL. An object which embodies, or refers to, an emotional or abstract meaning or complex of meanings.

SYNECDOCHE. A figure of speech which substitutes the part for the whole, the whole for a part, or the material for the thing of which it is made. For example, "the rolling wave" for the sea, and "canvas" for sails.

TERCET. A verse unit of three lines. Usually all three lines rhyme with each other, but in *terza rima* the middle line rhymes with the lines of a neighboring tercet.

Terza rima. A form of tercet in which the middle line of the first tercet rhymes with the first and third lines of the second one, and so on.

TONE. The mood or prevailing feeling in a poem, the result of the attitude toward the subject or toward the audience.

TROCHEE. A two-syllable *foot* or unit of rhythm. It consists of a stressed syllable followed by an unstressed one.

VILLANELLE. A prescribed form consisting of five tercets and a concluding quatrain. The villanelle uses the same rhymes throughout. The tercets rhyme aba, and the quatrain, abaa. The distinguishing feature of the villanelle is the repetition of its first and third lines as the concluding lines of the following stanzas alternately, and then as the two concluding lines of the poem.

INDEX OF TOPICS

INDEX OF POETS,
TITLES,
AND FIRST LINES